CARING FOR FUTURE GENERATIONS

Recent Titles in
Praeger Studies on the 21st Century

Vitality and Renewal: A Manager's Guide for the 21st Century
Colin Hutchinson

The Foresight Principle: Cultural Recovery in the 21st Century
Richard A. Slaughter

The End of the Future: The Waning of the High-Tech World
Jean Gimpel

Small is Powerful: The Future as if People Really Mattered
John Papworth

Disintegrating Europe: The Twilight of the European Construction
Noriko Hama

The Future is Ours: Foreseeing, Managing and Creating the Future
Graham H. May

Changing Visions: Human Cognitive Maps: Past, Present, and Future
Ervin Laszlo, Robert Artigiani, Allan Combs, and Vilmos Csányi

Sustainable Global Communities in the Information Age: Visions from
Futures Studies
Kaoru Yamaguchi, editor

Chaotics: An Agenda for Business and Society in the Twenty-First Century
Georges Anderla, Anthony Dunning, and Simon Forge

Beyond the Dependency Culture: People, Power and Responsibility in the
21st Century
James Robertson

The Evolutionary Outrider: The Impact of the Human Agent on Evolution
David Loye, editor

Culture: Beacon of the Future
D. Paul Schafer

CARING FOR FUTURE GENERATIONS

Jewish, Christian and Islamic Perspectives

Edited by Emmanuel Agius and Lionel Chircop

Praeger Studies on the 21st Century

Westport, Connecticut

Published in the United States and Canada by Praeger Publishers,
88 Post Road West, Westport, CT 06881.
An imprint of Greenwood Publishing Group, Inc.

Printed in the United States of America

The paper used in this book complies with the
Permanent Paper Standard issued by the National
Information Standards Organization (Z39.48–1984).

10 9 8 7 6 5 4 3 2 1

English language edition, except the United States and Canada,
published by Adamantine Press Limited, Richmond Bridge House,
417–419 Richmond Road, Twickenham TW1 2EX, England.

First published in 1998

Library of Congress Cataloging-in-Publication Data

Caring for future generations : Jewish, Christian, and Islamic
    perspectives / edited by Emmanuel Agius and Lionel Chircop.
        p.   cm.—(Praeger studies on the 21st century, ISSN
    1070–1850)
    Includes bibliographical references and index.
    ISBN 0–275–96501–5 (alk. paper).—ISBN 0–275–96502–3 (pbk. :
alk. paper)
    1. Judaism—Forecasting—Congresses.   2. Christianity—
Forecasting—Congresses.   3. Islam—Forecasting—Congresses.
I. Agius, Emmanuel.   II. Chircop, Lionel.   III. Series.
BM30.C37   1998
200′.1′12—DC21   98–37911

Library of Congress Catalog Card Number: 98–37911

ISBN: 0–275–96501–5 Cloth
        0–275–96502–3 Paperback

Copyright © 1998 by Adamantine Press Limited

Individual chapters copyright © 1998 by the contributors

Contents

Part IV - Islamic Perspective

Contributors

Anthony Abela studied at the University of Malta from where he graduated in Arts (1970) and then in Theology (1972). He continued his post-graduate studies at the Pontifical Biblical Institute in Rome, where he obtained a licentiate (M.A.) in Biblical Studies in 1978 while in 1986 he defended his doctoral thesis on the Abraham narrative in Genesis as a literary unit. Since 1988 he has been the Head of the Biblical Department of the Faculty of Theology at the University of Malta. At present he also works as Translation Consultant for the United Bible Societies. He is the author of several scientific articles and books.

Emmanuel Agius is senior lecturer in philosophical and religious ethics at the University of Malta. He studied philosophy and theology at the University of Malta and at the Catholic University of Louvain, Belgium, where he obtained an M.A. and a Ph.D. He pursued post-doctoral research in the field of bioethics at the University of Tübingen, Germany, as a Fellow of the Alexander-von-Humbold Stiftung, at Georgetown University, Washington, D.C. as a Fulbright scholar, and at the University of Notre Dame, Indiana. He is a member of Malta's National Bioethics Committee, co-ordinator of the Future Generations Programme of the Foundation for International Studies (University of Malta), editor of the *Future Generations Journal*, and member of the European journal *Medicine, Health Care and Philosophy*. He is the author of three books and co-editor of four publications on future generations. His articles have appeared in a number of international journals.

M. A. Zaki Badawi was born in Egypt in 1922. He was educated at the Al-Azhar University of Cairo and at University College in London from where he obtained his B.A. (Hons) in Psychology and Ph.D. In 1986 Dr Badawi was appointed Principal of the Muslim College in London, a post which he still occupies today. He is also Chairman of the Muslim Law (Shariah) Council, U.K., Vice Chairman of the World Congress of Faiths, Member of the the High Council of Islamic Affairs (Egypt), the World Council for Islamic Call (Libya), the Mu'tama Al Alam al Islami (Pakistan) and many other World Organisations.

Abubaker A. Bagader was born in Mecca, Saudi Arabia in 1950. He finished his post-graduate studies in sociology at the University of Wisconsin-Madison, where he obtained his Ph.D. in 1979. In the same year he joined the King Abdelaziz University as an assistant professor in the department of Sociology, where eventually he became a full-time professor. Prof. Bagader has published many articles and books in Arabic and English in the area of sociology of the family, urban sociology, sociology of knowledge and sociology in Islam. He has also worked as consultant for several government agencies in Saudi Arabia and has lectured in various American and European universities. He has also participated in several international conferences and congresses.

Joseph Calleja is a lecturer in New Testament studies at the University of Malta. He joined the Franciscan Conventuals in 1965 and later continued his studies at the University of Malta where he obtained a B.A. degree and a Lic.D. Dr Calleja followed his post-graduate studies at the Pontifical Biblical Institute in Rome where he obtained an S.S. Lic. He also obtained a diploma in Patristic Studies from the Pontifical Institute for Patristic Studies and an S.Th.D from the Pontifical Faculty at St. Bonaventure (Rome). From 1979 to 1989 he taught Biblical Studies at the Pontifical Faculty of Theology at the same Institute. He is the author of several books and articles mainly on the Gospel of St. John.

Lionel Chircop received his B.Phil from the Catholic University of Louvain (Belgium) and then pursued his post-graduate studies in Milltown Institute for Theology and Philosophy (Ireland) and the University of Malta from where he obtained a B.A. (Hons) in Theology and Human Studies. He is currently Project Officer with the Future Generations Programme of the Foundation for International Studies, University of Malta, and co-editor of the Future Generations Journal. He is currently reading for an M.Phil.

Saadia Khawar Kan Chishti obtained her Ph.D. in Education from Cornell University, New York, in 1974. From 1989 to 1990, she was the Director of Public Instruction (colleges) and Chairperson of the Women's University Commission (1990-3), in Punjab, Lahore. In Taplow Court, England, she helped draft the pre-UNCED Declaration. In 1993, she was nominated and designated Vice-Chancellor of the Proposed Women's University, Pakistan, by the Prime Minister of Pakistan. Dr. Chishti is a member of the Council of Islamic Ideology (Constitutional Body) and served the government of Pakistan for two three-year terms. She is the founder and President of the Pakistan Human Ecology Council, a chapter of the Commonwealth Human Ecology Council (CHEC), London.

Peter Crossman graduated with an M.A. in Theological Studies from Wheaton Graduate School, Illinois, United States, in 1978. He obtained his S.T.B./M.A. in Religious Studies (1983) and his Licentiate in Theology (1988) from the Faculty of Theology at the Catholic University of Leuven, Belgium. From 1975 to 1991, he worked for various religious organizations that provide relief to underdeveloped and developing countries, particularly in Africa. Since 1991, he has been the General Secretary of the European Ecumenical Organization for Development (EEOD) based in Belgium.

Hilal Elver holds an L.L.B. (1974) and Ph.D. (1985) from the University of Ankara. She has held high administrative posts, including that of Head of Legal Department and Director General in the Ministry for Environment and General Directorate for Women's Status, Turkey. She has taught courses in Roman Law, Comparative Law and Environmental Law and has published extensively on the subject of environmental law. She has been visiting Fulbright Professor at the University of Michigan in the United States from 1993 to 1994. Currently, she is the UNEP chair holder and Associate Professor of Law at the Mediterranean Academy of Diplomatic Studies at the University of Malta.

Joseph Farrugia was born in 1954 in the Island of Gozo, Malta. After his ordination in 1978 he continued his studies at the Gregorian University in Rome, where he acquired an S.Th.L. in Dogmatic Theology and a Doctorate in Fundamental Theology. He is the author of *The Church and the Muslims* as well as several articles of a theological nature. He is lecturer in Fundamental and Dogmatic Theology and Ecumenism at the Faculty of Theology of the University of Malta and at the Seminary of Gozo.

Ronald Gallagher is the Vice Chancellor of Betlehem University in the West Bank, Occupied Territories. He has previously been Assistant to the President, as well as Professor of English and Modern Languages at Saint Mary's College of California. He received his Ph.D. in Comparative Literature (Anglo-Irish and French) from the University of Washington. He has been a De La Salle Brother since 1964.

George Grima studied arts and theology at the University of Malta and at the University of Louvain, Belgium, (1972-1975) from where he obtained a licentiate in philosophy and a doctorate in theology. He did post-doctoral work in the field of social ethics at the University of

Tübingen, Germany, with the help of a Fellowship awarded by the Alexander-von-Humboldt Foundation. His research interests lie in the area of theology and human rights on which he has published several articles. He is at present Professor of Moral Theology and Dean of the Faculty of Theology at the University of Malta.

Stanislav Hubik is an Associate Professor at the Department of Sociology and Andragogy at the Palacky University in Olomouc and Head of the Department of Social Work at Ostrava University, Czech Republic. Almost all his scientific work has been conceived in research on culture, communication and global problems. He has published three (books), monographs and around sixty studies.

Raphael Jospe obtained his Ph.D. in Jewish Philosophy from Brandeis University, Massachusetts, United States. He was Associate Professor of Judaic Studies and Coordinator of the Centre for Judaic Studies at the University of Denver, Colorado, United States. Since 1985 he has been Senior Lecturer in Jewish Philosophy at the Open University of Israel, Jerusalem. Dr Jospe has written and edited a number of books as well as published several articles in Israeli, American, and European journals.

Manfred Kulessa is a director of the Association of the Churches' Development Services and of the Joint Conference Church and Development, an ecumenical working group of the German Churches. A retired staff member of the United Nations Development Programme, he is also a part-time lecturer at the University of St. Gallen, Switzerland. At the International Conference on Population and Development (ICPD), he served as a member of the German delegation.

Hans Küng was born in 1928 in Switzerland. From 1948 to 1957 he lectured in Theological Studies at the Gregorian University, the Sorbonne and the *Institut Catholique de Paris*. From 1963 to 1965 he was the official theological consultant (Peritus) to the Second Vatican Council appointed by Pope John XXIII. From 1960 to 1963 he was Professor of Fundamental Theology and between 1963 and 1980 he was Professor of Dogmatic and Ecumenical Theology at the Faculty of Catholic Theology and Director of the Institute for Ecumenical Research at the University of Tübingen. Since 1980 he has been Professor of Ecumenical Theology and Director of the Institute for Ecumenical Research at the University of Tübingen. Prof. Küng has honorary degrees from several universities, has written many books, and is co-editor of several journals.

Adel A. Megahed is a professor of Engineering Physics at Cairo University, Egypt, and was a visiting professor at several universities in Europe and the U.S.A. His research areas are in renewable energy, environmental physics, dispersion, gas and plasma dynamics.

Joseph Mercieca was educated at the Gozo Seminary. He obtained his S.Th.D. (Greg.) from the Gregorian University and his J.U.D. (Lat.) from the Lateran University in Rome. Mgr. Mercieca also obtained a B.A. from the University of London through a correspondence course. He was ordained priest in March 1952, was Rector of the Gozo Seminary from 1959 to 1969, and he was appointed Judge of the Sacred Romana Rota. He was also consultor to the Congregation of the Sacraments and of the Congregation for the Doctrine of Faith. On 27 July 1974 Mgr. Mercieca was appointed auxilliary bishop of Malta and consecrated titular bishop of Gemelle in Numidia on 29 September of the same year. Mgr. Mercieca was appointed Archbishop of Malta on 12 December 1976. On 11 June 1991 he was nominated member of the Supreme Tribunal of the Apostolic Signature in Rome.

Ugo Mifsud Bonnici graduated from the University of Malta with a B.A. in 1952 and an L.L.D. in 1955. He has been active in politics since 1966 and was a frequent contributor to the party papers. He was appointed Opposition Spokesman for Education in 1972 and was elected President of the Nationalist Party General Council in 1977. From 1987 until 1992 he was Minister of Education and the Interior, and from 1992 until 1994 he was Minister of Education and Human Resources. In 1994 he was appointed President of the Republic of Malta.

Salvatore Privitera achieved the doctorate in Theology at the Gregorian University in Rome and a degree in Philosophy at the Universita' Degli Studi (Palermo). He proceeded with his post-doctoral research at the University of Münster, in Germany, with the help of Alexander-von-Humboldt Stiftung. He is the Director of the Instituto Siciliano di Bioetica founded within the Faculta Teologica di Sicilia, where he is professor of Philosophy and Moral Theology. He is the author of various books and articles.

David Rosen is Professor of Jewish Studies at the Jerusalem Centre for Near Eastern Studies in Israel. He is the Director of Inter-Faith Relations in Israel for the Anti-Defamation League of B'nai B'rith and the League's liaison to the Vatican. He is president of the World Conference on Religion and Peace, and the Jerusalem Institute for Inter-Religious Research and Relations. He founded the Inter-Religious

Coordinating Council in Israel, the Clergy for Peace, and the Rabbinical Human Rights Organization, and is a member of the International Jewish Committee for Inter-Religious consultations. He was ordained Rabbi in Israel and served as Chaplain in Western Sinai. During 1975-1979 he was the Senior Rabbi of the largest Jewish congregation in South Africa and from 1979 to 1985 he was the Chief Rabbi of Ireland and lectured at the Irish School of Ecumenical Theology.

Jeremy Rosen obtained his Rabbinical Diploma from the Mir Academy in Jerusalem and his Ph.D. from Be'er Sheva. He has served as the Principal of Carmel College and as Rabbi of the Bulawayo Hebrew Congregation, Giffnock Synagogue, and Western Synagogue in the United Kingdom. He has also been a consultant on inter-faith issues to the Chief Rabbinate. Rabbi Rosen is a Lecturer and President of at the Faculty for the Study of Comparative Religion at F.V.G. Antwerp, Belgium.

Emilianos Timiadis graduated as a Doctor of Theology from Halki Theological Academy in 1949. As a priest, he served in Turkey, England, and the Netherlands. In 1959 he was ordained Bishop. In 1961 and 1967 he was appointed Metropolitian of Calabria and Metropolitan of Sylivria, respectively. He was the Ecumenical Patriarchate representative to the World Council of Churches in Geneva from 1959 to 1984, President of the International Ecumenical Fellowship from 1980 to 1985, and Co-Chairman of the Joint International Lutheran-Orthodox Commission on behalf of the Ecumenical Patriarchate. He has served as a visiting professor to various ecumenical institutes in Europe and the United States.

Preface

Central to our self-understanding as human beings, religion beats at the heart of culture, that collection of mores, myths and mystique which, binding a people together, imbues a given community with coherence and identity. Every society needs tradition with a common 'belonging' firmly rooted in a past which predicates the present and postulates the future.

In no area in the world, perhaps, is religion more essential to a proper perception of a given culture than in the Mediterranean region. Around the Middle Sea, on whose shores the "peoples of the book", Jews, Christians and Muslims, thrived and grew, there flourished those Judeo-Christian and Islamic values which characterize southern, eastern, northern and western Mediterranean societies and, almost by anthropological osmosis, much of "European" and "western" society.

It is, in fact, paradoxical that religious movements of the Mediterranean region have often been presented as a factor of tension and division rather than as one of unity. Yet religions essentially promote an interior change of heart and of society based on moral norms, offering in principle incentives for collaboration among their followers. An interreligious dialogue going beyond faith and spiritual fellowship to a common struggle for justice can enrich a holistic vision through complementarity of perspectives. Such a dialogue cannot be confined to the religious sphere but must embrace all dimensions of life: economic, socio-political and cultural. It must be more than an amicable sharing of views and experiences and should encompass mutual challenges leading to collaboration in the building of a new humanity. It is in their common commitment to the fuller life of the human community that religions discover their complementarity and the urgency and relevance of a transcendental dialogue.

Without dialogue it would be difficult to achieve that cooperation which would transform religions into a force for progress rather than reduce them to further competition. Dialogue, however, calls for a very positive sensitivity to the nuances of faith and, above all, to claims of truth. Openness to others entails respecting their sense of loyalty to tradition. Only the two values of faithfulness and openness are likely to ensure a lasting harmony of religions.

The three monotheistic religions are discovering more and more that what unites them is more important than what divides them. Moreover, the points of difference are of lesser consequence in many respects than those of convergence. They have, for example, a common conviction of the fundamental unity of the human family. The unity of past, present and future generations, as one community of humankind created by God, is embraced by Jews, Christians and Muslims. The leaders of these three religions have become more alive to their common mission to see that the goods of the earth, bequeathed by the Creator, are destined to be shared by all members of the human family, including unborn generations. This concept provides perhaps the most fundamental basis for all efforts of solidarity, cooperation and partnership, and offers a lasting security through peaceful co-existence and development between the peoples of the Mediterranean.

Indeed, that security must emerge from an abiding respect for human rights, an area that calls for deep understanding of differing, but far from contradictory, perception of human rights in biblical and kuranic acceptance. It may well be that in particular, the rights of future generations provides the necessary focus of convergence between dissimilar approaches to the dignity of the individual within the collective process of the unity and continuity of the human family.

It was this spirit of interreligious dialogue which inspired the Future Generations Programme of the Foundation for International Studies, in conjunction with the Faculty of Theology at the University of Malta, to convene a conference on Our Responsibilities towards Future Generations: Jewish, Christian and Islamic Perspectives. The conference was held at a time of growing awareness of socio-political and socio-cultural interdependence in the Mediterranean region.

During the three days of the conference, representatives from Judaism, Christianity and Islam met together and discussed the contribution of each religion to future generations. Participants shared their common concerns, commitment and mission to transmit to future generations a better Mediterranean than the one inherited from the past. The constructive dialogue thus generated revealed that the major monotheistic religions rather than fomenting potential conflict, enjoyed in their original conception a high potential for peace and reconciliation not only among present peoples but also between present and future generations.

The conference felt that the task of religious leaders is to educate the rising generations by instilling in them a sense of responsibility for posterity.They therefore found an encouraging convergence on many issues in the conviction that tomorrow, rather than being an arid criticism of yesterday, should guide their steps today.

These proceedings are offered in the hope that they will stimulate among religions further discussion on our responsibilities towards future generations. May God's promise made to Abraham, the father of Judeo-Christian and Muslim believers, be fulfilled among all generations.

Finally, it is with great satisfaction and hope for tomorrow that in this volume we are including as an appendix the new *Declaration on the Responsibilities of the Present Generations towards Future Generations* which was promulgated by UNESCO on 12 November 1997. If the ethical principles and objectives enshrined in this declaration were to find resonance in our hearts and come to permeate all our thinking and actions we would be safeguarding the wellbeing of future generations, conscious of the fact that they will one day be part of that unity we call humankind.

Emmanuel Agius & Lionel Chircop
Future Generations Programme
Foundation for International Studies
University of Malta

PART I

INTRODUCTION

1

Monotheistic Religions and Intergenerational Ethics

UGO MIFSUD BONNICI

Ethics are invincibly bound to human self-consciousness: morality exists without the elaborations of formal religious beliefs. Some have been tempted to see religion as a superfluous burden in that, in repetition of the pelagian heresy throughout the centuries, man can be good in reply to an innate natural code, without the grace of religious faith. One need not return to the repeated refutations, which might seem as anachronistic as this old heresy. Religions surely provide systems, drawing further conclusions from the simple atomic precepts, and the situations in life are so complex, and the intricacies of further civilisation and human society situations so interwoven, that few would begrudge the formal religions this contribution towards the evolution of ethical discernment.

The areas where it would be naive to rely on the primitive moral institutions are numerous, and the debates on matters of proper ethical conduct raging in many of these areas are usually strong. The limelight is stolen by controversies concerning interpersonal relations and sexuality, but the great monotheistic faiths' proposals on so many other *vexatae questiones*, ranging from euthanasia to the preservation of the natural and historical environment, are now capturing the world's attention. It is pertinent to examine the credentials of the great religions and their rights to speak out on what is right or wrong.

This "prophetic" stance of the three great religions is no longer accepted as valid. Indeed, there is a tendency in the first world to treat religious declarations about some of these issues as irrelevant, hieratic and boring, and yet surely, these religions have some history of ethical study and a primogeniture of moral *approfondissement*.

One of the areas where simple unsophisticated morals would have few answers, perhaps not even enough questions, would be precisely in the area of the rights of the unborn, as well as the rights of anonymous humanity. At the very first instance, the sense of history, of a becoming, of a collectivity beyond the immediate community or beyond the other visible or recognisable communities, this abstraction, is a product not only of cold reason or philosophical deduction; its spark is inspirational, basically religious in the widest sense.

We who have been brought up in the Judeo-Christian tradition have been accustomed to the typical patriarchal preoccupation with the future sons of Abraham. The then present sons of Abraham were writing, with some extrapolation, going backwards and forwards. Even if *ex-post facto* however, it was surely a great mental evolution to propose a vital interest in the yet unborn, far out into the future. In the Hebrew Bible, punishments as well as rewards were visited on succeeding generations. Indeed, the unity of a race or of the whole of humankind was traced back to a common experience of good or evil in the ancestors. One has to strain one's imagination to conceive of a moral preoccupation for future unseen generations or for distant and abstract humanity outside the religious perspective.

Even today, when so many of the Judeo-Christian moral concepts have permeated our culture to such an extent that even non-religious or agnostic morality may seem imbued with the basic theorems of that morality, the contestations to the conclusions occur precisely where there has been a *caesura* in the religious continuity.

Islam not only has been influenced by the Bible and the fundamental rules of conduct that emerge from the Old and New Testament, but is in a sense a reaffirmation of the unity of a merciful and all-powerful God, sanctioning that morality through a different source of revelation.

Lay (or should one say religiously uninformed) opinion may be astonished at the confluence on vital thinking of the Jewish, Muslim and Christian moral theology. Perhaps there is more differentiation in belief than in morality.

Essential to the three great religions is their view of each human being as an immortal, with terrible duties bound to his "salvation". Correspondence with God's plan of history is the trial at every moment in every individual's life. The obverse is the right of every person as against his fellow *personae*. We have duties towards future persons: they will have rights. What is ultimately only ascribable to religion is the actuality of future rights within the prospect of the plan of history as being ever present even if unfolding in time. The divine prism is also preformative in the spelling out of environmental responsibilities. Some have seen in the modern revival of the sentiments of sacred awe towards nature a return of the old pre-Christian pantheistic religion of pagan Europe. The sacred reverence towards animals and created things is a religious attitude in St. Francis of Assisi more than the return of the heathen spirits. Within the religious feeling as expressed in Psalm 19, the heavens and indeed all objects around us are manifestations of God, and, as expressed in Psalm 117, all nations are called upon to give glory to the Lord.

The universality of this religious feeling extending backwards and forwards in time and all-encompassing with regard to all peoples and all creation is a basic contribution to our civilisation. The formulation of the United Nations Human Rights Declaration is the best proof of its genesis, and Maritain's personal collaboration and what he has written about it are sufficient evidence of the natural law derivation in direct descent from the Judeo-Christian tradition as also in fact secularised by the Enlightenment. The extension of the recognition of the rights of future generations could not be understood without the humanistic humus, which in turn is grounded in the basic transcendental value of every human being.

The contribution made by the Enlightenment, that of distinguishing the role of law from that of morals, is still valid today. Legislation should not enforce morality, neither should morality depend on law. However, the influence of ethical thinking on the formulation of legislation and the recognition of rights and obligations can never be underestimated. Perhaps this important distinction should not mean a conscious effort to lessen that influence.

2

God as the Guardian of Future Generations

JOSEPH MERCIECA

The 1992 Rio Earth Summit has shown that the international community is deeply concerned about the wellbeing of unborn generations. The three major documents signed at Rio by many Heads of State pledge to safeguard the natural, cultural and genetic resources of our one and only Earth for the benefit of posterity. Fortunately, the international community is becoming ever more conscious and conscientious of its responsibilities towards generations yet to be born.

Caring for the wellbeing of future generations has become a moral duty in present-day society. We cannot live as if we are the last generations. We are obliged to respond to the ecological challenge and to think about the needs and interests of the humanity of tomorrow.

The ecological crisis requires world cooperation and responsibility because it has assumed global proportions. Men and women having no particular religious conviction, but with an accurate sense of their responsibility for the common good, recognise their obligation to contribute to the restoration of a healthy environment. All the more, men and women who believe in God the Creator should feel called upon to address the problem.

Common Belief

A belief common to the three major religious movements of the Mediterranean is that God created the Earth for the benefit of all generations. Both the Bible and the Qu'ran speak about the beauty of nature. Both sacred books confirm that God destined the Earth and all it contains for the use of every individual and all peoples. Judaism,

Christianity and Islam believe that the Earth is a common heritage, the fruits of which are for the benefit of all. Therefore, no generation enjoys an exclusive right to the resources of the Earth. Every generation has the right to enjoy what God created for the benefit of all humankind.

Religions can play an important role in today's commitment to build a culture of solidarity with all generations and with nature. We all know that religions cannot solve all the environmental, economic, political and social problems of the Earth. However, they can provide what obviously cannot be attained by economic plans, political programmes or legal regulations alone: a change in the inner orientation, the whole mentality, the 'hearts' of people; a conversion from a false path to a new orientation for life. Humankind needs social and ecological reforms, but it needs spiritual renewal just as urgently. The spiritual powers of Judaism, Christianity and Islam can offer a fundamental sense of hope for the future, a ground of meaning for our responsibility towards coming generations, and ultimate standards to judge today's consumeristic life-style.

The belief of these three world religions in one God should continue to act as a protest against the perennial tendency in man to fashion his own gods, which, though small and perishable, are capable of dividing man within himself and men among themselves. Monotheism, a characteristic feature of the Jewish, Christian and Muslim religions, represents a milestone in the religious history of humankind precisely in opening up man to a reality which is above individual, ethnic and national interests: it is not a God of this or that individual, group or nation but the one and only God to whom man and the world owe ultimately their being and existence and through whom all life will be renewed and will fulfil itself.

In the context of monotheistic faith, our responsibility for future generations acquires a new and deeper dimension. Besides pointing to the universal destination of all created goods, as I have already observed, it resists every attempt to take unfair advantage over the rest. The interests of present generations, of course, have to be properly identified and affirmed but they should never be pursued at the expense of coming generations.

Moderation in the use of resources is, therefore, more than a simple disposition which is to be promoted particularly at a time like ours, when awareness of the limits of our available and potential resources creates an urgent moral imperative to set and keep a limit to the use of goods that we may need or wish to use. Moderation is an indispensable attitude of those who want to serve God who is Lord and Father not only of present but also of future generations.

The Powerless

The power of God, according to Judaism, Christianity and Islam, is exercised in the interests of the powerless. This is the reason why God is presented as taking the side of the poor. In the Old and New Testaments as well as in the Qu'ran the poor are those whom the economic, political and social systems are excluding from and depriving of developing as free and intelligent human beings. Once born, however, every man and woman has some power, even though they may be victims of oppression, and big social changes often come about with the increasing consciousness of the hardships involved in an unjust state of affairs. Future generations, in so far as they are not even born, are absolutely powerless and their prospect of a dignified life depends in a radical way on the actions and permissions of present generations.

The argument that future generations have no rights because they are non-existent would have to be reviewed when seen in the context of the belief in God, who is always on the side of the powerless. God stands on their behalf and pleads their cause. He is the guardian of those who are living now and those who will be living in the future. The concept of a guardian representing the interests of future generations is altogether justified on the basis of our common belief in God as the protector and defender of those whose rights are not recognised and much less respected.

The Earth is put at our disposal. May followers of Judaism, Christianity and Islam, together with other world religions, be enlightened and respectful managers of a heritage which must keep its fruitfulness for the generations to come.

PART II

JEWISH PERSPECTIVE

3

The Contribution of Judaism to Humankind's Future

Over the years, religious teaching has signally failed to prevent interreligious conflict and intolerance. Memories of the fierce conflicts in ex-Yugoslavia and in Rwanda must, in the words of the Biblical Prophet, "make our ears ring". Moreover, we believe that more contact among people of different religions can only help bridge the gaps and bring about reconciliation. And yet, sadly enough, these are two examples that apparently seem to prove the very opposite.

On the other hand, neither can it be said that those secular traditions that have tried to supplant religions have been any more successful. And despite all of this we are all experiencing increased fervour and a return to religious life even though the manifestations may not always be to our liking. Under these circumstances I wish to explore Jewish thinking and see if it has something to say that might be helpful to our discussion and sense of direction. There are three themes I should like to raise:

- What does my religion expect of me with regard to humanity?
- How does my religion expect me to relate to other religions?
- What has my religion to say about our responsibility for the ecological future of our world?

Authority in Traditional Judaism

For the benefit of anyone unfamiliar with the self-perception of Jewish tradition, a few words about authority in Judaism from the point of view of what is often, but misleadingly, called Orthodoxy seem appropriate.

The Five Books of Moses, also known as the *Torah*, are the main source of Divine Revelation to the Jewish People and although they were given through Moses, he is, essentially, secondary to the actual message and is the equivalent neither of Jesus nor Mohammed in Jewish terms. These Five Books are referred to also as 'The Written Law'. But of course the actual text is and always was open to interpretation. "And God said" might or might not imply vocal chords!

The question of how the original text was understood at the actual time was traditionally clarified by 'The Oral Law'. In many ways, this power of clarification gave the Oral Law even greater authority than the actual Written Text. For example, if one takes the text in Exodus 21,24, "An eye for an eye", the Oral Law explains how one is to take the eye of a blind man who has impaired the sight of a less unfortunate being, or how one is obliged to compensate someone with a full set of teeth when one harms them. In such cases the Oral Law clarifies that the words, taken in their original context, refer to financial compensation. Or when Leviticus 23,40 states that on the Festival of Tabernacles, "You shall take the fruit of a good tree", we rely on the Oral Tradition to tell us what that 'Good Tree' was.

The Oral Law, despite its importance and the constant additions and accretions to it, was not written down for hundreds of years (and even then with great reluctance) after the emergence of The Five Books, as a response to increasing Roman dispersion of the centres of Jewish learning, in the second century. The compilation was called *Mishna* and the ensuing debate and ongoing developments, adaptations and additions were called *Gemara*. There were two versions, the Jerusalem version and the Babylonian version. But the latter, because of the power and dominance of the Babylonian community, became the authoritative one. Its compilation in the sixth century created a combined encyclopedia of Jewish Lore and Law that is known as the *Talmud*.

Within Judaism, different branches relate to the *Talmud* with varying degrees of respect; but the Orthodox world regards it as the primary source of current Jewish life in the widest sense.

Judaism may well share its written Bible with other religions but the *Talmud* is unique to Judaism and provides the source of the ideas I am presenting here. Yet I should like to emphasise that in my opinion the differences among world religions are not as great as some would have us believe. In the *Talmud* one finds statements that coincide with most of the major ideas and themes of other religious traditions. The differences lie not so much in ideas as in the different cultural ways that religious traditions express themselves; in the behavioural rather than the theoretical. In a way, if the ideological gaps are not so wide, this must give us cause for optimism. But on the other hand, one cannot simply ignore the power of human behaviour and its potential to create barriers. Rather, this is what we must try to understand if we are to find respectful ways of coming together.

The Essential Message

It has long been a tradition to try to encapsulate faiths in simple sound bites or slogans. The following simple statement by the prophet Mica (6,8) could probably be accepted by everyone: "It has been told to you, Mankind, what God seeks and what He requires of you ... simply to do justice and love kindness and to walk in humility with your God". But more particular to post-biblical Judaism is the debate in the Jerusalem *Talmud* (Nedarim 9) that took place nearly two thousand years ago.

Rabbi Akiva said, " 'Love your neighbour as yourself' (Leviticus 19) is the most important principle of the *Torah*". What he meant by this (as opposed to Hillel's famous line which Christians will be familiar with, namely "What is hateful to you, do not do to your neighbour") was that the community of believers, the sharers of the Covenant, should treat each other with shared responsibility and as equals, with concern and love. Akiva's position was strongly opposed by mainstream Pharisee Rabbinate and given his political views (he supported the Bar Cochba revolution against Hadrian in 134-136, considered him to be the *Messiah* and was martyred for his pains) we can take this to be an expression of Jewish nationalism. At this point it is important to note that the mainstream Pharisee Rabbinate strongly opposed Akiva's position at that time and he was regarded in a similar way that mainstream and ultra Orthodoxy regards religious Jewish Nationalists in Israel today - with distance and disapproval.

In reply, Ben Azai (the title 'Rabbi' was not given to an unmarried scholar, no matter how great his authority, as a sign of disapproval) disagrees and says that the fundamental principle is: "This is the record of the history of Mankind" (Genesis 5,1). In other words, all humanity is a unity with a common source. As the *Talmud* says (Sanhedrin 38): "Man was created as a single unit so as to show that everyone comes from one source and whoever destroys one Soul is virtually killing a whole Universe". In other words, we are all the children of one God and must show our shared Fatherhood in fellowship and concern.

This debate was a crucial one in Jewish History. The Pharisees, despite their awful press in the New Testament, were the popular party, the meritocracy "of the people, by the people and for the people". They had just seen off the threat of the Sadducees, who were the rich, privileged, priestly aristocracy and opposed the flexibility and adaptability of the more egalitarian Pharisees. But the Pharisee tradition itself was split (as the Hillel-Shammai controversy over conversion indicates), just as Christianity was split between Peter and Paul - between remaining a national religion to concentrate on intense, qualitative survival or expanding into a more universal and influential religion through adaptation to different cultural contexts.

As a matter of fact, after Constantine made Christianity the state religion of the Roman Empire in 323 A.D., Judaism (despite Julian's brief interlude) was deprived of all pretensions of becoming a universal religion. The First Council of Nicea and then the Pact of Omar in the seventh century A.D. effectively reduced Judaism to pariah status under the former and subservience (often benevolent) under the latter. As a result, Judaism turned in on itself and concentrated on survival. The poor Deacon of Oxford who was burnt at the stake in the twelfth century would have attested to the dangers of joining the Jewish religion, although it appears that a woman was involved and so we must blame the Romantic ideal instead!

This inevitably led to an emphasis on behaviour, on those elements that preserved identity and difference, and in effect, helped sustain the external antagonism imposed onto the stranger, the wanderer (and in Europe, the Christ killer), by refusing to go away and by remaining as a reproach and stubborn symbol of the survivability of a different and even despised religion - as the texts engraved on the sculptures along Charles Bridge, in Prague, attest.

But this emphasis on survival and self-preservation, and the subsequent influence of Judaism out of all proportion to its numbers, showed the force and viability of a behaviour-orientated religious tradition that permeated the home and the community as well as the synagogue. In effect, "God weighed His followers rather than counted them". 'Small and intense' seemed as viable as 'many but loose'.

Unfortunately, there was another side to this picture: the fomenting of a defensive attitude, a sort of 'paranoia' and 'siege mentality' that still sees enemies round every corner and is convinced that 'the World' is out to destroy it (a complex reinforced by global apathetic reaction to Nazi Genocide, only confirmed by the ongoing release of archive material). This siege mentality is one of the major barriers to inter-faith dialogue within the Orthodox world. We need to reiterate that self-preservation does not require self-imprisonment, nor withdrawal into a 'mental ghetto'.

State or Religion

The *Talmud* records another debate going on at that time concerning the relationship between states and religion. Of course the notion of statehood is a relatively modern one in the nationalist sense. Rabbi

Gamliel said: "Do not get close to Governing Authorities for they only appear friendly when it is in their interests" (*Avot* 2.3). The involvement of religion in government discredits religious authority by degrading it. Religion needs to preserve its idealism and impartiality. Does this mean, therefore, that Judaism does not see itself as permeating the whole gamut of human activity?

Chanania the Priest gives quite a different opinion when he says: "Pray for the welfare of government, for without people fearing it, they would swallow each other alive" (*Avot* 3.2). An impressive precursor of Hobbesian utilitarianism! Of course one would expect an aristocratic Sadducee with government connections to take this position! But in effect the *Torah* itself is a total constitution that governs every aspect of individual and community activity.

Judaism had no option under Roman control but to 'render unto Caesar what was Caesar's' and developed the principle that in civil matters "*Dina De Malchuta ... Dina*" - "The Law of the Land is The Law". This enabled Jewish communities to survive, but it was not the ideal.

For two thousand years Judaism was denied the political options that led to the debate about state and religion. Of course it could be argued that the whole issue of statism is a post-Enlightenment development. But control over one's own community was only granted to Jews, as in Poland, under very strict measures. The establishment of the state of Israel has revived these issues and indeed the conflict between democracy and religious autocracy. It seems to me that in the near future the divide will be less along religious lines and more on how states are to be run and the sort of societies they will be.

'Religious totalitarians' will have more in common with each other across the religions than their own secularists. I suspect that alliances of self-interest will soon emerge to change, and somehow to improve, the inter-denominational climate but leading to more 'Kultur Kampfs' of the sort we are witnessing in Algeria and amongst the Palestinians. But returning to my main theme, the first principle I derive from Jewish teaching is that we are all God's children and must work together for the benefit of all humanity, not just our own, particular vested interests.

How Do We Relate to Other Religions?

How would Rabbi Akiva have resolved the question of what Judaism has to say about those outside it? It is important to bear in mind here that Akiva was the child of converts himself. He was the archetypal Pharisee, poor and ignorant into middle age and raising himself through sheer hard work to a position of leadership.

Three times a day, Jews recite the *Aleynu* prayer whose text comfortably pre-dates Rabbi Akiva. Its central phrase is: *"Letaken Olam bemalchut Shaddai"* - "We look to God to rectify the world through His Kingship". How do we achieve this *'Tikkun'*, this rectification? One way is Messianic. Judaism has always been divided over whether Messianism is active or passive. For some it meant divine intervention in a miraculous way to correct abuses, oppressive government and improve upon the human condition. This position remains that of the Ultra Orthodox world today, both those who oppose Zionism and those who remain neutral. This view has tended to gain the upper hand at times of oppression, when things seem so bad that only a miracle can save the situation.

Others have taken Messianism to mean the active involvement in trying to rectify the situation and bring about change. This after all was Akiva's position in supporting Bar Cochba and considering him to be the Messiah. Temporarily, at least, he did remove the oppression of alien governments. This is the view of religious Zionism today. And it is a view that is in the ascendancy at times of Jewish empowerment.

But where does Messianism leave the rest of world? One response is that Judaism does indeed have expectations and standards for those beyond it, but in a very particular way.

The Other

People often refer to the Judeo-Christian tradition or ethic. I believe this to be erroneous and misleading. The Christian ethic is an amalgam of various influences, as is the Jewish ethic. Many ideas, such as the distinction between body and mind that led many to the paths of celibacy and monasticism, were derived from the Greek world view that the rabbis strongly opposed.

To understand Judaism, one has to look at it other than through the Western mind set that is so heavily reliant on Greek thought processes. For example Judaism works its world of ideas out of the *Midrash* (a tradition, parallel with and overlapping the *Talmud*), rather than theology. This mixture of Biblical exegesis, homiletics, folklore and wisdom literature is the major source book of Jewish thinking on what are called theological issues. Later philosophical traditions are more of an apologetic reaction to external currents.

A fundamental issue revolves around the now virtually universal concept of 'truth' as an absolute. This perspective finds no resonance in the pre-Greek Jewish world. 'Truth' (*Emet*) is only used empirically in the *Torah*: "Is it true, did these events really happen?" (as in Deuteronomy 17,4.) When it is used later in an abstract way, it refers to a kind of 'certainty' reached through experience and emotion rather than intellectual analysis. In the *Talmud* it is never used in an absolute sense, so that only a non-Jew could have asked Pontius Pilate's question: "What is truth?"

For Judaism there may be several truths and what is true for me may not necessarily be true for you. The Torah has the concept of *Ger Toshav*, "the stranger in your gates" who must be given civil rights, may participate in Temple activity provided he adheres to certain basic rules. These rules were later formulated in the *Talmud (Sanhedrin)* as The Seven Noachide Commandments (the Moral Code that according to tradition was in force at the time of Noah) that applied to every human being and gave everyone a similar spiritual status as the Jew. Specifically one was not to blaspheme, not to worship idols, not to murder, commit adultery or steal, not to be cruel to animals or to set up courts of law. Adherence to these gave one the status of "The Pious of the Nations". In other words, like the European Union, there were paces of progress at different levels!

Just as within historical Judaism the priests once had specific tasks but were not *ipso facto* superior to the 'common' people, and within *Halacha* there was and remains the option of taking the strict or the lenient path, so too outside Judaism there were different options, the minimalist and the maximalist.

The Meiri, a major Medieval Rabbinic authority living in Provence, was asked whether Christians who worshipped effigies counted as idol worshippers or not (Maimonedes, who was born in Cordova in the twelfth century but lived mainly in Egypt, thought that only Islam counted as Monotheistic with Judaism). He replied that the criterion was *Mugdar Be Nimussim*, "Constrained by Morality", and so long as a people had moral codes they were to be treated as "the stranger in your midst" or as a *Ben Noach*, a son of Noah, outside Israel (there being a question as to whether 'the stranger' applied only in Israel).

The role of the Jew in this wider context was *Kiddush Hashem*, that is, to sanctify God by behaving in an admirable way. Thus, he would increase the amount of spirituality and help make the world a better place for everyone. Thus 'Truth' has many faces and opportunities.

The obligation on the Jew is not so much to be a missioner but to witness, a concept that will resonate with Christianity even though the missionary tendency remains a powerful if controversial one. In a world of such sensitivity and easy access to the means of communication, people are often on the lookout to berate religion. Missionary activity is increasingly being singled out as an example of religious arrogance. There is little that is more insulting to a spiritual person than to be told there is something inadequate in his relationship with God and that only someone else's concepts can put it right! It seems to me to be one of the failures of religious thinking that we still have not gone beyond this sort of arrogance. Accordingly, the second principle I derive from Jewish thinking is that religions have a duty to bring more spirituality into this world, not by competing over each other's members but by respecting the work of each and trying to fill vacuums where no concept of God exists at all.

Ecology

Fortunately, ecological concerns are increasingly attracting our attention. However, ecological awareness is far from being a new phenomenon. On the one hand, international meetings such as the Cairo Conference raise the question of population control. Despite the Bible's command to "Be Fruitful and Multiply" the *Talmud* in *Taanit* lays down strict rules limiting procreation at times of famine and shortages of supply. Although the obligation to procreate is fundamental, the *Talmud* does not show the rigidity, in regard to either abortion or contraception, that is so central to Christian theology; and *Halacha* has more of a tendency towards relativism (for better or for worse!). Again it is a question of absolutes. In other words these concerns were indeed addressed by the Rabbis of the *Talmud.*

The twentieth-century authoritative Commentary *Meshech Chochma,* quotes the Jerusalem Talmudist Yochanan Ben Beroka as saying: "We are commanded to imitate God, just as God created plants, birds, fish and animals and only then created Adam. And just as God created the Garden first and then put man in it to tend it ... so too we must see that the plants and the animals are cared for before we take care of ourselves." Man was blessed, in the first chapter of Genesis, and told to "rule all creatures". Just as kingship implies responsibility and obligation, so does it with man in relation to Nature. Indeed man was placed in the garden "to tend it and to protect it" (Gen 2,15).

The law in Deuteronomy (22,6) that one must send the mother bird away before taking the eggs or the fledglings was the basis of another debate in the *Talmud.* Was the purpose of the law to show concern for the feelings of creatures or was it to teach humans to care for them? In other words, "Is the world anthropocentric or ecocentric?" The debate remains unresolved, for both elements co-exist in our sources. Although on balance, it has to be said that Judaism veers towards the anthropocentric/humanist approach. But either way it offers an important starting point for our discussion. Similarly the law (Deuteronomy 20,19) "Do not destroy fruit-bearing trees (even in war) because man is like the tree of the field" clearly states the position of mutual dependence inherent in the relationship.

But there is also the question of responsibility to our own children. One of the most popular of Talmudic stories is that told in *Taanit* of Choni Ha Meagel (the Jewish precursor of Rip Van Winkle) asking an old man why he is planting a carob tree that takes seventy years to bear fruit. The reply is: "My Grandfather planted that tree for me and I am planting this for my grandchildren". The tradition of care and responsibility for nature is so deeply rooted in the Jewish tradition, partly because of its loving connection with its Promised Land, a concept that is inseparable from the whole concept of the divine plan for the universe.

Yet, when all is said and done, there is no doubt that humanity, with its special relationship with God, is the priority. Human life remains the culmination of the creative process. Accordingly, the third principle is that as agents of God we have been entrusted with custodianship of the world and we must husband its resources with great care and responsibility.

Conclusion

I have outlined some basic areas where, I believe, Jewish teaching can help us to respond constructively to the crucial questions that concern us. And yet the theory is easy. As our Rabbis say (in *Avot*): "The words are not as important as the deeds." We are only too painfully aware of our failure to present religion as a unifying, curative force in the world.

I think we are also very conscious of the fact that we all know how to present the kindly face and the diplomatic impression of our own religions. We are all pretty good apologists. But in our hearts I believe we all realise how we are often undermined from within. There are deeds which, although we deplore them forcefully, still get done quite often in the name of religion.

We all have within our religious communities those with whom we share less than with others who live outside. We have amongst us those who want to reach out and co-exist and those only concerned with triumphalism.

Interreligious dialogue helps us reinforce each other's determination to work together in peace and friendship for a better world that benefits both present and future generations. And if we sometimes feel isolated within our own communities let us remain assured that there are people from all faiths who share our ideals and hopes and are committed to live up to them despite serious setbacks.

We are indeed the children of one God and we are the bearers of spiritual gifts to humankind. And if we do not strive to share them, who will? The following concluding quote from *Avot* (2.16) helps us maintain a healthy balance as we keep on striving to make our desires come true: "It is not for you to complete the work. But neither are you free to desist or to abandon your responsibility."

4

Educating for
Interreligious Responsibility

RAPHAEL JOSPE

There are various critical areas in which we are challenged to consider, from an interreligious perspective, our responsibilities towards future generations. However, in this paper I should like to limit myself to two main areas of concern, namely "Educating for Responsibility" and "Interreligious Dialogue". This is not to say that the other topics, such as the "Culture of Peace for Future Generations", "Environmental Obligations" or "Genetic Engineering", are not of vital and immediate importance. However, from a strictly interreligious perspective, these may well be areas in which our diverse religious traditions will agree readily on the common, universal dangers we all face, even if they do not (or do not yet) agree on the proper responses to those dangers. These include war and the proliferation of the means of mass destruction, environmental pollution which increasingly transcends national and even regional borders, and scientific and technical advances which have by far outpaced our wisdom in knowing their moral limits. How, when and where should these new advances in technology be applied responsibly?

Without in any way denegrating the urgency of these questions, I wish to address an area in which our religious traditions are far less in agreement with each other, namely "Inter-faith Dialogue on our Responsibilities Towards the Future of Humankind" and "Educating for Responsibility Towards Posterity", or what I prefer to call "Educating for Interreligious Responsibility: Ritual Exclusivity vs. Spiritual Inclusivity". By this phrase I simply mean this: How do our religions teach us to see ourselves in relationship with others, and what teachings do we wish to transmit to our children if they are to avoid the kind of interreligious (as well as intra-religious) strife and intolerance from which humanity has suffered for centuries? This is a danger which, paradoxically, may be growing rapidly with the spread of fundamentalist fanaticism in the closing years of this most secular of centuries. Religion, in short, has all too often been part of the human problem. What is our responsibility, in the context of interreligious dialogue, to ensure that religion will be part of the solution for future generations?

Permit me to note that I have no authorization to speak on behalf of the entire spectrum of the Jewish people - as if 'Jewish unanimity' were not more or less a contradiction in terms. I do think, however, that my perspective may be reflective of the concerns of that sector of the Jewish community which sees no contradiction in principle between fidelity to the Torah and enlightened commitment to modern culture.[1] While my perspective is thus necessarily only Jewish and an outsider has no right to speak on behalf of other traditions, I hope that what I propose in a Jewish context may be relevant to those who share parallel concerns within the Christian and Islamic communities.

My paper is divided into three sections:

1. From tolerance to acceptance: Moving from spiritual exclusivity to inclusivity, and from ritual inclusivity to exclusivity;
2. On the correlation between the ritual and the spiritual;
3. On the meaning of covenant and chosenness.

From Tolerance to Acceptance: Moving from Spiritual Exclusivity to Inclusivity, and from Ritual Inclusivity to Exclusivity

The thirty years since the Second Vatican Council have certainly witnessed major progress in interreligious dialogue and relations. Yet, we remain far from a true and mature relationship with each other. Tolerance, after all, however preferable it obviously is to persecution, consists both literally and practically of our willingness to "suffer" or "endure" deviant beliefs and practices. It implies, ultimately, no recognition of the other's position as inherently valid or true, in relation to God or to us.[2]

I am reminded, in this context, of the story of two religious leaders who returned in the same carriage from a state ceremony. "Isn't it wonderful", the first said to his religious fellow-traveller, "how we both worship God, each in his own way?" "Yes," replied the second, "it is wonderful. You worship God in your way, and I worship God in His way!"

Can we, as members of the human species, afford to continue, in the age of "the global village", to maintain such a religious "superiority complex"? Or, rather, has not the time finally come for us to recognize both the spiritual immaturity and moral irresponsibility of such religious exclusivity and competitiveness, and to develop instead a more mature interreligious relationship of inclusivity and cooperation?

The question was posed thus by Cardinal Joseph Ratzinger at the unprecedented International Jewish-Christian Conference on "Religious Leadership in Secular Society" in Jerusalem, in February 1994. Cardinal Ratzinger asked whether we can move religiously "from Tolerance to acceptance". It is highly significant that the question was posed by the Prefect of the "Congregation for the Doctrine of the Faith", a body once known as the Inquisition!

Unfortunately, in the past, and even today, all too often, religious "acceptance" has meant nothing more than acceptance on my terms. This is what I would refer to as "ritual inclusivity vs. spiritual exclusivity": world religions assert their claim to exclusive spiritual truth, to which others can have access only if they accept, whether voluntarily or through the coercive power of the state, inclusion in the rituals - of deed or creed - of the dominant group. This ritual inclusiveness, the desire to attain or impose a uniformity of religious belief and behaviour, follows logically from spiritual exclusiveness: there is only one form of religious truth, and I know it; there is only one key to the kingdom of heaven, and I possess it.

Now, in a sense, such ritual inclusivity is both a logical and a moral corollary of spiritual exclusivity. If, in fact, I possess the unique spiritual truth, without which there can be no salvation, then how would I serve my God or my fellow humans by keeping that exclusive truth to myself? Clearly, I should attempt to share it with others, so they may partake of the benefits conferred by membership in the ritual community, however defined in terms of creed or deed. However, I may recognize that assent to the truth must inherently be voluntary, and therefore I may refrain from seeking to impose my religious way of life on others, in the hope that they will eventually come to embrace it of their own free will.

Nevertheless, the proponent of religious Tolerance, on the one hand, and on the other hand, the religious fanatic or fundamentalist who seeks to impose his views on others, do not differ in their goals, but only in the means to attain them. Both of them share a spiritual exclusivism, which claims unique possession of religious truth and salvation. They differ only on the question of whether others should be actively coerced to conform, or whether one should passively await their voluntary conformity. Ultimately, however, they have the same vision, of universal religious uniformity on their terms.

Spiritual exclusivity, and its corollary of ritual inclusivity, can thus never advance beyond mere Tolerance, in the best of cases. In the worst of cases, they will continue to permit or even encourage the kind of barbaric outrages to which the human species seems to be ever more inclined, outrages fuelled by religious fervour. How often are we witness, all over the world, to a hatred of our fellow creatures, masquerading as a love of their creator, as if we serve God by destroying or desecrating the image of God, our brother or sister human being?

Facing the Challenge

The challenge we face, then, is to invert the relationship. Instead of spiritual exclusivity, and its corollary or ritual inclusivity, it means to strive for a spiritual inclusivity, by which we can accept the other as a valid and legitimate way of life, with the corollary of ritual exclusivity, by which we maintain and respect our diverse and unique religious ways of life, without actively seeking or even passively promoting uniformity. When we recognize and accept the spiritual validity of others, in other words, when we are spiritually inclusive, we can, and indeed should, be ritually exclusive, inasmuch as there is no longer any need or desirability to include others, whether by persuasion or by coercion, in our particular ritual requirements, or to seek ritual uniformity. Such ritual pluralism is thus exclusivistic in the positive sense of recognizing both the legitimacy of other approaches as they are, and the limitation of the particular demands that each tradition makes, whether of creed or of deed, to its own adherents.

The relationship, therefore, may be inverted. Instead of a spiritual exclusivity of truth or salvation, which ultimately delegitimates others (however tolerant we think we are of them), we now relate to others inclusively as spiritually legitimate. Instead of a ritual inclusivity, in which we seek to extend ritual conformity and uniformity externally, at the expense of the integrity of the others' ritual traditions, we now can foster a pluralistic ritual exclusivity, recognizing that the distinctive ritual requirements of a particular tradition, even our own, are binding exclusively internally on members of that community.

By inverting the relationship what do we gain, and how do we progress? What we gain is the possibility of a new interreligious relationship based on mutual acceptance of legitimate differences. We progress by recognizing that it is in the ultimate interest of each of our traditions to enhance, rather than to obliterate, religious pluralism. Religious distinctions are thereby strengthened, not undermined.

Historically, mutual religious fear and distrust may well have been inevitable; they were caused by, and in turn contributed to, greater competition and struggle for supremacy. Even today, we cannot deny the empirical fact that religion itself, or in combination with other factors such as national, ethnic, racial or ideological strife, remains all too often a source and catalyst of violence and oppression.

If, however, we wish religion to become a powerful force in meeting the global challenges we all face together, we shall have to find a religious way to re-educate ourselves as well as our children. When spiritual exclusivity is replaced by inclusivity, and when ritual inclusivistic uniformity is replaced by exclusivistic pluralism, the diverse religions should have little to fear from each other, and their ability as well as willingness to cooperate, rather than compete, should then be enhanced.

Judaism, Christianity and Islam, as the three claimants to the legacy of Abraham's covenant with God, have had historically much to argue about, given the mutual exclusivity of many of their claims. It is precisely because the three Abrahamic traditions have so much in common that they have had so much strife, but that they now also have the greatest opportunity for dialogue and cooperation.

This is not to preclude the possibility of and need for dialogue and cooperation with other, non-Abrahamic and non-monotheistic religions. The encounter should begin with, but not ultimately be limited to, the traditions which see themselves as the physical and/or spiritual children of Abraham. The common history, symbols and texts of Judaism, Christianity and Islam continue to fuel a bitter rivalry, and the contemporary political realities of life in my home city of Jerusalem aggravate those historic tensions.[3] However, these undeniable tensions and even the violence and terrorism to which they sometimes lead, while they make our task much more difficult, do not free us from seeking a genuine interreligious encounter; they render it all the more vital and urgent. In the words of Rabbi Tarfon (late first - early second centuries of the common era): "You are not obligated to complete the task, nor are you free to shirk it" (*Mishnah*, *Avot* 2:21).

On the Correlation between the Ritual and the Spiritual

It would be naive optimism to see in religion an unquestioning positive potential for meeting global challenges, especially in the light of past historical records, and present, shattering atrocities committed in the name of religion, or worse still, with religious sanction.

We would like to think of religion as restraining and refining our base instincts. Indeed, the English word "religion" is derived from the Latin "religio", which some scholars think to be derived from "religare", to bind or tie. The Hebrew word often used for religion, "dat", actually means "law". And in Arabic, at least one usage of the term "din", religion, also denotes "judgement".[4]

So if our three western cultures are in agreement, at least etymologically, that religion involves some kind of restraining influence, it would appear that religion has failed people miserably. That, at least, is a popular contemporary conclusion.

Our problem, however, is not a modern one. The biblical prophets of ancient Israel considered the same problem but arrived at the opposite conclusion, that the people had failed religion. Their eloquent criticism of the ritual behaviour of their contemporaries is typified by Isaiah:

What is the multitude of your sacrifices to me? says the Lord. I am satiated with the burnt offerings of rams and the fat of fed beasts, and I do not desire the blood of bullocks and lambs and goats. When you come to appear before me, who requested this of you, to trample my courtyards? ... My being hates your new moons and festivals; they have become a burden to me [which] I am weary of bearing. When you spread your hands, I will hide my eyes from you; even when you make many prayers, I do not hear, [for] your hands are full of blood (Isaiah 1,11-15).

The people's attempt to repent ritually is equally perverse. In the words of Isaiah read to this day in the synagogue on *Yom Kippur*, the Day of Atonement, which dramatically epitomizes the problem of the correlation between the ritual and the spiritual dimensions of life:

Call out, spare not, lift up your voice like the ram's horn, and tell my people of their crime, and the household of Jacob their sins. They seek me every day, and desire to know my ways. Like a nation which has done righteousness and has not abandoned the ordinances of its God, they ask me for righteous ordinances and desire the nearness of God, [saying] "Why have we fasted, and you have not seen; why have we afflicted ourselves, and you have not known?"... Is such the fast I have chosen, a day on which a person afflicts himself, bowing his head like a bullrush, spreading sack-cloth and ashes? Is this what you call a fast and a day acceptable to the Lord? Is not this the fast which I choose: Open the fetters of evil, loosen the bonds of the yoke, let the oppressed go free, break every yoke. Is it not to offer your bread to the hungry, and to bring the homeless into your home? When you see someone naked, to cover him, and not to ignore your fellow flesh? Then will your light break forth like the dawn, and your healing will quickly flourish; your righteousness will go before you, and the glory of the Lord will follow you. Then you will call, and the Lord will answer, you will cry out, and He will say, "Here I am" (Isaiah 58,1-9).

We would be sadly mistaken, however, if we were to interpret Isaiah here, and other prophets elsewhere, as opposing ritual, and as favouring some kind of vague and abstract ethic, as if people in their day - as in our day - did not have a basic need for ritual. What the prophets like Isaiah opposed was not ritual *per se*; throughout the prophetic literature we find constant and consistent reaffirmation of ritual and of the Temple cult. What the prophets of Israel opposed was the desecration and violation of proper ritual by treating it as magic, as if a ritual act itself has some kind of power to force God to do one's will without any inherent correlation to one's ethical obligations. The problem, then, is not ritual behaviour in worshipping God. The problem, rather, is the perversion of ritual by ignoring its ethical and spiritual dimension.

The rabbis of the Talmud (in the centuries immediately preceding and following the time of Jesus) correctly understood the earlier message of the prophets when they chose for the Torah portion read in the synagogue on *Yom Kippur* morning an extremely ritualistic passage from Leviticus 16, describing the atonement ceremonies of the High Priest in the Temple, and then complemented that Torah portion with Isaiah 58. For the two passages, Leviticus and Isaiah, are not opposed, and they do not teach different lessons. The rabbis, like the prophets before them, intuitively understood that the ritual dimension of Leviticus and the ethical dimension of Isaiah are, in fact, complementary.

Think, for a moment, of such categories as "universal and particular", "mountain and valley", "heads and tails". These are not opposite but correlative notions. They do not contradict or negate each other. Rather, each is necessary for the other to exist; neither notion is complete, or can even exist, without the other. Their true existence is co-existence.

That is also, I suggest, the relationship of the ritual and the spiritual (including ethical) dimensions of religion, as demanded by the Torah and the prophets. Clearly, when we, today, follow the ritual letter of the religious law while ignoring its ethical spirit, we, like our ancestors, are guilty of perverting the very meaning of religion, and engaging in impotent magic rather than true worship of God.

For ritual cannot function alone. It has no independent magical power to change the baseness of our lives into something spiritually precious. It is only in concert with a genuine spiritual commitment, based first and foremost on ethical responsibility, that ritual has any power in our lives. Like a catalyst in a chemical reaction, ritual can bring about a change in us only when the proper spiritual and ethical ingredients are present. Without those ingredients, no spiritual reaction takes place, and we remain unchanged. Indeed, if anything at all has changed, it is for the worse, because like the people fooled by the false gold of alchemy, we have deluded ourselves into thinking that we have been refined, whereas in fact we have not truly changed at all.

The Ritual Dimension

Let us now consider the question from the opposite perspective. The prophets, of course, condemned the Jewish people's perversion of ritual.

But if the function of ritual is to be a spiritual and ethical "catalytic converter" in our lives, perhaps we can attain the ethical and spiritual ends without resorting to the ritual means. Why is the ritual dimension important or necessary, especially when so often it has been, and continues to be, perverted?

If we were disembodied spiritual beings, some kind of angels in the medieval cosmology, perhaps one could argue the point successfully. However, we are not. We are fundamentally creatures of this earth, albeit in the image of God, and we have our basic material, physical, emotional, social and political needs.

This does not mean, however, that our being terrestrial creatures, with all kinds of differing and occasionally conflicting needs and desires, necessarily condemns us to violating our ethical responsibilities. Such a view would scarcely be compatible with the imperative of *teshuvah*, literally a turning or returning, a change in ethical direction, the repentance which is at the heart of much of the ritual behaviour prescribed in the Torah, and which implies the ability to change radically and for the better.

Contrary to much of the classical Christian interpretation, and to some minority Jewish interpretation, of original sin, according to which sin is the condition in which we all live, and all humans inevitably sin because of Adam and Eve's original sin in Eden, the concept of *teshuvah* taught in the Bible, Talmud and later Jewish literature offers ethical encouragement.

Understood in this light, what the story in Genesis teaches is not the inevitability of sin, but the opportunity to sin. As Martin Buber interpreted this story, we do not sin because Adam and Eve sinned, but we sin as they sinned. "If you do not do well", God says to Cain, "sin lies at the door". The door is open, but where does the Torah say here that the person must inevitably pass through it? To the contrary, the Torah assures Cain and us that evil's "desire is for you, but you can control it" (Gen 4,7).[5]

Since the opportunity to sin is a constant of our complex lives, we need regular, if not constant reminders of our ethical obligations, and we need to set aside fixed, regular times in our lives for the kind of periodic review and reappraisal that constitute true *teshuvah*.

We humans seem to need ritual in many areas of our lives. We celebrate birthdays and anniversaries, to express our love for our family, and to give ourselves a feeling, at least one day a year, of being special. Husbands and wives often wear a ring or have some other tangible reminder of the exclusivity of the marital relationship and of their devotion to each other. Nations have flags which provide a symbolic focus for patriotic feeling, and they observe national days celebrating their independence and victories and mourning their losses.

Indeed, those nations which, in the twentieth century, often attempted to deprive their people of genuine religious ritual often invested their national rituals with a religious sort of fervour.

So ritual, whether religious or secular, and on whatever level - personal, familial, social or national - seems to fulfil basic human needs for regular and symbolic expression of some of our deepest feelings.

Granted, then, that our external rituals, such as the Jewish rituals of *teshuvah* on *Yom Kippur*, are all too often devoid of inner spiritual content, and fail to change our ethical direction, would we really be more likely to experience a genuine spiritual *teshuvah*, personal and collective, purely spontaneously, without any tangible or symbolic reminders? The ritual catalyst may, unfortunately, lead only a fraction of the time to a spiritual reaction, but unless we try the many times, we shall not succeed even the few times. Again, the ritual alone has no independent or magical power to change anything. It can only bring about the desired reaction when we provide the necessary spiritual ingredients.

Matter of Recognition

The correlation of the ritual and spiritual dimensions of ritual, again as exemplified by *Yom Kippur*, was emphatically recognized, not only by later Jewish philosophers but by the earlier Talmudic rabbis of classical times. One of the key biblical verses recited repeatedly in the rituals of *Yom Kippur* is Leviticus 16,30: "For on this day will there be atonement for you, to purify you from all of your sins, before the Lord be pure."

The Torah does not say here that "this day (*ha-yom*) will atone for you", but "on this day (*ba-yom*) will there be atonement for you". The ritual observance of the Day of Atonement itself cannot effect the atonement. What, then, happens "on this day"?

The interpretation of this verse of Rabbi El'azar ben 'Azariah (late first century - early second century of the common era) teaches a fundamental lesson about the ritual-spiritual correlation: "From all of your sins, before the Lord be pure." *Yom Kippur* can atone for the transgressions between a person and God (*bein adam la-maqom*), but *Yom Kippur* cannot atone for transgressions between a person and another person (*bein adam le-havero*) until he satisfies the other person.[6]

In other words, when the offence is purely ritual, and involves no harm to another person, the atonement rectifying the offence is also purely ritual: the ceremonial observance of *Yom Kippur* itself suffices. First one has the ritual ceremonies (the first half of the verse: "For on this day will there be atonement for you, to purify you"), and then one is ritually pure before God (the second half of the verse: "From all of your sins, before the Lord be pure").

However, ritual, again, is not magic, and when the offence has involved harming another person, the ritual cannot take effect, and cannot even be initiated, until the offender rights the wrong and satisfies the person he has harmed. Only then can he engage in the ritual ceremonies of atonement.

Rabbinic Judaism thus sees our verse as teaching both the importance of ritual (the ceremonies of *Yom Kippur* can lead to purity before God) and also the limitations of ritual (the ceremonies of atonement cannot, in themselves, have any effect until the prior ethical conditions are fulfilled).

What is essential here, and cannot be over-emphasized, is that the ritual-spiritual correlation, with its ethical dimension, is not superimposed upon Leviticus by later Judaism - whether of the biblical prophets, the Talmudic Rabbis, or the medieval philosophers; it is a fundamental feature of the Levitical system itself.

The Book of Leviticus, which epitomizes more than any other section the Bible's concern for formal, external ritual behaviour, begins by describing various types of sacrifices to be offered on different occasions and for various offences. Then, in Chapter 5,20-26 in the Hebrew Bible (in Christian Bibles, Chapter 6,1-7), the Torah cites for the first time the case of an offence involving harming another person:

The Lord spoke to Moses, saying: When a person sins and commits a trespass against the Lord by dealing deceitfully with his fellow in the matter of a deposit or a pledge, or through robbery, or by defrauding his fellow, or by finding a lost object and lying about it; if he swears falsely regarding any one of the various things that one may do and sin thereby, when one has thus sinned and, realizing his guilt, would restore that which he got through robbery or fraud, or the deposit that was entrusted to him, or the lost thing that he found, or anything else about which he swore falsely, he shall repay the principal amount and add a fifth part to it. He shall pay it to its owner when he realizes his guilt. Then he shall bring to the priest, as his penalty to the Lord, a ram without blemish from the flock, or the equivalent, as a guilt offering.

In other words, the person could not bring his guilt offering to the Lord until he had first compensated the person he had harmed, adding a 20% penalty to the principal owed. Only then, when he had righted the ethical wrong, could he begin his ritual ceremony of atonement before God. The ethical dimension of the ritual-spiritual correlation is thus built into the very structure of the ceremonies of Leviticus.

Although many people have ignored or overlooked this fact, in a sense it really need not surprise us. Ritual was, and is, after all, a fundamental feature of the covenant between Israel and God, a covenant the foundation of which was always, from its very inception with Abraham, ethical.

Consider the contrast between Noah and Abraham. When Noah was informed of the impending destruction of the whole world, he uttered no protest, and simply made the necessary preparations to save himself and his family. In the case of Abraham, on the other hand, when God was about to destroy the wicked towns of Sodom and Gomorrah, the Torah states that:

The Lord said: Shall I cover up from Abraham what I am about to do? For Abraham will surely become a great and mighty nation, through whom all the nations of the earth will be blessed. I have known him, that he might command his children and his household after him, to observe the way of the Lord, to do righteousness and justice (Gen 18,17-19).

Ethics is not tangential to the covenant; it lies at its very foundation, and it gives it ultimate direction and meaning. That is why Abraham, and not Noah, could legitimately challenge God, as God's ethical covenantal partner: "Forbid it to you, to do such a thing, to kill the righteous together with the wicked, so that it would be the same for the righteous and the wicked. Forbid it to you. Will the judge of all the earth not do justice?" (Gen 18,25).

On the Meaning of the Covenant and Chosenness

The issue of the ethical foundation, direction and meaning of the covenant brings us back to our original question of spiritual and ritual exclusivity and inclusivity. As I have suggested elsewhere,[7] the Jewish concept of the chosen people, and its correlative concept of the covenant (*berit*, which etymologically also denotes choice), while exclusive in the ritual sense that the laws of the Torah apply only to the Jewish people, is by no means spiritually exclusive. On the contrary, the overwhelming textual evidence throughout Jewish literature from the Bible down to our own day leads to the conclusion that chosenness implies no spiritual exclusivity, specifically with regard to salvation, however defined.

This is in sharp contrast with Pauline Christianity's understanding of Genesis and of the human condition. According to this view, because of Adam and Eve's original sin, all people are in a state of sin, which precludes their meriting salvation. Paul then interpreted Habakuk 2,4, "the righteous will live by his faithfulness" as meaning it is through faith (*pistis*) that a person can attain the eternal life of salvation.[8] In the words of Paul: "For I am not ashamed of the Gospel; it is the power of God for salvation to every one who has faith, to the Jew first and also to the Greek. For in it the righteousness of God is revealed through faith for faith, as it is written, 'He who through faith is righteous shall live'"(Romans 1,16-17). "Now it is evident that no man is justified before God by the law; for He who through faith is righteous shall live" (Galatians 3,11).

The Pauline logic is consistent: because of original sin, salvation cannot be merited by the deeds of the law, but is attainable only through faith in Jesus as the Christ. This doctrine, combined with Jesus's explicit statement that "I am the way and the truth and the life; no one comes to the father except by me" (John 14,6) accordingly leads, in much of classical Christianity, to an exclusivistic view of salvation.

The consistency of the Pauline view notwithstanding, even those minority Jewish views which draw some kind of causal connection between what Adam and Eve did and how we behave, do not, and could not, thereby conclude that the precepts of the Torah are to be replaced by a system of faith as the basis for salvation. Rather, from a Jewish perspective, the exclusivity of the Christian scheme of salvation is understood to be inconsistent with divine justice. Even such an early modern proponent of enlightened Jewish-Christian dialogue as Moses Mendelssohn (Germany, 1729-1786) minced no words on this Christian spiritual exclusivism: "Inasmuch as all men must have been destined by their Creator to attain salvation, no particular religion can be exclusively true ... A revelation that claims to be the one and only road to salvation cannot be true, for it is not in harmony with the intent of the all-merciful Creator."[9]

The statement of the ancient Talmudic sages, which became normative in rabbinic Judaism, and was codified by Rabbi Moses Maimonides (1135- 1204), is that "the righteous of the nations of the world have a portion in the world to come" (*hasidei umot ha-'olam yesh la-hem helek la-'olam ha-ba*).[10]

Who are these righteous gentiles who share in this spiritually inclusive view of salvation? According to Maimonides,[11] they are non-Jews who follow what the Talmudic rabbis called "the seven commandments of the children of Noah". These seven principles, which the rabbis deduced from Genesis, are (1) the prohibition of idolatry, (2) the prohibition of blasphemy, (3) the prohibition of murder, (4) the prohibition of incest and adultery, (5) the prohibition of theft, (6) the prohibition of eating a limb of a living animal, and (7) the requirement to establish a legal system of justice.[12]

Regardless of how these principles were specifically deduced by Jewish tradition, and whatever their precise meaning and authority, what is clear is that they are consistently regarded not as Jewish laws but as universal. They were given to Adam and Noah, the progenitors of all humans. Their universal priority to the national laws given to the Jewish people in the Torah is thus both logical and chronological. In basic terms, from a Jewish perspective, they are the laws upon which any just and ethical society must be founded, and they provide the standard to which all people are expected to adhere.

Special Obligations

The Jewish people, however, because of their particular covenant with God going back to Abraham, have the additional obligations of the Torah, which according to Jewish tradition embodies 613 commandments. So when a Jew violates his ethical responsibilities, he has, in effect, transgressed doubly. The ethical violation is always inherently wrong for anyone. But for a Jew, who has special covenantal responsibilities, the violation is also of obligations imposed by the Torah.

The difference between Jew and non-Jew, however, is not merely quantitative, in other words: the non-Jew is obligated by the seven commandments of the children of Noah, whereas the Jew is obligated by the 613 commandments of the Torah. The difference is also, in another sense, qualitative. Even in reference to the violation of the basic ethical precepts common to Jews and non-Jews, the Jew should know better, because of the special obligations of the covenant.

On the one hand, all people are equally precious, and equally obligated ethically. Therefore, according to the prophet Amos, "Are you not like the Africans to me, Israel, says the Lord" (Amos 9,7). On the other hand, the same prophet also refers to Israel's unique covenantal relationship with God: "Only you have I known among all the families of the earth; therefore I will inflict on you all of your transgressions" (Amos 3,2). These two statements are not at all inconsistent, as might at first appear. In the first case, Amos is saying that the Jews are in fact no better, and no more precious to God, than anyone else. In the second case, the prophet is challenging the Jews to be better, not than others, but than they themselves are. Because they have a special relationship with God, they are more accountable for their failures. The covenant grants no special privileges; it imposes special responsibilities.

This perspective on chosenness can perhaps be understood in terms of the standards that parents apply to their children. When the child comes home, and the parents find out the child has done something wrong, and ask, "You know that's wrong. Why did you do it?", to which, if the child doesn't say, "I don't know", he or she is likely to respond, "But everyone was doing it.", typically, then, the parents will reply, "It doesn't matter what everyone else was doing. You are our child, and we expect more of you." The point here is not that the child is, in fact, better than the other children. In fact, he or she is not. Rather, the parents are telling the child that because they love him or her, they expect more, whatever others may do. It is this love which imposes special responsibilities.

Similarly, it is the covenantal love between God and "Abraham, my lover" (in the phrase of Isaiah 41,8) which makes for the difference not only between Noah and Abraham, referred to previously, but also between Job and Abraham. Job, like Noah, is described as innocent (*tam* or *tamim*).[13] Neither, however, is a member of the chosen people. Noah, of course, antedates the covenant. In the case of Job, there is no evidence to indicate his precise identity, although his country 'Uz and the ethnic background of the other characters in the book are not Israelite. In any event, the ethical dilemmas raised by Job are not specifically Jewish. The problems of evil, injustice and the suffering of the innocent are fundamental human problems of universal import.

We have already noted that Noah does not argue with God over the impending destruction of the world. Job, like Abraham, does argue with God. But contrast God's response to Job with the response to Abraham. God replies to Job "out of the storm", saying: "Who is this who darkens counsel by words without knowledge? . . . Where were you when I founded the earth?" (Job 38,2-4). Why does God resort to such an *ad hominem* argument to disqualify Job's challenge, whereas Abraham's challenge is accepted? Abraham also was not present at the creation, and was equally ignorant of the sky's measure.

The answer, I believe, is that the intimacy of the covenant permits, and the higher ethical responsibility of the covenant requires, Abraham to challenge divine injustice. God, as the source of justice, must be just, and as Abraham's loving covenantal partner, God must respond to the challenge.

The ritual and the spiritual dimensions of the covenant are thus intertwined and correlative. The Jews are expected to be "a kingdom of priests and a holy nation" (*mamlekhet kohanim ve-goy kadosh*), in the words of Exodus 19,6. The Hebrew term *kadosh*, usually translated as "holy", denotes something distinctive, different or special. That is why it is the term for the marital relationship (*kiddushin*), in which the husband and wife "sanctify" or "hallow" each other by the exclusive nature of their relationship, which makes them "special" to each other and "different" from all others.

The ethical imperative follows from, but also requires, a sense of being special or distinctive: behaviour which may be permitted or at least tolerated in someone else is unacceptable in someone special. Therefore, the code of holiness begins with the Israelites being told, "You be holy, for I, the Lord your God, am holy" (Leviticus 19,2).

Such distinctiveness is fostered by rituals, such as the dietary laws of *kashrut*, which effectively distinguish the Jews from their neighbours. Indeed, in sharp contrast with later theories which allege various

physical benefits as accruing to those who observe the laws, the Torah
never promises "lengthening of days" for the observance of the ritual
laws of *kashrut*, as it does for some other laws of a moral nature
elsewhere. All the Torah itself says is that kashrut serves to distinguish
the Jews as a "holy nation":

Differentiate between the pure beasts and the impure, between the impure
birds and the pure, and do not make yourselves abominable with any beast or
bird or whatever crawls on the earth, which I have differentiated from you as
impure. You should be holy for me, for I the Lord am holy, and I differentiate
you from the nations to be mine (Leviticus 20,25-26).

For you are a holy people to the Lord your God, and the Lord has chosen you
from all the peoples on the face of the earth to be his special people. Do not eat
any abomination ... For you are a holy nation to the Lord your God; do not cook
the kid in its mother's milk. (Deuteronomy 14,2-3. 32; cf. Exodus 22,30 and
Leviticus 11,44-47).

This sense of ritual distinctiveness, engendered by exclusive
ceremonial laws, can foster a distinctive sense of ethical responsibility,
a kind of *noblesse oblige*. Ethical responsibility, in turn, requires a sense
of distinctive obligation, not to follow prevalent, popular patterns of
behaviour, which again reinforces the need for ritual distinctions. The
ritual and the spiritual dimensions of the covenant are thus correlative:
neither is prior to the other. The ritual and the spiritual are mutually
necessary and interdependent.

The Alternatives

What are the alternatives to this view of ritual-spiritual correlation?
The first is to suggest that ritual behaviour does not have any inherent
relationship to spiritual meaning and ethical behaviour. This option
would mean that ritual is a kind of pagan magic. No matter how we live,
no matter how much we may harm other people as well as ourselves by
our behavior, this view holds that there are ritual ways in which we can
force the divine records to be cleansed, without any further human effort
or ethical responsibility on our part. It is magic because it suggests that
we can change reality without any regard for natural or ethical
causality and consequences. It is pagan because it affirms divine forces
which lack any unitary coherence; forces which either are capricious, or,
conversely, can be manipulated to one's own whims. Unfortunately
there are still many pagans in the world, who unknowingly practise
ritual magic, including some nominally religious Jews.

The second option, if my view of the ritual-spiritual correlation is incorrect, is to suggest, along with various philosophers, including most prominently the late Professor Yeshaiah Leibowitz in Israel, that ritual behaviour is simply and purely a matter of obeying divine commandments. The commandments have, or need have, no inherent spiritual or ethical meaning, nor need they offer us any utilitarian benefit. They are given in order to be observed, out of a loving obedience to the divine will, the obedience of one who serves God out of love, without any expectation of reward. This view, while popular in certain Orthodox circles, is rejected out of hand by Maimonides,[14] for whom the ideal person is also the one who serves God out of love, without expectation of reward. For Maimonides, however, the person's motivation to serve out of love, rather than out of a selfish concern for reward, should not be confused with the purpose of the commandments, which are beneficial to people. Leibowitz's view of obedience for its own sake also fails, to my way of thinking, because it reduces us to automatons blindly following orders, and renders our religious behaviour totally mechanical. I should prefer to think that behaviour in which we invest so much time and effort has some inherent worth.

If both these options, which sunder the ritual-spiritual correlation and render ritual either pagan magic or inherently meaningless, are unacceptable, then we are left with the view, which is also that of Maimonides, that ritual behaviour is supposed to benefit, enhance and refine the lives of the people who sincerely engage in it. Thus, commandments preventing cruelty to animals, for example, are motivated not by concern for the animals *per se*, but by the need to refine human behaviour.[15] As Rabbi Moses ben Nahman (1194-1270) extended Maimonides's argument,[16] ritual commandments cannot be construed as benefiting God, as if God needed the light of the candelabrum (*menorah*) in the Temple, or the food of the sacrifices, or to be reminded of the miracles He had performed. In all these cases, "there is no benefit to [God], except that we should know the truth." The purpose of such commandments as prohibiting the slaughter of an animal and its young on the same day (Leviticus 22,28) and the requirement to chase away the mother bird before taking its chicks or eggs (Deuteronomy 22,6) similarly cannot be simple compassion for the animals, "for in that case it should have prohibited slaughtering" animals altogether.

Rather, the reason for the prohibition is to teach us the quality of compassion, so that we might not be cruel ... These commandments concerning beasts and birds are not compassion for them, but rather are injunctions for us, to guide and teach us good qualities.

The ritual-spiritual correlation, which is so fundamental to the concept of the covenant, can aid us in clarifying a popular misunderstanding, among Jews and non-Jews alike, of the related concept of the chosen people. Chosenness, as presented in the classical sources from the Bible down to our day, is not an externally directed, comparative category, in which the Jews, individually and collectively, are compared to other people and nations. Even such an ardent nationalist as the great medieval Hebrew poet and philosopher Judah Ha-Levi (1085-1141) recognized, in all honesty, that Jews are, in fact, no better ethically and no more intelligent or wiser than any other people.[17]

Indeed, if I may be permitted a digression on this point, one of the pleasures of interreligious dialogue today is the recognition that our partners in dialogue are no less fully human, no less intelligent, reasonable, educated, sensitive or moral than we would like to think we ourselves are. Many people, children or spiritually and morally immature adults, when they first learn of the beliefs of other people, react instinctively by saying (or at least thinking), "How can anyone seriously believe that?" Genuine interreligious dialogue should teach us to be rather less smug about our own beliefs and assumptions, which turn out to be not quite as self-evident as we had previously thought, and rather more respectful of the spiritual and intellectual, as well as the moral integrity of the beliefs and assumptions of others.

Which of us, after all, can be absolutely certain that he or she, as an individual or as a member of a particular religious community, has attained perfect knowledge of the objective truth? Is this what the Psalmist expected of us when he said, "The Lord is close to all who call Him, to all who call Him in truth (*be-emet*)" (Psalm 145,18)? We often misunderstand the qualifier "in truth" (*be-emet*), which the Septuagint rendered literally as *en aletheia*, and the Vulgate similarly as *in veritate*. Luther correctly avoided translating the qualifier cognitively, rendering it instead as "*die ihn mit Ernst anrufen*", although I don't think the Psalmist meant "earnestly". Moses Mendelssohn was more on the mark when he translated it as "*die aufrichtig ihn anrufen*".[18] This rendition of *be-emet* as "sincerely" reflects the comment of the medieval rationalist Bible exegete and grammarian Rabbi David Kimhi (c. 1160-1235), with whose commentaries Mendelssohn was familiar, as were Christian Hebraists at the time of the Reformation. Kimhi, whose exegetical works are replete with anti-Christian polemic, nevertheless interprets "the Lord is close to all who call Him" as meaning: from whatever nation he may be, so long as he calls him in truth, that his mouth and heart may be the same. The Psalmist, then, does not limit God's accessibility and proximity to those who know the truth, but extends it to all who are sincere in their approach.

Returning, then, to chosenness, it is not externally directed. Rather, chosenness is internally directed. It does not mean that Jews are in fact better than others, but challenges them to better themselves. Chosenness reminds Jews that they should become better people.

Chosenness and covenant thus understood as internally-directed challenges to the Jewish people are fully compatible with spiritual inclusivity and genuine acceptance of other religious traditions.

On one level the covenant thus sets the Jews as a people apart from other nations. On a ritual level, its exclusivity is explicit, in the positive sense that Jews have no reason to expect others to adopt exclusively Jewish ritual obligations, and can, within the context of their own particular covenant, accept other religious traditions as legitimate and valid for their own adherents. Of course, such recognition and acceptance will only be complete if they are genuinely mutual.

Thus it is precisely this ritual exclusivity which permits, and even mandates, a spiritual inclusivity, since the "seven commandments of the children of Noah" provide a pluralistic paradigm for universal knowledge of the truth, basic moral obligation, and participation in salvation. This is not a universalism of uniformity but of diversity, a diversity ever enhanced and furthered by mutual respect, so that in the words of the prophet Micah: "Let all the peoples walk, each one in the name of its God, and we will walk in the name of the Lord our God forever" (Micah 4,5).[19]

Notes

1. For the discussion of these points, see Jospe, R. (1981), 'Faith and Reason: The Controversy Over Philosophy' in Jospe, R. & Wagner, S. (eds.) (1981), *Great Schisms in Jewish History*, New York, Ktav: pp. 73-117; rev. edn., 'Faith and Reason: The Controversy Over Philosophy in Jewish History' in Kajon, I. (ed.) (1993), *La Storia della Filosofia Ebraica*, Milan: pp. 99-135.

2. In his seminal essay 'Auto-Emancipation: An Appeal to His People by a Russian Jew' (1882), Leo Pinsker (1821-1891) similarly argued that emancipation and tolerance are no less degrading than persecution, because whether tolerated or persecuted, the status of the Jews as a minority everywhere is always determined by the majority. Even a tolerated minority thus never attains equality with the majority, because it never enjoys self-determination, and remains dependent on the good will of the majority.

3. Cf. Jospe, R. (1993). 'Jerusalem's Significance in Scripture and Tradition: A Jewish Perspective', pp. 38-56 in Ucko, H. (ed.) (1994), *The Spiritual Significance of Jerusalem for Jews, Christians and Muslims*, Geneva, World Council of Churches.

4. *The Oxford English Dictionary* lists possible derivations for "religion". The Hebrew term "dat" (law) is found exclusively in such late biblical books from the Persian period as Esther and Ezra, with the problematical exception of the phrase "esh dat" (a fiery law?) in Deuteronomy 33:2. The Arabic "din" generally means religion, but is

also used in the Qur'an for judgement, as in the phrase "king of the Day of Judgement" (*yaum al-din*) (Surah 1:4, Al-Fatihah). For a discussion of this term, and the possibility of its being borrowed from the Hebrew *yom ha-din* or Aramaic cognates, cf. Jeffery, A. (1938),*The Foreign Vocabulary of the Qur'an,* Baroda: pp. 131-133.

5. Note the similarity of phrasing here with Genesis 3,16, where the woman's "desire is for your husband, and he will rule over you".

6. Mishnah, end of tractate *Yoma,* Ch. 8:9, and Midrash, Sifra on Leviticus, Aharei Mot, Ch. 8 (Venice ed.), p. 166.

7. For a more complete discussion, see Jospe, R. (1994), 'The Concept of the Chosen People: An Interpretation', *Judaism: A Quarterly Journal* 43 (2): pp. 127-148.

8. For a different reading of this passage and concept in a Jewish context, see the discussion in my 'Faith and Reason' article, see note 1 above: pp. 76-77 (rev. edn.: pp. 102-103), and in 'The Concept of the Chosen People', see note 7 above: pp. 131-133.

9. Cf. Mendelssohn, M. (1969). 'Letter to Prince Karl-Wilhelm', pp. 126-127 in Jospe, A. (ed.). *Jerusalem and Other Jewish Writings*, New York, Schocken; Jospe, E. (ed.)(1975), *Moses Mendelssohn: Selections From His Writings*, New York, Viking: pp. 116-117.

10. Maimonides, M. (1927). *Mishneh Torah* (Code of Law), Book of Knowledge, Laws of Repentance 3:5. English trans. (1927), New York, Simon Glazer: p. 397; and Hyamson, M. (1937/1971). *Jerusalem*, vol.1, Feldheim Publishers: pp. 84-86.

11. Maimonides, M. (1979): *Mishneh Torah* (Code of Law), Book of Judges, Laws of Kings 8:11, New Haven, Yale University Press; cited in Twersky, I. (1972), *A Maimonides Reader*, New York, Behrman House: p. 221. Cf. Zuckermandel and Lieberman (eds.). *Tosefta*, 'Avodah Zarah' 8:4: p. 473; and Babylonian Talmud, Sanhedrin 56a.

12. Cf. the extensive treatment of the seven Noachide laws in Novak, D. (ed.) (1983), *The Image of the Non-Jew in Judaism,* New York. For a brief survey, cf. 'Noachide Laws', *Encyclopedia Judaica* , vol. 12: pp. 1189-1191.

13. Genesis 69 and Job 1,1.

14. Maimonides, *Guide of the Perplexed* 3:48, rejects "the opinion of those who think that there is no reason for the Law except only the will [of God]". Cf. English trans. (1963), Chicago, University of Chicago Press, Shlomo Pines: p. 600. Maimonides also strongly argues (in *Guide of the Perplexed* 3:31) that to deny that the law has some reason and serves some beneficial purpose, whether or not immediately evident to us, is to impute imperfection to the Torah. A law which serves no beneficial purpose is clearly imperfect, and may, Maimonides suggests, even be harmful. Moreover, according to Maimonides (in *Guide of the Perplexed* 3:25), the notion that God does things merely as an expression

of His will which serve no such beneficial purpose is to render God's actions either futile (aiming at no real end) or frivolous (aiming at some low or meaningless end). Cf. Pines edn.: p. 504.

15. *Guide of the Perplexed* 3:26. Cf. Pines edn.: p. 508.

16. Ben Nahman, M., *Commentary to Deuteronomy* 22:6.

17. Ha-Levi, J., *The Kuzari* 2:48 and 3:7. On Ha-Levi's theory of Jewish particularity, see my article 'Jewish Particularity from Ha-Levi to Kaplan: Implications for Defining Jewish Philosophy', pp. 307-325 in Jospe, R. and Fishman, S. (eds.) (1980), *Go and Study: Essays and Studies in Honour of Alfred Jospe*, New York, Ktav; Jospe, R. (1982), *Forum on the Jewish People, Zionism and Israel* 46-47 (Fall-Winter): pp. 77-90.

18. On Mendelssohn's Psalms translation, see Altmann, A. (1973), *Moses Mendelssohn: A Biographical Study,* University of Alabama: pp. 242-244.

19. Micah 4,5. This verse is problematical, because it appears to contradict the earlier verses in the chapter, asserting that all nations will come to worship God in the Temple in Jerusalem. Some (including the Aramaic Targum and Rashi) therefore interpret this verse in a negative light: the nations are idolators, whereas we worship the true God. Others see this verse as referring to the present state of affairs, whereas the earlier verses refer to the ideal state in Messianic times. Still others interpret the verse in the pluralistic sense in which I am citing it. Admittedly, the pluralistic reading of the verse puts it into a dynamic tension with the other verses, but it seems to me that this is precisely the tension the prophet may have intended to create, and it is certainly the tension in which we live, between a universalism which must not be too monolithic and a pluralism which must avoid complete relativism.

Eloquent precedents for such religious pluralism without relativism may be found in the political philosophy of the Age of Reason in the eighteenth century, which gave rise to such interrelated developments as the Enlightenment and emancipation of the Jews in Europe and the American Revolution in the New World. It need, therefore, not surprise us to find similar arguments in the writings of such diverse authors as Moses Mendelssohn (1729-1786) in Germany and Thomas Jefferson (1743- 1826) in the U.S.A. Mendelssohn, who took an active interest in the American Revolution, concludes his *Jerusalem, Or On Religious Power and Judaism* (1783) with an argument against uniformity (having already argued against the possibility of religious coercion). Addressing Christian rulers, Mendelssohn says:

A union of faiths, if it were ever to come about, could have only the most disastrous consequences for reason and freedom of conscience ... If the goal of this universal delusion were to be realized, I am afraid man's barely liberated mind would once again be confined behind bars ... If you care for true godliness, let us not pretend that conformity exists where diversity is obviously the plan and goal of Providence. Not one among us thinks and feels exactly like his fellowmen. Why, then, should we deceive each other with lies? ... Why should we use masks to make ourselves unrecognizable to each other in the most important concerns of life, when God has given each of us his own distinctive face for some good reason? ... A union of faiths is not tolerance. It is the very opposite. For the sake of your happiness and ours, do not use your powerful prestige to give the force of law to some eternal truth that is immaterial to civic well-being; do not transform some religious doctrine to which the state is indifferent into a statute of the land! Concentrate on what men should or should not do; judge them wisely by their actions; and let us retain the freedom of thought and speech with which the Father of all mankind has endowed us as our inalienable heritage and immutable right ... Let no one usurp a right which the Omniscient has reserved to Himself. If we render unto Caesar what is Caesar's, then let us also render unto God what is God's. Love truth! Love peace!

Cf. Jospe, A. (ed.), *Jerusalem and Other Jewish Writings*, see note 9 above: pp. 108-110.

Thomas Jefferson similarly wrote in his "Notes on Virginia", Query 17:

The rights of conscience we never submitted, we could not submit. We are answerable for them to our God. The legitimate powers of government extend to such acts only as are injurious to others ... Reason and free inquiry are the only effectual agents against error... It is error alone which needs the support of government. Truth can stand by itself ... Is uniformity of opinion desirable? ... Difference of opinion is advantageous in religion. The several sects perform the office of a *censor morum* of such other. Is uniformity attainable? Millions of innocent men, women, and children ... have been burnt, tortured, fined, imprisoned; yet we have not advanced an inch towards uniformity. What has been the effect of coercion? To make one half the world fools, and the other half hypocrites.

In the same year (1786) that Mendelssohn died, Jefferson authored the "Act Establishing Religious Freedom Passed in the Assembly of Virginia", which he regarded as one of his greatest accomplishments:

Well aware that Almighty God hath created the mind free; that all attempts to influence it by temporal punishments or burdens, or by civil incapacitations, tend only to beget habits of hypocrisy and meanness, and are a departure from the plan of the Holy Author of our religion, who being Lord both of body and mind, yet chose not to propagate it by coercion on either, as was in his Almighty power to do ... That it is time enough for the rightful purposes of civil government, for its officers to interfere when principles break out into overt acts against peace and good order; and finally, that truth is great and will prevail if left to herself ... Be it therefore enacted by the General Assembly, that no man shall be compelled to frequent or support any religious worship, place or ministry whatsoever, nor shall be enforced, restrained, molested, or burthened in his body or goods, nor shall otherwise suffer on account of his religious opinions or belief; but that all men shall be free to profess, and by argument to maintain, their opinions in matters of religion, and that the same shall in no way diminish, enlarge or affect their civil capacities ... That the rights hereby asserted are of the natural rights of mankind, and that if any act shall be hereafter passed to repeal the present or to narrow its operation, such act will be an infringement of natural right".

Cf. Padover, S. (ed.) (1954). *Thomas Jefferson on Democracy*, New York, Mentor Books: pp. 109-114.

5

Abraham's Legacy to Future Generations

ANTHONY ABELA

The Lord said, 'Shall I hide from Abraham what I am about to do', seeing that Abraham shall become a great and mighty nation, and all the nations of the earth shall bless themselves by him? No, for I have chosen him, that he may charge his children and his household after him to keep the way of the Lord by doing righteousness and justice; so that the Lord may bring to Abraham what he has promised him (Gen 18,17-19) (RSV).

This aside comment dropped by the Lord as he leaves Abraham's and Sarah's encampment in order to embark on the last stage of his 'reconnaissance' journey to Sodom and Gomorrah, encapsules a value judgement made by the writer of Israel's 'primary history' inclusive of Genesis - 2 Kings,[1] located as it is at a crucial junction within the Abraham Narrative of Genesis.[2] *Yhwh's* commentary offers clues as to the strong attraction exercised by the figure of Abraham on our historiographer and his generation as to motivate the composition of this 'larger unit'[3] with the patriarch as a main character.[4] The Lord's panegyric sketches the character of the patriarch as *Yhwh's* confidant just as the prophets were (v.17, cf Jer 23; Amos 3, 7),[5] as mediator of universal blessing[6] and especially as called to be teacher and guide to future generations.[7] This is how the writer of Gen 11, 27- 25,18 expressed the relevance of Abraham to his and to subsequent generations.

Two questions come to mind immediately: What was Abraham's message? What important word could he communicate to all his descendants for which he received a divine commission? Who was the writer who composed the Abraham Narrative and for which audience? Modern scholarship conceives of the biblical writers not as simple tradents but as authors and composers who shaped the material they considered worthy of forming the subject-matter upon which to exercise their literary genius. So the question of the writer and his original audience is indispensable to answer if we mean to approach seriously the other query of Abraham's message to future generations contained in his narrative about him. The problem is that neither the question of the historical context in which this unit was written, nor that of Abraham's message, is easy to answer.

Historical Context

We cannot discuss the history of the literary composition of Gen 11, 27-25,18 in complete isolation. It forms part of a larger literary context that comprises at least the Pentateuch and, for some specialists, what scholarship has termed the Deuteronomistic History, that is, Joshua-2 Kings. Although the art of interpreting Scripture goes back to the biblical period itself, a scientific approach in the study of the Bible developed in the eighteenth and nineteenth centuries with the so-called historical-critical method.[8] The development and refinement of this critical study of the Bible, especially the Hebrew Bible, are closely though not exclusively attached to the analysis of this historiographical section.

We shall refrain from recounting in detail the history of this critical research, for which we refer the reader to the accounts in Otto Eissfeldt,[9] Henri Cazelles,[10] Albert de Pury/Thomas Römer,[11] Anthony F. Campbell/Mark A. O'Brien[12] and Joseph Blenkinsopp.[13] Summarising to the extreme we may say that scholarship identified two models of the compositional process that could have occurred as these Scriptures came into being.[14] One model envisages the final form of Genesis-2 Kings as the outcome of a long and slow process of composition, starting with oral traditions that extended back hundreds of years before they finally crystallized into script,[15] and passing through literary units called by scholarship 'documents'. Hence the "Documentary Hypothesis" which in its classical formulation by Julius Wellhausen isolated and identified at least four documents for the Pentateuch[16] and several for the Deuteronomistic History.[17] Till the 1970s, there was consensus as to the relative chronology of the sources/documents and the general consistency of each; but agreement as to the mutual relationship of the sources was not wide-ranging: some would conceive this compositional process as a series of subsequent redactions (Martin Noth);[18] others as the sewing together by presumed 'Redactors' of originally independent documents.[19] According to this model the earliest document/level of redaction called the Yahwist was pre-exilic (possibly Salomonic)[20] while the latest was the 'Priesterkodex' (P) or priestly redaction.[21] Since 1970, the consensus about the pre-exilic origin of the earliest redactions (J or better JE) was shaken, and today while recognizing that the Pentateuch, as we know it, went through at least two (J and P) redactions, this line of research holds that the entire corpus, together with the Deuteronomistic history, was addressed to the exilic and post-exilic communities.[22]

An Alternative Hypothesis

There has been a slow growing consensus[23] among scholars that:

(a) "the essential cohesion of the Pentateuch story" (Blenkinsopp) is owed to the literary activity of one individual writer. This essential cohesion would involve the presence of one basic theme,[24] an evolving narrative thread, and a thinly disguised historical function.[25]

(b) The Pentateuch, as we know it from tradition, was not composed as an independent literary unity but as part and parcel of a wider historiographical opus that would have included both the Pentateuch and the Deuteronomistic history.[26] The present writer is currently engaged in proving that this hypothesis is not only tenable but the best explanation offered to date on how this corpus came into being. In this paper we shall approach the Abraham Narrative in Genesis from this perspective, namely, that Gen. 11, 27-25,18 was composed by an individual who:

• had lived the bitter experience of the Babylonian exile and was writing from the perspective of those who sat down by the "waters of Babylon" and wept when they would remember Zion (Psalm 137,1); [27]

• addressed his opus to the exilic community probably in the second half of the sixth century BCE as the scenario of international politics was changing with the rapid disintegration of the Neo-Babylonian (Chaldean) empire and the rise of the Persian empire.[28] We owe to this changing political situation the basic optimism that characterizes this historiographical work, something which it shares with such contemporary writings such as Ezek. 40-48 and Deut.-Isaiah's canticles (Is. 40-55). These literary creations offer cultural projects that envisage the return of the deportees to the land of Israel, the land of their fathers;

• addressed the issue of ethnic and cultural identity of the exilic community by tracing back their origins to their forebears and narrating their traditional history seen essentially as a "history of salvation".[29] He offers his readers/listeners a cultural project just like one of his main personages, Moses, in the Book of Deuteronomy, while the people prepare to cross over the Jordan to the Promised Land. This cultural programme serves also as incitement not to integrate completely into the dominant culture of Babylon since the 'sons of Israel' did not belong there. The literary genre adopted allowed the writer to employ the rule of 'statement by indirection', so that, for instance, God's injunctions to the patriarchs to leave Mesopotamia to go and settle in Canaan may be read as a thinly disguised invitation to the writer's implied audience[30] to return to their homeland as soon as a good opportunity offers itself.[31]

• Our historiographer was not operating in a cultural vacuum. He wrote his work just as Herodotus was writing his *Histories* in order to establish the responsibility for the Persian War. Although we cannot yet establish whether there were some direct contacts between our writer and Greek historiographers, resemblances between biblical historiography as represented by Genesis-2 Kings and ancient Greek historiography regarding narrational and compositional techniques have led a number of scholars to search for an explanation that would not appeal to sheer fortuity.[32] This work has been described as the primary, national history of ancient Israel.

• This historiographer divided his national history first in two parts: the Mosaic period and the post-Mosaic period, depending upon the role played by his central character, Moses. Among the human figures that feature in the first half of this opus, Moses plays the role of chief spokesman and leader (not uncontested, Num 12,16) as the people are prepared to enter the land that had been promised to them. When Moses dies, leadership is assumed by successors who give their share to the realization of the project outlined by the great mediator in his long farewell speech (Deuteronomy). As the dynamics of the narrative demand, our writer sets all the legislative material that he found in the first part of his work as though it is narrating the foundational period in the historical experience of the people. All the important religious and civil institutions are either founded during the Mosaic period or are envisaged as corollaries to appear on the horizon of history some time in the not-so-distant future. A case in point is the monarchy: it is envisaged in Moses's programmatic speech (Dt 17, 14-20), deemed necessary for smooth political administration (Jdg 21,25), and finally established when certain cohesion has been attained by the tribes (1 Sam 8). The narration of the various periods is stopped at crucial moments to make room for commentary by main characters (Abraham: Gen 24,7; Jacob: Gen 49; Moses: Ex 15; Moses: Deuteronomy; Joshua: Jos 1; Joshua: Jos 23; Samuel: 1 Sam 12; Solomon:1 Kgs 8) or by the narrator[33] himself (Jdg 2; 2 Kgs 17).[34]

• The writer of this historiographical work tends to focus the narration of the several periods of this history on specific principal figures whose stories are skilfully woven into narrative units that give the impression of being self-contained, almost independent unities.[35] These "hero-oriented historiographic" units (Thompson) often open with the entrance of the hero and come to a close with his death or with his dismissal to forgetfulness. This is very clear with Exodus-Deuteronomy, which has Moses as the central figure. The Abraham Narrative in Gen 11, 27-25,18 offers another sure example. Each of the larger literary unities shares with the rest a number of literary features which narratologists[36] have helped us to discover and appreciate. But each has to be read as a story on its own, with literary and theological peculiarities, even though the several larger units are woven into one unifying global design of which historiographical progression is the visible marker.

The Abraham Narrative in Genesis

This sketchy presentation of the writer presumed to have composed Genesis-2 Kings brings us to a closer scrutiny of one of its several larger units, the Abraham Narrative. In style it tends to differ from the other units that make up Genesis, that long introduction to the 'history of the $b^e n\hat{e}$ $yirsa^c el'$. It is episodic in character, with each episode apparently forming a short story on its own.[37] Cohesion within the Abraham Narrative is achieved through an overarching structure that respects the poetic properties of each episode while redirecting them teleologically,[38] an evolving characterization,[39] and thematic coherence.[40] Probably due to the complexity of the message to be communicated, the overarching structure that keeps the episodes together and offers them a richer hermeneutical platform is complicated.[41] It basically consists of two parallel panels (a: 12,10-13,1; b: 13,2-18; c: 14,1-24; d: 15,1-21 corresponding to a^1 20,1-18; b^1 21,1-21; c^1:21,22-34; d^1: 22,1-19), a concentric central block of episodes (a: 16,1-16; b: 17,1-27; c: 18,1-33; b^1: 19,1-28; $a^{1:}$ 19,29-38), the whole being flanked by an introduction (11,27-12, 9) and a concluding block (22,20-25, 18). The structure was designed in order to create two semantic movements: "One is linear and chronological, following the evolvement of the plot, the other is circular assuming the use of the analogy principle by which episodes are mutually illuminating owing to corresponding location within the overarching structure."[42]

This "redactional structuring"[43] serves the narrator well as he sounds the depth of his argument, the experience of faith, which he sees embodied in the two protagonists of this literary unit, Abraham and his wife Sarah. The circular movement to which the global structure hints and the *caesura* after Gen 19, with Gen 20,1-18 marking a fresh beginning after a climax has been reached in Gen 18 where *Yhwh* comments favourably upon Abraham (why not upon Sarah as well?),[44] testifies that for the narrator Abraham is a complex personal character and that the experience of faith does not imply linearity of development and commitment. Abraham resumes with his role of trickster (Gen 20) even after his great encounter with *Yhwh* when he dared counsel "the Judge of all the land" (Gen 18). One would expect Abraham to become a different person after this meeting, a 'holier' individual. The narrator would answer that *Yhwh's* influence upon the individual believer does not obliterate personal characteristics and traits; it may redirect these tendencies; it may provoke a quicker process of maturation within the individual man of faith. Personal features, though, may remain with the believer long after he/she has had his/her deep experience with *Yhwh*.

Yhwh's Commentary

A closer observation of *Yhwh's* words concerning Abraham in Gen 18,17-19 cannot be avoided at this point. *Yhwh* utters his soliloquy in the presence of only his two companions, who as yet appear as 'men', and of Abraham, who accompanies his Guests as they leave his encampment.

(a) Gen 18,17-19 Constitutes a Commentary on Abraham

Diachronical and synchronical readings converge in taking these verses as commentary. Ever since Julius Wellhausen,[45] diachronical approaches viewed vv.17-19 as secondary and redactional in toto or in part[46] to the source material pre-existing the present text.[47] The problem with these approaches is that we do not know for sure the nature of the sources which the writers and redactors presumably found and employed.[48] Synchronical approaches insist that these verses are essential to the structure and purpose of the episode as a whole and have to be read as congenital with 18,1-16 and 18,23-33.[49] Whether as an interpolation into an already constituted text or as an organic part of a compositional unity, these verses are read today as commentary on *Yhwh's* behaviours[50] or on Abraham himself as the principal character and as the embodiment of the message which the writer would like to communicate.

(b) Commentary within the Abraham Narrative Is not an Absolute Novelty

The narrator has at times employed his characters[51] to comment upon some event involving Abraham [12,17-18 (Pharaoh); 16,5 (Sarai)]; on other occasions he has abandoned narration to embark upon short hermeneutical enterprises: in 15,6 he wedges in his comment in order to enlighten the reader about the patriarch's state of mind after hearing *Yhwh's* promises in vv.45. "And he believed the Lord; and he reckoned it to him as righteousness."[52] In closing that episode, the narrator intervenes once again to explain the mysterious ceremony he has just described and which has seen *Yhwh* as protagonist (v.17): "On that day the Lord made a covenant with Abraham" (v.18a). The novelty in Gen 18 consists in presenting *Yhwh* himself giving the commentary, and in *Yhwh's* commenting not on some event in which Abraham plays a role, but on the patriarch himself, or rather the system of values that this personage embodies. Naturally the location of *Yhwh's* interpretative contribution at this junction of the Abraham Narrative reflects conscious narrative strategies: in redactionally structuring his material, the narrator has chosen Gen 18, where *Yhwh* himself "enters the scene", as the fulcrum of the complex structural framework.[53] One should consider adding *Yhwh's* soliloquy in 18,17-19 among the writer's "retrospective and anticipatory reflections" (Noth) that span his entire historiographical opus.

(c) Yhwh's Soliloquy Has Its Own Internal Structure

Scholarship has not been over-generous in treating Gen 18,17-22. The prejudice passed down from generation to generation that some elements in these verses are secondary has exempted scholars from attempting to read *Yhwh's* soliloquy (singular not plural, contra Coats) as a unity. And yet this methodological stance offers the key to a proper and full understanding of what *Yhwh*, and the narrator, means to say here. In our discussion formal analysis comes first. Verses 16 and 22 are evidently transition verses marking "change of scene". In vv.17-21 we have Abraham and his three Guests all together while in vv.23-33 Abraham is alone with *Yhwh* as the (two) '*anashim* set out for Sodom. In vv.17-21 it is only *Yhwh* who talks; presumably he addresses the other characters "on stage" including Abraham, although we are not told whether this soliloquy is 'internal' or 'external'. Two incomplete introductory formulae in vv.17 and 20 have a structuralising function in that *Yhwh's* intervention is clearly divided in two parts. Other elements serve as markers to the narrator's intention of relating the two parts as opposite (Coats). A clear marker is the verb *ʿasah* , which appears three times in this short passage, with three different subjects: in v.17 the subject is *Yhwh*, the speaker; in v.19 it is Abraham's sons and household, while in v.21 Sodom and Gomorrah. The last two instances stand in contrasting position as one may deduce from the objects of the verb: Abraham's descendants are supposed to do "righteousness" (*sedaqah*) while Sodom and Gomorrah are said to be doing "outcry" (*za°aqat*). The narrator therefore intends to compare and contrast the two groups of people; this intention may offer the clue to what the narrator means to communicate through *Yhwh's* intervention.

Yhwh's soliloquy follows a rather rigid pattern. After an introductory statement in which *Yhwh* confesses he cannot in anyway hide anything from Abraham (v.17; A) there follows a BCB¹C¹ structure where the Bs inform reader of actions of the subjects of verb*°asah* with the Cs telling of initiatives to be carried out in the future. B states the reasons why *Yhwh* cannot hide from Abraham his intentions (v.18): Abraham is to become a great and strong nation with nations drawing blessings from associating themselves to him (*bô*). B¹ says about Sodom and Gomorrah that their 'outcry' and 'sin' were great indeed (v.20). Both B and B¹ are bicola, with each colon being introduced by an emphatic particle.[54] C (v.19) is a cluster made up of four cola; two are introduced by the preposition and conjunction *l°ma°an* outflanking two parallel clauses. C¹ refers instead to the sentence in v.21 where *Yhwh* spells out his programme of "going down" to verify the rumours that reached him (*ra'ah*) and have a clearer picture of what is happening in Sodom (*yada°*). This structure gives rise to a number of questions which, when answered, will hint to the narrator's mind about Abraham as teacher of future generations. We have to establish (i) the grammatical relationship between the verb *y°da°tîw* and the two *l°ma°an* clauses; (ii) the real meaning of the verb *y°da°tîw*; (iii) the grammatical relationship between the first *l°ma°an* clause and the clauses that begin with *ûsham°rû* and *la°asôt* in v.19; (iv) the meaning of *derekh Yhwh* and *s°daqah ûmishpat* in v.19.

A Question of Correct Parsing

Parsing the various terms and verbal clusters in verse 19a may sound to the uninitiated a pretty straightforward *tedium*, as none would appear irregular or rare. On the other hand it is this normalcy that attracted so little commentary in scholarly studies. Most readings were diachronical, noticing strong similarities in vocabulary and theology to Deuteronomy.[55] A synchronic approach would read these avowals of the Deuteronomic style and contents as anticipatory harpings of what is central to this historiography.

The linking particle *kî* that sews verse 19 to *Yhwh's* description of Abraham's glory (v.18) is usually parsed and translated as explicative (*"for", Jerusalem Bible 6*); yet one hardly misses a nuance of emphasis: "Certainly, I have known ..."[56] The governing word in verse 19, *y°da°tîw* comes from a root which is extraordinarily common in the Hebrew

Bible[57] and to isolate and identify its precise semantic value in our text would require the thorough examination of each and every occurrence of the term. This would take us too far astray, so that we have to limit our area of study to our immediate textual context, which is the Abraham narrative, and the larger literary unit that precedes this narrative (Gen 1-11).

Within this limited textual extension *YD^c* features twelve times in differing syntactical groupings.[58] Particularly relevant to our research are texts where the verb governs a direct object through the accusative marker *'et* (Gen 4, 1. 17.23). "Now Adam knew (*yada^c*) his wife Eve" (Gen 4,1, RSV); "to know" here refers to sexual intimacy.*YD^c* often means the sexual act in the Old Testament. The verb does not mean a recognizing or a knowing in the objective sense, recognizing or knowing something, but recognizing as the result of an encounter".[59] Gen 18,19 resembles in parsing this group of texts since the verb *YD^c* governs a personal pronoun as its object. The problem is that the subject of *YD^c* is *Yhwh* himself with Abraham being the object, and the Lord's knowing Abraham cannot carry the sexual connotations of the *YD^c* in Gen 4,1 and other texts. But the verb does imply special, close knowledge and relationship. *Yhwh* acknowledges that He could not conceal his plans from the patriarch who enjoyed a special status before him (perhaps in view of his future glory, v.18). Jewish savants often adopted this backward looking interpretation of *y^eda^ctîw* though they would nuance its force to avoid the sexual implications of the verb *YD^c*.[60] Deep respect for and admittance to intimate relationship were seen at least since the ninth and eighth century BCE as markers of the prophetic call (Ex 33, 5.17; Dt 34,10; Amos 3,2; Hos 13,5)[61] and Abraham will soon be described by God himself a prophet (Gen 20,7). Syntax, however, opens the way to a different interpretation; *y^eda^ctîw* is syntactically linked to the *l^ema^can* clauses and assumes the meaning of "choosing", "selecting" present in a number of texts where *YD^c* features (Jer 1,5; Hos 13,5; Amos 3,2). "For I have singled him out ..." (*Jerusalem Bible*). "For I have chosen him ..." (*Revised Standard Version*).[62] In this case *y^eda^ctîw* is pregnant with meaning. *Yhwh* emphasises not merely that Abraham was the object of his special care, but that He has chosen the patriarch for a special mission.

This nuance in *y^eda^ctîw* of "selecting, choosing for a mission" would require the final meaning in the conjunction *l^ema^can 'asher* of verse 19, "I have chosen him so that ... ", but would call for a different nuance in its second instance in v. 19b.[63] Rabbi Moshe Ben Nahman (1194-1270 CE) has already envisaged this possibility for *l^ema^can* of Dt 29,18;[64] a number of commentators[65] and modern grammarians accept that *l^ema^can* here introduces a result clause.[66] In this case the fulfilment of *Yhwh's* promises (*'asher dibber ^caltaw*) is presented as consequent to Abraham's *banîm* and household obeying their father's command.

The principal verb of the *l^ema^can 'asher* clause, *y^essawweh*,is mainly to be found in the primary history.[67] This action word appears very often in the Piel form and carries two basic meanings: "to give charge to somebody" and "to command somebody". For the former meaning the verb usually employs the services of a preposition *'el* or *^cal* (cf Gen 2,16; 12,30). When it means 'to command' *siwwah* governs a direct object in the accusative. In our text it also governs an object clause introduced by a waw consecutive: *w^esham^crû derek Yhwh* ... (cf Num 35,2 for a similar syntactical cluster). Gen 18,19 is one of two texts in Gen 1-21 where the verb has a human for subject; otherwise God is the subject of the verb, cf 3,11; 3,17; 6,22; 7,5.9.16; 21,4 and in all cases it means "to command". Abraham, therefore, has been selected by *Yhwh* in order that he may command ... Naturally we should not separate this mission of Abraham from his role as teacher within his household, since the father was supposed to be the principal teacher within the family circle, and its chief imparter of tradition (Dt 6,7.20-25).[68]

Abraham's direct recipients of his educational efforts are identified by *Yhwh* as *banaw* and *bêtô 'aharaw*. This phrase is novel for the Abraham Narrative, but not the idea of future descendants. In the introduction to the Abraham Narrative (11,27-12,9) we read the Lord's promise to give "this land" *l^ezar^caka* (to your descendants) (12,7). The same promise is made after the Egypt adventure (12,10-20) to Abraham and his "seed" (13,15.17, cf 15,18). The narrator makes *Yhwh* promise again and again that these descendants are to multiply exceedingly (13,16; 15,5; 17,4-5). In Gen 17 the collective noun *zera^c*, "descendants", is often qualified by the preposition *'aharîm*, "after", returning to Abraham (vv. 7.8.9.10) and to Izaak (v.19), making it clear that the narrator is thinking of future generations and not the immediate relatives of the (two) patriarchs (cf Gen 21,12). Whenever reference is made to close relatives in the Abraham Narrative different designations are employed, especially the term *ben*, son.[69] This would shed light on the meaning of *banîm* in verse 19; for while we cannot exclude in an absolute manner the nuance 'distant descendants' in the word as employed here,[70] its present literary context is narrowing its semantic range. *Banîm* on *Yhwh's* mouth cannot mean but Abraham's natural sons who have been mentioned together by the same protagonists (Gen 17,18-21). Abraham's mission as teacher has first to touch his (two) sons, even though they have been marked by God himself for different destinies.

The other object of the verb *y^esawweh* is rather rare in the literary unit dedicated to the history of humanity (Gen 1- 11) but quite common in the Abraham Narrative.[71] In the former it appears twice, both times in the Deluge Narrative. Once it is used in a technical sense within the cluster *mibbayit* which stands in opposition to the phrase *mihûs* "from outside" (Gen 6,14). Noah is asked to pitch the ark from within (*mibbayit*) as from without (*mihûs*). In Gen 7,1 Noah's *bayit* evidently refers to his immediate family circle. In the Abraham Narrative the term *bayit* may be said to be carrying various nuances. In Gen 19,2-3.4.11 (and perhaps 12,15) it may mean house as dwelling, habitation. In other several instances *bayit* appears to mean 'household' to which slaves belong because they are born within it or are bought into it [Gen 14,14; 15,2.3; 17,12.13.23; in v.12 it is specified that the *yelîd bayit* as well as the *miqnat kesef* (bought by money) are not Abraham's *zera*ᶜ]. But *bayit* may also mean descendants as an organized body just as one would find in Dt 25,9, where the widow of the deceased is allowed to revere the dead husband's brother who "would not build his brother's house" by observing the levirate law. Or in 2 Sam 7,27 where King David speaks of *Yhwh's* revelations that he will build the King a house (*bayit 'ebhneh lak*) meaning a dynasty (cf vv.11-16). *Bayit* in Gen 18,19 carries the same meaning: it refers to Abraham's future descendants taken not as individuals, but as a collectivity. That these descendants were to belong not simply to Abraham's children but to all subsequent generations is brought out by the preposition *'aharaw* "after him".

The contents of Abraham's instruction (Westermann) are described by the clause *wᵉshamᵉrû derekh Yhwh* which depends syntactically upon the verb *yᵉsawweh*, and an epexegetic phrase which is attached to it by grammar: *laᶜasôt sᵉdaqah ûmishpat*.[72] The three words that constitute this clause are quite common in the Hebrew Bible; but defining their precise semantic values is arduous. The verb *shamar*, for instance, in the Qal Indicative form appears 424 times[73] carrying one of the nuances "keep, watch, preserve".[74]

Much more frequent is the substantive *derekh*,[75] the direct object of the verb *shamar*, employed here without the usual accusative marker *'et*. *Derekh* is capable of several nuances, as can be seen from an essay into its uses in the history of early humanity and in the Abraham Narrative. Its basic meaning is that of "path, way, road," but assumes a metaphorical sense in a few of the twelve occurrences in Gen 1-25. In Gen 3,24 we read how *Yhwh* would bar "the way of the tree of life" while in 6,12 the narrator laments that all flesh has corrupted its "way" (*darkô*). In 16,7 *derekh* serves topography: "at the spring along the road (*bᵉderekh*) to/of Shur". In a number of texts *derekh* means "journey" (19,2; 24,21.27.42). The metaphorical meaning "custom" is to be found in 19,31.

The term *derekh* in *derekh Yhwh* of 18,19 has generally been interpreted metaphorically. What is particular about the term in this verse is the cluster in which it is situated. According to *BDB* in only five instances in the entire Hebrew Bible does the verb *shamar* take *derekh* for direct object. The 'way of *Yhwh*' has normally been given a moralistic interpretation and seen as referring to the ethical code which the Lord commanded: *kol hadderekh 'asher siwwah Yhwh* ("follow the whole way that *Yhwh* has marked for you and you shall live") (Dt 5,39, *JB*). Very often *derekh* with this nuance appears in the plural: *w^eshamarta 'et miswôt Yhwh 'elohêka laleket bidrakaw* ("And keep the commandments of *Yhwh* your God, and so follow his ways ... " Dt 8,6, *JB*). For this use consult Dt 10,12; 11,22.28; 19,9; 26,17; 28,9; 30,16; Jos 22,5; Jdg 2,22; 2 Sam 22,22; 1Kgs 2,3; 3,14 etc. An ancient targumic manuscript labelled "Addendum 27031",[76] attempts to make *derekh* understandable by converting it to the plural and translating the cluster as "to observe the ways that are straight in front of the Lord."[77] The substantive *derekh* "became a favourite word later for pious observance of the law and finds expression above all in the Psalms (Ps 119)".[78] But it is possible that *derekh Yhwh* focuses on God's own behaviour and evokes the theme of the *Imitatio Dei*. Benno Jacob comments on the phrase in this manner: "*Gottes richterliches Verhalten und Verfahren, und sie daraus lernen selber Gerechtigkect und Recht zu üben.*"[79] The stress on *Yhwh's* performance is probably being put in v.19 as this theme is going to predominate in the forthcoming dialogue between the patriarch and *Yhwh* (vv.23-32). Judicial justice is basically meant here.[80] Abraham is to teach his sons and his future descendants how to imitate the Lord's just behaviour. In view of this injunction one may understand Abraham's retort when confronted with the possibility that the Lord may act unjustly *vis-à-vis* the innocent in Sodom and Gomorrah.

The last element to be scrutinised in this study is the phrase *la^casôt s^edaqa ûmispat*. Some read this phrase as parallel to *w^esham^erû derekh Yhwh* "to observe the way of Yahweh and to do what is just and right" (Westermann). The cluster *la^casôt*, however, does not necessarily express finality. "It is with the preposition *l^e* that the infinitive construct is mainly used. The *l^e* can have various nuances: strong, weak, or even almost nil; thus *la^casôt* may have the following nuances: in order to do, in doing, by doing, and simply to do."[81] In our text the *l^e* together with the infinitive construct carries the weak nuance "in doing / by doing" as the phrase *la^casôt s^edaqa ûmispat* has an epexegetic function, it explains the meaning of *derekh Yhwh*. At the same time it delimits the semantic field within which we should situate the two terms *s^edaqa* and *ûmispat*.

Both taken singly and in their present combination these two terms are not among the most frequent in the narrative sections of the primary history. According to VOT[82] *s^edaqa* and *ûmispat* appear three times each in Genesis, two instances of which are in the Abraham Narrative; *s^edaqa* features in Gen 15,6; 18,19 and 30,33; *mishpat* is to be found in 18,19; 18,25 and 40,13. Their combination has been parsed as hendiadys;[83] their sequence is usually inverted (Loader). The present order can be found also in only two sapiential texts (Ps 33,5; Prov 21,3 though we should perhaps include Dt 33,21).[84] What may explain the

unusual order of the terms in 18,19 is the identical sequence of *saddîq* /
saddîqim and *mishpat* in the ensuing dialogue between Abraham and
Yhwh.

Isolating the precise nuance of the word *sᵉdaqa* in 18,19 requires that
we take into consideration both its occurrence in Gen 15,6 as well as its
use as an attribute of the judge and of God. In Gen 15,6 we read how
Abraham believed *Yhwh*'s promise of numberless progeny (v.5) and how
wayyahshᵉbeha lô sᵉdaqa "and he reputed it to him as *sᵉdaqa*".
Westermann defined 'righteousness' in this verse as "the correct
comportment in a critical situation" and cites Dt 24,13 as the first
occurrence of *sᵉdaqa* in this sense.[85] The two instances of *sᵉdaqa* in 15,6
and 18,19 are not read, therefore, as carrying identical meanings; but we
cannot accept Westermann's interpretation of Abraham in 18,19 as "father
of *mishpat* and *sᵉdaqa* " rather than as father of faith as he appears in Gen
15,6.[86] *Sᵉdaqa* differs in significance from that of 15,6 because while in the
latter the term stands for an interior act of the patriarch, in the former
sᵉdaqa is supposed to stand for an attribute of *Yhwh*. This theme is not a
rarity in the Hebrew Bible. Righteousness is described as God's sovereign
attribute in Pss 36,7; 71,19; in P. 99,4 and Jer 9,23 God is said to be
exercising justice and righteousness (*ᶜoseh mishpat ûsᵉdaqa*) as he governs
the world (cf Job 37,23; Is 1,27; 5,15; 10,22; 28,17 etc).

No less complex is arriving at a definition of *mishpat*. In our case we
may not ignore that the term forms part of the hendiadys *sᵉdaqa ûmishpat*
and that in a number of texts in the Hebrew Bible it is presented as the
attribute *par excellence* of the judge (*shophet*) and of God to denote justice,
right, rectitude (cf Is 30,8; Dt 32,4; Pss 111,7; 33,5; 37,28; 99,4; Hos 2,21;
Job 8,3; 34,12; 40,8 etc.).[87] Nehama Leibowitz follows E.Z. Melamed's
parsing of *sᵉdaqa ûmishpat* as hendiadys and translates it "righteous
justice". "Abraham was chosen therefore to teach his seed to execute just
judgement and that constitutes the way of the Lord."[88] The immediate
context (Gen 18,1-33) would spell out what the Lord's *derekh* in doing just
judgement means. Taking its place within *Yhwh's* speech one can say that
this *derekh* looks back both to *Yhwh's* faithful dealings with Abraham, his
promises and their would-be fulfilment *kaᶜet bayyah* "this time next
year",[89] as well as his behaviour as 'judge of the world' in not sweeping
away the just with the wicked (18,23) as we shall soon learn from his
interview with the patriarch.

Conclusion

What lesson could Abraham impart to future generations according to
our historian? A lesson in faith seen not so much as a purely interior
behaviour but as concrete action of historical and social connotations

patterned on God's dealings with man. Rather than "father of *s⁰daqa and mishpat*" seen in contradistinction to "father of faith" (Westermann), Abraham is the "son of *s⁰daqa* and *mishpat*" he saw realized in *Yhwh* (reading "son", *ben*, here as *nomen relativum* joined to a word denoting some quality or characteristic as *ben hayil* meaning "mighty man", *ben mesheq* "son of possession", that is heir). But insofar as he imitated God, Abraham became "father of righteous justice", which no longer stands in contrast to being a man of faith. *Genesis Rabbah* intuits rightly in reading *laᶜasôt s⁰daqah ûmishpat* as referring to the patriarch himself. In paragraph LIX:I, it narrates an anecdote of Rabbi Meir on a visit to Mamala. He saw only young people among his audience and wondered what could have happened to the old folks, whether there had happened in that community what 1 Sam 2,33 pronounced of Eli's family. "They said to him, 'Rabbi, pray for us'. He said to them, 'Go and carry out works of righteousness (charity), and you will gain the merit of enjoying old age'. 'What is the biblical verse that indicates it?' 'The hoary head is a crown of glory, it is found in the way of righteousness' (Prov 16,31). 'From whom do you learn that lesson?' It is from Abraham. Because concerning him it is written, 'To do righteous deeds' (Gen 18,19), he had the merit of attaining old age: 'Now Abraham was old, well advanced in years' (Gen 24,1)".[90]

Notes

1. For this concept of "primary history" cf. Freedman, D. N. (1962), 'Pentateuch', pp. 711-727 in Bottrick, G.A. et al. (eds.), *The Interpreter's Dictionary of the Bible*, vol. 3, New York; *Id.* (1963), 'The Law and the Prophets', *Vetus Testamentum Supplement* 9: pp. 250-265, *Id.* (1987), 'The Earliest Bible', pp. 29-37 in O'Connor, M. P. and Freedman, D.N. (eds.) (1987), *Backgrounds to the Bible,* Indiana, Winona Lake.

2. See below.

3. I borrow this concept from Rendtorff, R. (1990), 'The Problem of the Process of Transmission in the Pentateuch' (John J. Scullion, trans.), *Journal for the Study of the Old Testament (JSOT)* Supplement 89, Sheffield, Sheffield Academic Press: pp. 31-42, 181-188, but Rendtorff gives the phrase a slightly different meaning.

4. In a subsequent study I shall show that Sarah shares with Abraham the role of protagonist in Gen 11,27 - 25,18.

5. Cf. Leibowitz, N. (1993), 'Studies in Bereshit in the Context of Ancient and Modern Jewish Commentary', pp. 164-169 and Coggins, R. J. (1993), 'Prophecy - True and False', pp. 80-94 in McKay, H. A. and Clines, D. J. A. (eds.), *Of Prophets' Visions and the Wisdom of Sages,* JSOT Supplement 162. On the prophetic role of Abraham, I would refer

to Neher, A. (1983), *L'Essenza del Profetismo,* Casale Monferrato, Marietti: pp. 145-151.

6. For a discussion on the meaning of *w^{e}nibr^{e}kû bô kol gôyyê ha arez* in 18 cf. Westermann, C. (1985), *Genesis 12-36 A Commentary,* London, SPCK: pp. 151-152.

7. See below.

8. For an overview history of Scripture interpretation cf. Grant, R. M. and Tracy, D. (1984), *A Short History of the Interpretation of the Bible,* London, SCM Press. For detailed accounts of the development of the historical-critical method cf. Kraus, H. J. (1969), *Geschichte der historisch-kritischen Erforschung des Alten Testaments* , Neukirchener Verlag, Neukerchen-Vluyn; Rogerson, J. W. (ed.) (1993), *Old Testament Criticism in the Nineteenth Century,* Sheffield, Sheffield Academic Press. For an easy description of this method cf. Hayes, J. H. (1979), *An Introduction to Old Testament Study,* London, SCM Press; Hayes, J. H. and Holladay, C. R. (1982), *Biblical Exegesis. A Beginner's Handbook*, London, SCM Press. For appreciation of this scientific approach cf. Barr, J. (1983), *Holy Scripture.:Canon Authority Criticism,* Oxford, Clarendon Press: pp. 105-126. For an approach that differs from the critical method developed in Europe cf. Taylor, M. A. (1992), *The Old Testament in the Old Princeton School (1812-1929),* San Francisco, Mellen Research University Press.

9. Eissfeldt, O. (1974). *The Old Testament: An Introduction*, Oxford, Blackwell: pp. 155-211.

10. Cazelles, H. (1973). *L'Ancien Testament. Introduction Historique et Critique,* Paris, Desclée: pp. 5-244.

11. de Pury, A. and Römer, T. (1989). 'Le Pentateuque en Question: Position du Problème et Breve Histoire de la Recherche', pp. 9-81 in de Pury, A. (ed.), *Le Pentateuch en Question,* Geneva, Labor et Fides.

12. Campbell, A. F. and O'Brien, M. A. (1989). *Sources of the Pentateuch,* Minneapolis, Fortress Press: pp. 1-20.

13. Blenkinsopp, J. (1992). *The Pentateuch: An Introduction to the First Five Books of the Bible,* New York, Doubleday: pp. 1-30.

14. Cf. Abela, A. (1993), 'Min kiteb il-Pentatewku?', *Sijon* 6: pp. 12-21.

15. Noth, M. (1948). *Überlieferungsgeschichte des Pentateuch,* Stuttgart; McKane, W. (1979), *Studies in the Patriarchal Narratives,* Edinburgh. For a critique of this view cf. Whybray, R.N. (1987), *The Making of the Pentateuch: A Methodological Study, JSOT* Supplement 53: pp. 133-222.

16. Wellhausen, J. (1883). *Prolegomena zur Geschichte Israels* ; *Id.* (1899), *Die Composition des Hexateuchs und der historischen Bücher des Alten Testament,* Berlin.

17. Cf. Noth, M. (1981), *The Deuteronomistic History,* JSOT Supplement 15; Nelson, R. D. (1981), *The Double Redaction of the Deuteronomistic History,* JSOT Supplement18.

18. Noth, M. (1948). *Überlieferungsgeschichte des Pentateuch;* cf. Campbell and O'Brien,*Sources IX-XV*, see note 12 above.

19. For a critique of source and literary criticism cf. Whybray, R. N., see note 15 above: pp. 17-132.

20. Von Rad, G. (1966). 'The Problem of the Hexateuch', pp. 1-78 in *The Problem of the Hexateuch and Other Essays,* London, SCM Press; *Id.*, (1972), *Genesis*, London, SCM Press.

21. Eissfeldt, O., see note 9 above: pp. 204-208; Ska, J. L. (1989), 'Quelques rémarques sur Pg et la dérniére rédaction du Péntateuque', pp. 95-128 in de Pury, A. (ed.), *Le Péntateuque en Question,* Génève, Labor et Fides.

22. Van Seters, J. (1975). *Abraham in History and Tradition,* London, New Haeven; Schmidt, H. H. (1976), *Der Sogenannte Jahwist* , Zurich; Rendtorff, R. (1990), *The Problem of the Process of Transmission in the Pentateuch*, see note 3 above. The whole issue was debated by various authors in the *Journal for the Study of the Old Testament* 3 (1977).

23. Cf. Whybray, R. N. (1987), *The Making of the Pentateuch*, see note 15 above: pp. 221-242.

24 Clines, D. J. A. (1978). 'The Theme of the Pentateuch', *JSOT* 10.

25. For the concept of 'historical function' cf. Clines, D. J. A. (1978), see note 24 above: p. 97.

26. Cf. Blenkinsopp, J. (1992), See note 13 above: pp. 20-21. By the time this essay was finished the present author received a copy of Yehoshua Honigwachs' first of a four volume work *The Unity of the Torah. A Commentary on the Organization and Purpose of the Five Books*, Jerusalem/New York, Feldheim (1991). He could not consider the contribution of this volume for the purpose of this paper.

27. On the exilic community cf. Ackroyd, P. R. (1968), *Exile and Restoration,* London, SCM Press.

28. Cf. Noth, M. (1958), *The History of Israel,* London, Adam & Charles Black: pp. 289-316; Siegfried, H. (1981), *A History of Israel in Old Testament,* London, SCM Press.

29. This concept should be read together with the reflections of Westermann, C. (1979), *What does the Old Testament say about God,* Atlanta, John Knox Press.

30. For this concept cf. Iser, W. (1972), *The Implied Reader,* Baltimore/London; Ska, J. L. (1990), *Our Fathers have told us. Introduction to the Analysis of Hebrew Narratives*, Rome, Pontifical Biblical Institute: pp. 42-43.

31. Cf. Clines, D. J. A. (1978), see note 24 above: p. 98.

32. Van Seters, J. (1983). *In Search of History. Historiography in the Ancient World and the Origins of Biblical History*, New Haven/London, Yale University Press: pp. 8-54; Whybray, see note 15 above: pp. 225-230; Blenkinsopp, see note 13 above: pp. 37-42.

33. For the concept of 'narrator' as understood in this paper cf. Bar-Efrat, S. (1989), *Narrative Art in the Bible,* Sheffield, Almond Press: pp. 13-46; Ska, J. L., see note 30 above: pp. 39-64.

34. Martin Noth considered "this practice of inserting general retrospective and anticipatory reflections at certain important points in the history" as a characteristic which strongly supports the thesis that the Deuteronomistic History was conceived as a united and self-contained whole; see note 17 above: p. 6. But he failed to consider as falling under the same rubric Gen 49, Ex 15 and Deuteronomy.

35. Thomas L. Thompson seems to consider these "narrative blocks" as originally independent from each other. He describes them as a "genre" he calls "traditional complex-chain narrative". The greater part of what he says about the literary qualities and dynamics of these narratives is valid. Cf. Thompson, T. L. (1987),*The Origin Tradition of Ancient Israel, JSOT* Supplement 55: pp. 155-188. The present writer is not completely sure whether Thompson's outline of the formation process of Genesis-Exodus 1-23 which sees the crystallization of the traditional complex-chain narrative as the middle stage (*ibid.*: pp. 61-66), is less hypothetical than other (Noth's for instance) versions of this formation history. This outline does not appear in Thompson's important contribution *Early History of the Israelite* People (1992), London, E. J. Brill: ch. 8, where he discusses "the literary nature and historicity of the tradition".

36. To the works of Shimon Bar-Efrat and Jean-Louis Ska I would add two 'classics': Alter, R. (1981), *The Art of Biblical Narrative,* New York, Basic Books; Sternberg, M. (1987), *The Poetics of Biblical Narrative. Ideological Literature and the Drama of Reading,* Bloomington, Indiana University Press.

37. Cf. Bar-Efrat, *Narrative Art,* see note 33 above: p. 136.

38. Abela, A. (1991). 'The Redactional Structuring within the Abraham Narrative in Genesis', pp. 35-86 in Borg, V. (ed.), *Veterum Exempla. Essays in Honour of Mgr. Prof. Joseph Lupi,* Malta, Melita Theologica Supplementary Series 1.

39. Cf. Abela, A. (1993), 'Who is Sarah of the Abraham Narrative?', Münster. A paper read at the Society of Biblical Literature International Seminar (forthcoming publication).

40. Cf. Abela, A. (1989), *The Themes of the Abraham Narrative,* Malta.

41. Abela, A., 'Redactional Structuring', see note 38 above: p. 81.

42. *Ibid.*

43. The present writer borrows this phrase from Sasson, J. M. (1980), '"The Tower of Babel" as a clue to the Redactional Structuring of the Primeval History (Gen 1 1-11,9)', pp. 211-219 in Rendsburg, G. A. (ed.), *The Bible World, Essays in Honour of Cyrus H. Gordon,* New York. By

redactional structuring he means giving the narrative material a purposeful literary structure.

44. In the paper mentioned in note 39 an attempt is made to show not merely that Sarah is protagonist together with Abraham, but that she represents 'wisdom', reason, inquisitive and rebellious *vis-à-vis* the demands of faith. Abraham on the other hand embodies utter obedience.

45. *Die Composition*, see note 16 above: p. 28.

46. Noth, M., *Überlieferungsgeschichte*, see note 15 above: in note 259 considered only verse 19 as secondary. He has been followed by von Rad, *Genesis*, see note 20 above: p. 208, and others. For criticism cf. Westermann, *Genesis*, see note 6 above: pp. 12-36, 287-288; Loader, J. A. (1990), *A Tale of Two Cities,* Kamden, Kok Publishing House: p. 27.

47. Cf. Westermann, *ibid.*: p. 287.

48. Unless one accepts as proven the JEPD hypothesis.

49. Coats, G. W. (1983). *Genesis* , Michigan, Grand Rapids, Eerdmans: pp. 139-141.

50. "The passage of Gen 18,16-22 is best understood as a commentary or gloss of a story, which explains Yahweh's behaviour to the audience", Thompson, *The Origin Tradition*, see note 35 above: p. 92.

51. On the employment of characters by the narrator to express specific viewpoints cf. Berlin A. (1983), *Poetics and Interpretation of Biblical Narrative,* Sheffield, Almond Press: pp. 43-82; Sternberg, *Poetics of Biblical Narrative*, see note 36 above: ch. 5.

52. For a closer look at Gen 15 cf. Abela, A. (1986), 'Genesis 15. A Non-Genetic Approach', *Melita Theologica* XXXVII/2: pp. 9-40.

53. Abela, A., 'Redactional Structuring', see note 38 above: pp. 77-80.

54. On emphasis in Hebrew cf. Muraoka, T. (1985), *Emphatic Words and Structures in Biblical Hebrew*, Jerusalem.

55. Cf. von Rad, G., *Genesis*, see note 20 above: pp. 209-210; Schmidt, L. (1976), '*De Deo*'. *Studien zur Literarkritik und Theologie des Buches Jona, des Gesprächs zwischen Abraham und Jahwe in Gen 18,22ff und von Hiob 1*, Beihefte zur ZAW 143, Berlin: pp. 134-136; Blenkinsopp, *Pentateuch*, see note 13 above: pp. 121-124.

56. For this nuance in *kî* cf. Aejmelaeus, A. (1986), 'Function and interpretation of *kî* in Biblia Hebraica', *Journal of Biblical Literature* 105: pp. 193-209; Joüon/Muraoka, *A Grammar of Biblical Hebrew*: par. 164b.

57. Andersen, F. I. and Dean-Forbes, A. (1992). *The Vocabulary of the Old Testament,* Rome, Pontifical Biblical Institute, (henceforth *VOT*), registers 919 appearances.

58. Cf. Lisowsky, G. (1958.1993), *Konkordanz zum Hebräishen Alten Testament,* Stuttgart, Deutsche Bibelgesellschaft: p. 573.

59. Westermann, C. (1984). *Genesis 1-11. A Commentary*, London, SPCK: p. 288.

60. Cf. le Déaut, *Genèse*, pp. 188-189; Jacob, B. (1934), *Das erste Buch der Tora. Genesis,* Berlin: p. 447; Raschi (1985), *Commento alla Genesi,* Casale Monferrato, Marietti: p. 148; Leibowitz, *Studies*, see note 5 above: p. 169.

61. Cf. Blenkinsopp, J. (1983), *A History of Prophecy in Israel,* Philadelphia, Westminster Press: pp. 80-137.

62. Cf. Moberly, R. W. L. (1983), *At the Mountain of God,* Sheffield, *JSOT* Supplement 22: p. 70; Gelston, A. (1993), 'Knowledge, Humiliation or Suffering: A Lexical, Textual and Exegetical Problem in Isaiah 53', pp. 131-132 in McKay, H. A. & Clines, D. J. A. (eds.), *Of Prophets' Visions and the Wisdom of Sages,* Sheffield, JSOT Press.

63. Cf. *Gesenius' Hebrew Grammar* (1910.1980), Oxford, Clarendon Press: par. 1140; 165b-c; Joüon/Muraoka, *Grammar*: pp. 168.169.

64. Cf. Leibowitz, *Studies*, see note 5 above: p. 168.

65. Skinner, J. (1910). *A Critical and Exegetical Commentary on Genesis,* Edinburgh, ICC: p. 304.

66. Brongers, H. A. (1973). 'Die Partikal lemacan in der hebräischen Sprache', *Oudtestammentische Studien* 18: pp. 84-96; Joüon/Muraoka, *Grammar*: 169g.

67. Cf. *VOT*, see note 57 above: p. 405.

68. Cf. Wolff, H. W. (1975), *Antropologia dell' Antico Testamento,* Brescia, Queriniana (German original 1973): pp. 229-237; de Vaux, R. (1973), *Ancient Israel: Its Life and Institutions,* London, Darton, Longman & Todd: pp. 48-50.

69. Cf. Abela, A. (1989), *The Themes of the Abraham Narrative,* Malta, Studia Editions: p. 44.

70. Cf. Brown, F., Driver, S. R., Briggs, C. A. (1907. 1974), *A Hebrew and English Lexicon of the Old Testament,* Oxford, Clarendon Press: pp. 120-121. The volume is henceforth referred to as *BDB*.

71. Cf. Lisowsky, *Konkordanz*, pp. 213-228, especially pp. 213,225.

72. For parsing consult Joüon/Muraoka, *Grammar:* pars. 124l; 177j.

73. Cf. *VOT*, see note 57 above: p. 250.

74. Cf. *BDB*, see note 70 above: pp. 1036-1037.

75. *VOT*, see note 57 above: p. 81.

76. Cf. le Déaut, *Genèse*: pp. 29-37.

77. *Ibid.*: p. 189.

78. Heiler, F. (1961). *Erscheinungsformen und Wesen der Religion*: p. 148 as quoted by Westermann, *Genesis,* see note 6 above: pp. 12-36, 288. It is significant that the latest dictionary of Biblical Hebrew, Schökel, L. A. (1994), *Diccionario Biblico Hebreo-Espagñol,* Madrid, Editorial Trotta: pp. 184-185 has entered *derekh* in Gen 18,19 under the rubric "conducta, proceder, comportamiento, costumbres" and not under the title "Caminos de Dios".

79. Jacob, B., *Genesis*, see note 60 above: p. 447.

80. The bibliography on these verses is rich indeed. I refer the reader to Westermann's commentary *ad hoc* and to a couple of texts: Schökel, L. A. (1987), 'Uccidere l'innocente con il colpevole, lungi da te! (Gen 18, 16-23)', pp. 90-106 in *Dov'è tuo Fratello,* Brescia, Paideia, (Spanish original 1985); Coats, *Genesis,* see note 49 above: pp. 139-142.

81. Joüon/Muraoka, *Grammar*: par. 124l.

82. Cf. *VOT,* see note 57 above: pp. 160-209.

83. Cf. Melamed, A. Z. (1945), *Tarbiz* 16/4: pp. 173-198; Schökel, L. A., *Diccionario,* see note 78 above: p. 467.

84. Jacob, B., *Genesis,* see note 60 above: p. 447.

85. *Genesis 12-36,* p. 233. On this difficult text one may read von Rad, G. (1966), 'Faith Reckoned as Righteousness', pp. 125-130 in *The Problem of the Pentateuch and other essays, London,* SCM Press, (the German original belongs to 1951); Lohfink, N. (1967), *Die Landverheissung als Eid. Eine Studie zu Gn. 15,* Stuttgart, Verlag katholiche Bibelwerk: pp. 58-60. For a synchronical reading of Gen 15 see Abela, A. (1986), 'Genesis 15: A non-genetic approach', *Melita Theologica* No 37: pp. 9-40.

86. Westermann, C., *Genesis,* see note 6 above: pp. 12-36, 288-289.

87. Cf. *BDB,* see note 70 above: p. 1048.

88. On the basis of parallelism in two texts of Jeremiah (9,20; 22,15-16) Leibowitz identifies the 'way of the Lord' with "knowledge of the Lord", see note 5 above: pp. 169-170.

89. Westermann, *Genesis,* see note 6 above: pp. *12-36*, 273-274.

90. Cf. Neuser, J. (1985), *Genesis and Judaism. The Perspective of Genesis Rabbah. An Analytical Anthology,* Brown Judaic Studies 108, Atlanta, Georgia, Scholars Press: p. 81.

6

Judaism and Ecology

DAVID ROSEN

How manifold are thy works O Lord!
In wisdom hast thou made them all:
The earth is full of thy possessions.

These words make up the central verse of Psalm 104 which is full of detailed praise for the wonder, beauty and wisdom of the divine creation. At the heart of this adulation is the recognition that is most succinctly expressed at the beginning of Psalm 24: "The earth is the Lord's and the fullness thereof."

Indeed, fundamental to Biblical teaching is the affirmation that our world is created by God and thus belongs to Him. Human ownership can, in fact, be no more than tenancy. However, also central to Biblical teaching is the idea that the human being is more than simply the summit of this creation, and is in fact of such a special divinely endowed nature as to make the wanton destruction of a human life the most terrible and condemnable of deeds.

This special nature and privilege naturally bring with it special duties, responsibility and purpose, precisely in relation to creation itself. The human person is placed in the world in the Garden of Eden "to work and preserve it" (Genesis 2,15). Jewish tradition describes this task as a divinely mandated "partnership" with God in His creation.

Humanity's challenge is, therefore, to "work and preserve it", that is, to develop and to protect creation, our ecosystem. Genesis, however, also teaches us that at the heart of humanity's task and purpose is obedience to God's moral law and will, upon which depends humanity's success and well-being.

Furthermore, in reference to Abraham, the beloved of God, the prototype and example for all, it is stated even more categorically: "For

I know him that he will command his children and his household after him that they will keep the way of the Lord to do justice and righteousness". Accordingly, the task of the children of Abraham, and indeed of humanity, is to develop and protect our world physically, morally and spiritually.

The integration of these ideas may be perceived most profoundly in the Biblical concept of the Sabbatical year.

Sabbatical Year Dimensions

The teleology of the Sabbatical observance is precisely the recognition that "the earth is mine (says the Lord) and you are strangers and sojourners with me" (Leviticus 25,23). This recognition is expressed in three ways: During the seventh year, the land is to lie fallow (Exodus 23,10). The land rests and recuperates its natural vitality. Ownership of land in the sense of exclusive utilisation falls away for the year and the land and its natural produce are available for all and especially for the poor. Indeed as far as the land is concerned - and in an agricultural society the land is the very source of status - the Sabbatical year emphasizes that poor and rich alike are the same before God.

The connection between natural ecology and social ecology goes one stage further, precisely in relation to the vulnerable, in the second dimension of the Sabbatical year - in the cancellation of debts (Deuteronomy 15,1). Of course, this Biblical requirement has to be understood in the context of the agrarian society of Biblical times. This was not a commercial society in which monies were lent as part and parcel of economic life. Rather, loans were only necessary if the farmer had fallen upon hard times and had had a poor harvest or even none at all and lost his resources to guarantee the continued harvest cycle. In such a case, he borrowed from another, and when his harvest prospered, he could return the loan. The release of debts in the Sabbatical year prevented any unfortunate farmer from being caught up in a poverty trap and ensured a socio-economic balance between the more and the less fortunate and successful in society.

For a similar purpose, the Sabbatical year also required the release of slaves (Exodus 21,2-6). A Hebrew would enter into slavery within Israelite society if he had no means of providing a livelihood for himself or for his family. In this manner, he in fact sold his own employment to another. However, the requirements imposed upon those who maintained such slaves were so demanding that the Talmud declares that "he who had a Hebrew slave, in fact had a master over him!" The Bible indicates that an unmarried slave would be provided not only with all basic material needs but even with a wife. Understandably, in ancient Israel, there were not a few such Hebrew slaves who were very content to be in that situation. However, in the Sabbatical year, all such slaves were to be set free. "But if the slave plainly says 'I love my master, I will not go free', then his master shall bring him to the doorpost ... and shall pierce his ear with an awl ..." (Exodus 21,5-6).

Our sages of old ask, why should the ear be pierced and why against the doorpost? And they answer, let the doorpost over which God passed over in Egypt when He delivered the children of Israel from slavery and the ear which heard Him say at Sinai 'for unto me, the children of Israel are slaves' and not that they should be the slaves of slaves; let these testify that the man voluntarily relinquished his God-given freedom! Even then, according to Jewish law, the slave still had to go free in the Jubilee year, even if he still did not want to!

Thus the Sabbatical year emphasises not only the principle of divine ownership of His Creation and human custody of the natural ecology, but also the principle of God-given inalienable human dignity of all members of society as the foundation of a social ecology - what Pope John Paul II has described as a "human ecology".

Indeed, while the land itself and the earth's natural resources are to be respected and not over-exploited let alone destroyed, nevertheless, such respect and non-exploitation must be expressed above all in our social conduct, in our respect for human dignity and care for the vulnerable.

Significantly, therefore, the most extensive passage in the Bible dealing with the Sabbatical year, Leviticus 25, is followed by a chapter warning the children of Israel that if they hearken to God's commandments, they would live securely in the land and enjoy the rains in their season, the produce of the land and the bounty of the fruit trees. Whereas, if they failed to observe the commandments, (their) seed shall be sown in vain ... (their) land shall not yield its produce (nor) the trees of the land ... their fruit (Leviticus 26,16 & 20).

Fundamental Link

The twelfth-century Jewish scholarMaimonides understood these passages metaphorically and not literally. However, in our times, we may return to a literal understanding of these Biblical passages more obviously than ever before. For much of the pollution and destruction of our ecosystem are the result of human greed: insensitivity to the needs of other people as well as of other creatures, and unbridled exploitation and arrogance. In effect, much of the harm that is done to our land, our water sources, our air supply, and so on, is the result of our failure to hearken to God's ethical commandments and observe His moral will. As a result, we can no longer "live securely in the land" and our very survival on this planet is threatened. Only if we behave towards one another with justice and righteousness, with compassion and sensitivity; if we keep the Divine charge to "develop and preserve" our world, will we be able to enjoy the Creation that God has given us and be able to "live securely in the land". There is indeed a fundamental and inextricable link between our moral conduct and our ecosystem, and a human ecology is essential in order to preserve the natural ecology as a whole.

This demands of us to develop global perspectives on resources and responsibilities, for the human race is more interdependent than ever before. Indeed we live today, as it has been said, in a global village. A famous modern Jewish thinker, Abraham Joshua Heshel, declared that "parochialism has even become untenable". We might add that parochialism has even become self-destructive. Today, we who live in this global village are so interdependent that we are simply no longer able physically to avoid the moral challenge of our mutual responsibility. This recognition, if we were not able to see it as the Divine spiritual imperative that it is, now reveals itself as a socio-economic reality, demanding that we work together to address the global ecological challenges of our times. The inextricable relationship between moral and physical well-being has never been more evident.

One of the most popular texts concerning the idea of responsibility towards future generations precisely relates to the natural ecology. The Talmud, in tractate *Ta'anit* 23a, tells the story of a sage by the name of Honi who came across a man planting a carob tree. Honi asked the man how long it took for a carob tree to bear fruit and the man answered, seventy years. "Do you think you'll live to eat that fruit?" asked Honi. The man answered, "Just as my forefathers planted for me, so I plant this tree for my children and for theirs".

Of course, this story conveys more than just our responsibility for the natural ecology. It simply, yet powerfully, emphasises our religious, moral duty to consider and plan the consequences of our actions for the welfare of others and for the future of generations to come; to help create a sustainable, healthy, natural and moral human ecology for the future of humankind as a whole.

PART III

CHRISTIAN PERSPECTIVE

7

World Peace -
World Religions - World Ethic

HANS KÜNG

We all know that in the framework of the modern paradigm, specifically in the course of the French Revolution, the wars of the princes became wars of the nations. And with the end of modernity the wars of the nations became wars of the ideologies. Just consider: 1918 had already offered our century a first opportunity to replace the world of nationalistic modernity, which had collapsed with the first world war, with a new, more peaceful global world order. However, this was prevented by the ideologies of Fascism, Communism, National Socialism and Japanism, all of which had their foundations in modernity. In retrospect, they proved catastrophic false developments even for their supporters and set the whole world back by decades. Instead of a new world order there was world chaos.

Then, in 1945 (because of the obstruction caused by the Stalinist Soviet Union), the second opportunity for a new world order was missed. Instead of a new world order there was a division of the world.

In 1989 all these reactionary ideologies (including that of a self-righteous anti-Communism) came to an end; the age of the great ideologies seems to be over. Again, a new world order was propagated, though nothing was done towards realizing it. The wars (the Gulf War followed by the war in the Balkans) brought people back to earth. Has this third opportunity already been wasted? Instead of a new world order do we now have a new world disorder?

What Future Generations Have to Avoid: A War of Civilizations

Will not wars also be inevitable in the future? Certainly, but the wars in a new world epoch will no longer be wars of ideologies, but primarily wars of civilizations. This, at any rate, is the thesis of Samuel P. Huntington, the Director of the Institute of Strategic Studies at Harvard University, which is being much discussed at present. It is developed in his striking article on "The Clash of Civilizations?"[1] By "civilizations", Huntington, following Arnold Toynbee,[2] means the "cultural groupings", which extend beyond regions and nations. These are defined both by the objective elements of language, history, religion, custom and institutions and by the subjective self-identification of men and women. According to Huntington, there are today eight "civilizations" (with possible sub-civilizations): the Western, Confucian, Japanese, Islamic, Hindu, Slavic-Orthodox, Latin American and (perhaps also) African. So, in the future we are to expect political, economic and military conflicts, say, between Islamic civilization and the West, possibly combined with an "Islamic-Confucian connection" of the kind that can already be seen in the constant flow of weapons from China and North Korea to the Middle East. "The next world war, if there is one, will be a war between civilizations".[3]

If we survey the discussions which have taken place so far, especially in America,[4] it seems to me that some objections to Huntington's thesis do not even get off the ground. He has also explicitly affirmed:

- that even after the Cold War, nation states will remain the most powerful actors in world politics;
- that even future conflicts will be about political, economic and military power interests;
- there were, are, and will be numerous conflicts even within the civilizations concerned which cannot be explained as conflicts between civilizations.

Huntington has also been accused of interpreting political and economic conflicts *a priori* as ethnic and cultural conflicts and giving them a religious charge (as the un-religious Saddam Hussein attempted retrospectively to do in the Gulf War, adopting a cynical tactic). Here, a distinction must be made: of course, most conflicts, from Berg Karabach to the Gulf War, and from Bosnia to Kashmir, are not primarily about civilization and religion but about territories, raw materials, trade and money, in other words they are for economic, political and military interests. But the ethnic and religious rivalries form the constant underlying structures for territorial disputes, political interests and economic competition, structures by which political, economic and military conflicts can be justified, inspired and accentuated at any time. Great civilizations, therefore, do not necessarily appear to be the dominant paradigm for clashes in world politics, rather they offer the deeper cultural dimension or cultural resource to all antagonisms and conflicts between peoples which are always there and are in no way to be neglected. To this degree, Huntington is right in suggesting that in world politics, the Cold War paradigm and the First-Second-Third World pattern is to be replaced by a paradigm of civilizations.

Here I ask myself whether, when it comes to this cultural dimension, we should not begin more from the great religions and their different paradigms rather than civilizations, which are often difficult to define. In fact even Huntington is using religions to define civilizations when he speaks of an Islamic, Hindu, Confucian, or Slavic-Orthodox civilization. But there are two difficulties:

• Can one separate Orthodox Christianity as a distinctive civilization from 'Western' Christianity, as Toynbee has already done? A majority of Slavic Orthodox East Europeans and indeed Russians will protest that they do not belong to the European 'West'; in a broad analysis of the Christian paradigm, I try to show that Western and Slavic Orthodox Christianity are not two completely different religions or civilizations, but "only" two paradigms of one and the same Christianity (P II and P III). Certainly, these went their separate ways in the second millennium, but a reconciliation in the future is in no way to be ruled out.
• May one distinguish between Western North American and Latin American civilization so sharply? On both continents, politics, economics and culture were given a Christian stamp, from Europe, at almost the same time - with the cruel elimination of the native Indian population. The difference is that for Latin America the Latin Catholic paradigm (P III) was to be normative, whereas the normative paradigm for North America was to be Anglo-Saxon Protestant (P IV) and at a very early stage the modern Enlightenment paradigm (P V).

However, it must be said that Huntington is right on two decisive points:

i) As Toynbee already noted, contrary to all superficial politicians and political theorists, who overlook the depth-dimension in world political conflicts, religions are to be given a fundamental role in world politics: "In the modern world, religion is a central, perhaps the central force that motivates and mobilizes people ... what ultimately counts for people is not political ideology or economic interest. Faith and family, blood and belief, are what people identify with and what they will fight and die for".[5]
ii) Religions are not growing (and here Huntington differs from Toynbee) into a single unitary religion with Christian, Muslim,

Hindu and Buddhist elements in the service of a single human society. It is much more realistic also to take into account their potential for conflict as rivals: "Nation states will remain the most powerful actors in world affairs, but the principal conflicts of global politics will occur between nations and groups of different civilizations".[6]

Indeed, it will strike anyone who is not blind to history that the modern state frontiers in Eastern Europe (and in part, also in Africa) seem to pale in comparison with those age-old frontiers which were once drawn by peoples, religions and confessions: between Armenia and Azerbaijan, between Georgia and Russia, between the Ukraine and Russia, and also between the different peoples in Yugoslavia. We can understand the complexity of the problems in Yugoslavia only if we are aware that for a millennium - as a result of the division between the Western and Eastern Roman empire - two different paradigms of Christianity have been meeting in Yugoslavia, and that since the Turkish conquest 600 years ago, the Muslims (the only autochthonous Muslims in Europe) have also been a factor.

According to Huntington, we shall also have to reckon in the future with conflicts between civilizations. Such conflicts also threaten in the future; indeed, we must fear that "the most important conflicts of the future will occur along the cultural fault lines separating these civilizations from one another".[7] Why? Not only for geo-political reasons: because the world will become smaller and smaller, the interactions among people of different civilizations will become increasingly numerous, and the significance of the regional economic blocks will become increasingly important. But also for reasons of culture and religious politics:

1) the differences between the civilizations are not only real but fundamental, often age-old and all-embracing, from the upbringing of children and the constitution of the state to the understanding of the nature of God;

2) many people are once again reflecting on their own religious roots as a result of the cultural alienation and disillusionment with the West brought about by the process of economic and social modernization;

3) human cultural characteristics and differences are less changeable and dispensable than political and economic characteristics and differences (an Azerbaijani cannot become an Armenian and vice versa) and because religion divides mostly men and women even more sharply and exclusively than membership of a people: "A person can be half-French and half-Arab and

simultaneously even a citizen of two countries. It is more difficult to be half-Catholic and half-Muslim."[8] Particularly among people who are related in religion (what H.D.S. Greenway calls the "kin-country syndrome"), e.g. between Orthodox Serbs, Russians and Greeks, religion plays an underlying role which should not be neglected.

Countries where large parts of the population come from different civilizations, like the former Soviet Union or former Yugoslavia, may disintegrate over such conflicts. Other countries like Turkey, Mexico and Russia, which are culturally to some degree a unity but are inwardly at odds over which civilization they belong to (torn countries), will cause the greatest difficulties in any cultural reorientation that is necessary. A cultural redefinition is possible only if: first, the elite of such a country is vigorously committed to it; secondly, the people go along with it; and thirdly, the other civilization is prepared to receive the "convert". All three conditions seem to be fulfilled for Mexico in relation to North America; only the first two for Turkey in relation to the European Community; and perhaps none at all for Russia. But in the face of such possible conflicts even of civilizations and religions, does not the future of humankind look very dark? How are we to react to this situation?

What Future Generations Have to Strive for: Peace between Religions as Presuppositions for Peace among Nations

Not without justification, Huntington has been accused of deep pessimism and even an irresponsible fatalism; if conflicts in the future are to be primarily conflicts between civilizations, then these are as it were given by nature and therefore even unavoidable; in that case the future of humankind will be constant, endless war. Indeed, in that case, in addition to the "coming anarchy" because of "scarcity, crime, over-population, tribalism and disease" which the political journalist Robert D. Kaplan prognosticates in a striking and gloomy article in *Atlantic Monthly*,[9] there would ultimately and inevitably be a Third World War of civilizations which would necessarily lead to the end of our human race. Is there no alternative to this? Is it only the "West"?

Certainly, and this is not just Huntington's view, since the collapse of the Soviet system, the West has become excessively powerful - in military, economic and political terms - as a result of its wide-ranging control of the UN Security Council, the IMF, the "world community". But it has not succeeded in also winning over the young political, economic and intellectual elites in the rest of the world. The central axis of future world politics would be what has been called "the West and the

Rest". People in the West realize all too little that the basic Western concepts are fundamentally different from those of other civilizations. Individualism, liberalism, constitutionalism, democracy, separation of church and state, and human rights are concepts of which others find little resonance today in other cultures; these would tend, rather, to provoke the reaffirmation of their own traditional values. So what is to be done?

Despite everything, Huntington thinks also that these conflicts of civilizations must be avoided. In the short term there is a need to strive for a growing unity of the West, the increasing incorporation of Latin America and Eastern Europe, co-operation with Russia and Japan, a limitation of the military strength of the Islamic and Confucian states ... However, in the longer term, it is necessary to accommodate those non-Western civilizations which are preserving their traditional values and cultures and yet want to modernize themselves, and whose economic and military power will doubtless further increase. Huntington calls for this long-term strategy not only to maintain the economic and military power of the West in order to protect its own interests. Rather, Huntington's whole analysis culminates in a demand which is unusual for a political theorist.[10]

Now this is precisely what I am doing in my project on "The Religious Situation of our Time", under the slogan "No World Peace without Religious Peace". So it is now possible to formulate the pragmatic antithesis to the "clash of civilizations". This runs: "Without peace between religions, war between the civilizations. Therefore, no peace among the religions without dialogue between the religions. No dialogue between the religions without investigation of the foundations of these religions ...".

It is my conviction that the analyses of the political theorist are partly confirmed by those of the philosopher and the theologian. And at the same time, they also are partly differentiated. Here, I would mention just four important points:

- Firstly, if we recognize that Western and Eastern Christianity do not represent two religions/civilizations but two different constellations, albeit very different, two paradigms of the one Christianity (P II and P III), the convergence of, and mutual understanding between, which had already been considerably advanced by John XXIII, the Second Vatican Council and Patriarch Athenagoras of Constantinople, then we can also recognize that an ecumenical understanding among the churches (in Yugoslavia, the Ukraine, with Russia) could have prepared the way for mutual understanding among the peoples in them. (Why should what was possible between French and Germans be impossible, say, between Serbs and Croats?)

- Secondly, if we work out that even three religions like Judaism, Christianity and Islam, which historically have been mostly in confrontation, nevertheless have numerous common features of faith and even more, of ethics, then we need not give up hope that the tensions which naturally there have always been between religions and civilizations will not necessarily lead to a clash, even to a military collision. In that case, peace is possible (why should not an agreement like that between the Israelis and the Palestinians be also possible between Armenians and Azerbaijanis, Indians and Pakistanis?).
- Thirdly, if in each religion one attempts to work out the different paradigms - the original, the ancient, the "medieval", the modern paradigms - which (origins excluded) have all usually been preserved to the present day, we can see better how the fundamentalist option is nowhere the only one, but that in all the great religions (and quite especially in Judaism, Christianity, and Islam) several options are on offer, at least some of which make understanding easier. In fact, today every religion is unavoidably confronted with modernity, with modern science, technology, industry, democracy and generally, with modern culture.
- Fourthly, if Western politicians, diplomats and lawyers had a better knowledge of the other religions, then they would be in a position not only to negotiate but also to carry on dialogue. At international negotiations and conferences like, for example, the most recent conference on human rights in Vienna, they could point out to the Chinese Communists (and other autocratic Asian governments) that human rights are not something exclusively Western, but that the concept of "jen", the "humanum", is quite a central concept of Chinese tradition which could very well be a basis for human rights at the present time.[11] And there is no disputing the fact that from China, Tibet, Burma and Thailand through Indonesian Westirian and from the Philippines to Kenya and the Congo, human rights express something deeply longed for by subjects from their rulers.

With freedom of opinion, a man like Ying Sheng in China could activate the millions that the brave Nobel prizewinner Aung San Sun Kyi could mobilize in Burma through free elections. Yet, without a doubt, a better basis for human rights, for peoples of the non-Western world, could be found in their own ethnic and religious traditions than simply in the Western notion of natural law.

Lastly, if people in the West had a better knowledge of other religious and cultural traditions, they would understand why many Asians, who are open to the West and affirm modernization, are still sceptical about the Western system of values. Thus, for example, many Asians are unwilling to accept, say, unlimited individualism (with no concern for community) and absolute freedom (with all the phenomena of Western decadence connected with it); rather, as always, they attach importance to strong families, intensive education, strict work, frugality, a lack of demands and national teamwork (thus, the diplomat Tommy Koh, who is Director of the Institute of Policy Studies in Singapore).[12]

Does the West also practise the values which it preaches to the "rest"? All this brings us to my third point, which has not had its due in the discussion of Huntington so far, the question of an ethic, given the lack of orientation which is nowadays rampant everywhere.

The Great Danger for Future Generations: Lack of Orientation

What should human beings hold on to - in all circumstances and everywhere? The vacuum in orientation is a world problem.

Everywhere in the former Soviet block after the collapse of Communism and under the surface even in Communist China, still as oppressive as before: "To cope with this moral and spiritual vacuum is a problem not only for China but for all civilizations".[13]

In the United States, where the population has increased by 41% since 1960 but violent crimes have increased by 560%, single mothers by 419%, divorces by 300%, children growing up in one-parent families by 300%,[14] and shootings are the second most frequent cause of death after accidents (in 1990, 4,200 teenagers were shot).

In Europe, where after the murder of a two-year-old child by two ten-year-olds in Liverpool even *Der Spiegel* lamented in a cover story on the "orientation jungle" and a lack of "tabus" unprecedented in cultural history: "The youngest generation must cope with a confusion of values the extent of which is almost impossible to estimate. For them, clear standards of right and wrong, good and evil, of the kind that were still being communicated by parents and schools, churches and sometimes even politicians in the 1950s and 1960s, are hardly recognizable any more."[15]

Modern men and women who are alienated from themselves, who have "killed" God, are wandering aimlessly and with no resting place, threatened with nihilism, through a time and a world which are less and less easy to survey. What Friedrich Nietzsche, the most clear-sighted critic of modernity (though he did not overcome it), saw already arising in the nineteenth century, namely, man "beyond good and evil", obligated only to his "will to power",[16] the "death of God" and overturning the "whole of European morality", has become a fatal reality in the twentieth century: not only in figures of terror like Stalin and Hitler, not only in the Holocaust, the Gulag Archipelago and in two world wars ending with atomic bombs, but also in everyday life, in the unprecedented scandals involving leading politicians, businessmen and trade unionists in our industrial nations, or in the egocentricity, consumerism, violence and xenophobia of so many people, young people in particular.

It is amazing that *The Book of Virtues* by William Bennett, formerly adviser on drugs to the American president, which argues for a "reasonable mean between a charter for vandals and torture" also reached the top of the bestseller list in America.[17] It is again possible to talk of responsibility, honesty, loyalty, courage, compassion, friendship, tenacity and self-discipline. Today, it should be clear, without further justification that if, in the new world constellation which is coming into being, humankind on our planet is going to have any further guarantee of survival, there is urgent need for a universal basic consensus on humane convictions. A question which is thousands of years old is also unavoidable in our time. Why should one do good and not evil? Why are people not just obligated to their will to power, to success, riches, consumer goods, sex? Fundamental questions are often the most difficult of all, and all over the world much about morals, laws and customs was taken for granted down the centuries because it was backed by religious authority which is no longer automatically accepted. A worldwide dialogue, a global dialogue, has already been set in motion which is to lead to a consensus over shared values, standards and basic attitudes, which should lead to a global ethic.

For the fundamental question is: why should human beings - understood as individuals, groups, nations, religions - behave not in a bestial way, merely ruled by their physical urges, but in a human, truly human, humane way? Why should they do this unconditionally, in other words in all circumstances? And why should everyone do this, and no class, clique or group, no state or party be excepted? The question of an obligation which is both unconditional (categorical) and universal (global) is the basic question for any ethic in a society which is shaped by tendencies towards increasing scientific and economic globalization (one need think only of the international financial market or satellite television).

It should be evident that there is a fundamental problem here particularly for modern democracy, which has now also been adopted by Eastern Europe, about which we should not moralize in a self-righteous way but on which we should reflect self-critically. The mediaeval clerical ('black") state and then again the modern totalitarian ("brown" or "red") state prescribed the world view and punished any deviation with corresponding penalties, even to the point of burning or gassing people. But the self-understanding of the free democratic state, which recognizes freedom of conscience and religion, is that it must be neutral in its world-view, and must tolerate different religions and confessions, philosophies and ideologies. Yet, for all that, this state should not decree any meaning to life or any lifestyle; it should not set down any supreme values and ultimate norms in law if it is not to violate its ideological neutrality. Is this not quite manifestly the basis of the dilemma of any modern democratic state, whether in Europe, America, India or Japan?

People normally feel an unquenchable desire to hold onto something, to rely on something. In a technological world which has become so complex, and in the confusion of their private lives, they would like to have somewhere to stand, a line to follow; they would like to have criteria, a goal. In short, people sense an unquenchable desire to have something like a basic ethical orientation.

But all experiences show that human beings cannot be improved by more and more laws and precepts, nor, of course, can they be improved simply by psychology and sociology. In things both small and great we are confronted with the same situation: knowledge of things is not yet knowledge of meanings, rules are not yet orientations, and laws are not yet morals. Even the law needs a moral foundation. And security in our cities and villages cannot be bought simply with money (and more police and prisons). The ethical acceptance of laws (which provide the state with sanctions and can be imposed by force) is the presupposition of any political culture. What is the use to individual states or organizations, whether these be the European Community, the United States of America or the United Nations, of constantly new laws, if a majority of people or powerful groups or individuals have no thought of observing them and constantly find enough ways and means of irresponsibly imposing their own or collective interests? *Quid leges sine moribus*?, runs a Roman saying: "What are laws without morals?"

Towards a Global Ethic Binding Future Generations

Certainly all states in the world have an economic and a legal order, but in no state in the world will this order function without an ethical consensus, without an ethic for its citizens by which the state with a democratic constitution lives. Already in the French Revolution there were those who wanted to have human duties formulated from the start along with human rights. The international community has already created transnational, transcultural and transreligious legal structures (without which international treaties would in fact be sheer self-deception). But if it is to exist, a new world order needs a minimum of common values, standards and basic attitudes, an ethic which, for all its time-conditioned nature, is binding in all senses of the word, for the whole of humanity, in short, a global ethic.

It was at the Parliament of the World's Religions, meeting in Chicago on 4 September 1993, that the Declaration Toward a Global Ethic[18] was passed. For the first time in the history of religions, a minimal basic consensus relating to binding values, irrevocable standards and fundamental moral attitudes was formulated. This basic ethical consensus can be:

- affirmed by all religions despite their "dogmatic" differences, and
- supported by non-believers.

Now, of course, that does not mean that such a global ethic would make the specific ethics of the different religions superfluous. The global ethic is no substitute for the Sermon on the Mount or the Torah, the Qur'an, the Bhagavadgita, the Discourses of the Buddha or the Sayings of Confucius. On the contrary, it is precisely these age-old "sacred texts", which are important for billions of people, that can give a global ethic a solid foundation and make it concrete in a convincing way.

Let me end by quoting what the Global Ethic Declaration has to say about non-violence:

Numberless women and men of all regions and religions strive to lead lives not determined by egoism but by commitment to their fellow humans and to the world around them. Nevertheless, all over the world we find endless hatred, envy, jealousy and violence, not only between individuals but also between social and ethnic groups, between classes, races, nations, and religions. The use of violence, drug trafficking and organized crime, often equipped with new technical possibilities, has reached global proportions. Many places are still ruled by terror "from above"; dictators oppress their own people, and institutional violence is widespread. Even in some countries where laws exist to protect individual freedoms, prisoners are tortured, men and women are mutilated, hostages are killed.

(a) In the great ancient religious and ethical traditions of humankind we find the directive: *You shall not kill!* Or in positive terms: *Have respect for life!* Let us reflect anew on the consequences of this ancient directive: all people have a right to life, safety and the free development of personality in so far as they do not injure the rights of others. No one has the right physically or psychically to torture, injure, much less kill, any other human being. And no people, no state, no race, no religion has the right to hate, to discriminate against, to "cleanse", to exile, much less to liquidate a "foreign" minority which is different in behaviour or holds different beliefs.

(b) Of course, wherever there are humans there will be conflicts. Such conflicts, however, should be resolved without violence within a framework of justice. This is true for states as well as for individuals. Persons who hold political power must work within this framework of a just order and commit themselves to the most non-violent, peaceful solutions possible. They should work for this within an international order of peace which itself has need of protection and defence against perpetrators of violence. Armament is a mistaken path; disarmament is the commandment of the times. Let no one be deceived; there is no survival for humanity without global peace.

(c) Young people must learn at home and in school that violence may not be a means of settling differences with others. Only thus can a *culture of non-violence* be created.

(d) A human person is infinitely precious and must be unconditionally protected. But, likewise, *the lives of animals and plants* which inhabit this planet with us deserve protection, preservation and care. Limitless exploitation of the natural foundations of life, ruthless destruction of the biosphere and militarization of the cosmos are all outrageous. As human beings we have a special responsibility - especially with a view to future generations - for Earth and the cosmos, for the air, water and soil. We are all *intertwined* in this cosmos and we all are dependent on each other. Each one of us depends on the welfare of all. Therefore the dominance of humanity over nature and the cosmos must not be encouraged. Instead, we must cultivate living in harmony with nature and the cosmos.

(e) To be authentically human in the spirit of our great religious and ethical traditions means that in public as well as in our private life we must be concerned for others and ready to help. We must never be ruthless and brutal. Every people, every race, every religion must show tolerance and respect - indeed high appreciation - for every other. Minorities need protection and support, whether they be racial, ethnic or religious.

I am convinced that the new world order will be a better order only if as a result we have a pluralistic world society characterized by partnership, which encourages peace and is nature-friendly and ecumenical. That is why, even now, many people are committing themselves on the basis of their religious or human convictions to a common world ethic and are calling all people of good will to contribute to a change of awareness in matters of ethics.

Notes

1. Huntington, S. P. (1993). 'The Clash of Civilizations?', *Foreign Affairs* 72(5): pp. 22-49.

2. Toynbee, A. (1934-1961). *The Study of History*, vols. I-XIII, Oxford: p. 61.

3. Huntington, S. P., see note 1 above: p. 39.

4. Ajami, F., Bartley, R. L., Binyan, L., Kirkpatrick, J. J., Mahbubani, K. (1993). 'The Critical Responses to Huntington', *Foreign Affairs*, 72(4). Huntington's 'Response', *Foreign Affairs* 72(5): pp. 186-94.

5. Huntington, S. P., "Response', *Foreign Affairs* 8: pp. 191-94.

6. Huntington, S. P., see note 1 above: p. 22.

7. *Ibid.*: p. 25.

8. *Ibid.*: p. 27.

9. Kaplan, R. D. (1994). 'The Coming Anarchy', *Atlantic Monthly* (February): pp. 44-76.

10. Huntington, S.P., see note 1 above: p. 49. Jacques Delors, (ex) President of the European Community Commission, is also convinced that "future conflicts will be sparked by cultural factors rather than economics or ideology". And he warns: "The West needs to develop a deeper understanding of the religious and philosophical assumptions underlying other civilizations, and the way other nations see their interests, to identify what we have in common" (quoted in Huntington, S. P., see note 4 above: p. 194).

11. Shu-Hsien, L. (1993). 'Das Humanum als entscheidendes Kriterium aus der Sicht des Konfuzianismus', pp. 92-108 in Küng, H. and Kuschel, K. J. (eds.), *Weltfriedent durch Religionsfrieden*, Munich.

12. Koh, T. (1993). 'The Ten Values that Undergird East Asian Strength and Success', *International Herald Tribune* (12 December).

13. Binyan, L. (1993). *Foreign Affairs* 72(4): p. 21.

14. Mahbubani, K. (1993). 'The Critical Responses to Huntington', *Foreign Affairs* 72(4): p. 14.

15. Cf. *Der Spiegel* 9 (1993).

16. Küng, H. (1984). 'The Rise of Nihilism: Friederich Nietzsche' in *Does God Exist? An Answer for Today*, London: ch. 1.

17. Bennett, W. (1994). *The Book of Virtues,* New York.

18. Küng, H. and Kuschel, K. J. (eds.) (1993). *A Global Ethic: The Declaration of the Parliament of the World's Religions*, London, SCM Press.

8

Responsible Parenthood for
Future Generations

EMILIANOS TIMIADIS

One of the evils threatening human intelligence is the superficial approach to, and reading of, what is known as "history". It is not enough to recall past events chronologically without scrutinising, with a critical mind, the "whys" of those events and drawing the appropriate lessons. Etymologically, history, ιστορια, comes from the classical Greek verb οιδα, meaning going deeper into the casual reasons of events. In such a way the great historian Thucydides invites us to read the Peloponnesian Wars critically so that future generations avoid grave mistakes committed in the past.

For the Greek historian Polybios (200-120 B.C.), an objective analyst of national and political upheavals, history implies a continuous schooling and learning for all from happy or unhappy events. Thence, his diptych: παθημα, μαθημα, "Knowledge of history constitutes a unique education and exercise-*paideia* and *gymnasia*" (Hist. I, 1, 2).

What happens today as the understanding of history is fragmentary and discouraging? We should shape education in such a way that contemporaries study the past of humanity carefully and find out the interrelationship and interdependence of events with the future. If we start our inquiry from the first generation (the first couple in the Old Testament) we find two key statements by God: that this Earth should be kept carefully, and that continuous work should be done for its maintenance and progress (Gen 3,23). This means that while we enjoy all the blessings of creation, we cannot overlook those coming after us, for the earthly resources and spiritual values are established for the benefit of both present and future generations.

The trouble is that we do not have a holistic picture of humanity as a universal family embracing past, present and future generations. Each human being living now somehow belongs also to future generations. We have inherited so many monuments from our ancestors. Similarly we should bequeath to posterity a healthy heritage that goes beyond environmental richness, and includes also spiritual values, cultural traditions and technological advancement.

When one approaches the issue of future generations from the perspective of human beings in the process of becoming, one cannot avoid raising the problem of birth control and population growth. These could be seen as a violation of the natural link between human generations in the ongoing process of humanity's development in history. The following pages offer a careful examination of the issues of birth control and population growth.

A New Mission

Demography, birth-control and a right solution to such pressing problems preoccupy all of us. We may differ on secondary details, but as regards the essentials there is a consensus, in spite of different wordings and formulations. Such is the case of a recent book by Abdel Rahim Omran, professor of the conservative Moslem University of Al Azhar in Cairo.[1]

It is time to underline an aspect often forgotten: the human person is a referential being whose wellbeing depends on past values, who at the same time transmits values to posterity. And the question is: What quality of values will we leave for future generations? Aristotle uses the term πολιτικος (politikos) in order to show the inner connection of one citizen to the precedent and to the descendant κοινωνικον και πολιτικον ζωον (Politika A2, 12 53, 3). This important affirmation was repeated by St. Basil of Caesarea, widening the horizons of contemplative life, showing the *unus nullus* (Great Rules, quest. 3). We have, by all means, to fight any self-centred view of man and of Creation, which was known as Narcissism, so well refuted by Louis Lavelle: *"Narcise s'enferme dans sa propre solitude pour faire société avec lui-meme; dans cette parfaite suffisance qu'il espère, il éprouve sa propre impuissance."*[2]

In each age we must think not only of the problems emerging from the state of our current needs and challenges concerning our pleasure and comfort, but also of what eventual repercussions these may have for future generations. Let us take a hypothetical example. We are born and around us there are no trees, no vegetation and no water. It is terrible, catastrophic, and certainly such a new inhabitant would rightly want to repeat the wish of Job not to have been born at all. Fortunately, such is not the case: after our birth, we do find a smiling and most beautiful Nature. But our age undergoes changes that threaten not only the future but even the present generations. In addition to the natural devastations and moral deviations, the worst are errors with regard to family health, to the right education, to a decline in most fields of leisure time, music, art, the very meaning of life, sexual behaviour, with an unbalanced attention to "having", "possessing", "enjoying" and less to the "being" of our interior world.

We risk passing on to those who are to come after us a distorted picture of life: hedonistic, self-indulgent, superficial, rather than a deep spiritual metamorphosis. We must declare openly that in the most fundamental ethical issues, the differences amongst Judaism, Christianity and Islam are morphological rather than essential. The same thing is formulated in different languages but is almost identical. It is not fair to try to insist upon the same expression. Above all, what counts is the essential. We all may agree that none of us advocates the excesses of hypertrophied nationalism; nobody claims that such illogical stands convey the spirit of our respective religions. It is impossible that one God in whom we all believe could dictate to us to consider the other as an enemy, an opponent, an unbeliever.

We need a new mission, to reduce tensions, confessing that all of us, in spite of our differences, are children of God, that this Earth is common to us, to feed all; that the same God demands a common effort to restore the family's dignity, the woman's respectability, to improve the education given to our children and to provide all with human values. For such targets, it is easy to find parallel references in our sacred books. We all agree that the very centre of the decline or renewal in man is in our heart. In it is played the whole problem of the right choice, of the right interpretation of so many vital questions. Hearts need a cathartic operation regarding humility and true penitence.

Crisis within Families

In a short theatrical sketch played in Athens recently, the focus was on the causes of wars. A little child was asking his father: "How do wars begin?" The father said: "Listen carefully. Let us take a comparison, supposing that England and America disagree". But at that moment, the mother, hearing this intervenes and remarks sharply: "This is nonsense! These two countries can never disagree. It is shameful to tell such lies to our child!"

The father gets angry and says: "Who claimed the contrary? I just expressed a hypothetical case which of course does not correspond with reality." But the mother, fuelled by such an argument, becomes more aggressive: "You do not know how to explain to our child and discuss it with him!" Of course, the dialogue deteriorated into a quarrel, increasing the tension and the words exchanged became more bitter. The young boy, surprised and shocked, intervenes, to put an end to this quarrel: "Father, I thank you. Now, I do know well how wars start!"

Hence, the origin of conflicts, disputes, enmities. Not only among nations, but among friends, neighbours, within the same family. The most insignificant thing can upset one, almost accidentally. Most disputes begin by a small spark, from a violent expression, from nothing. And yet, behind this "nothing" is hidden a greater evil: an excessive egoism, a self-reliance. It is this spark fuelling our anger and passion, escalating into conflicts, rupture, division, hostility. This happens in every other field. Our heart is already weakened, vulnerable, receptive to any kind of evil. In view of such considerations and aware of dangerous symptoms, explosive for the future, we have to re-educate ourselves, thus preparing for a better future generation. Without such an ontological, deep inner renewal, peaceful co-existence (as idealized by international organisations) would remain a pure dream. What St. James in his letter has to say on this matter can certainly be found, with equal meaning but differently formulated, both in the Old Testament and in the Qu'ran:

What causes wars, and what causes fightings among you? Is it not your passions that are at war in your members? You desire and do not have: so you kill. And you covet and cannot obtain; so you fight and wage war. You do not have, because you do not ask. You ask and do not receive, because you ask wrongly to spend it on your passions ...(James 4, 1-4).

What is vital to a continuous and everlasting education of the present and the next generations is the basic truth: that man is not the exclusive owner on Earth but only a steward, an administrator, *oikonomos*. God entrusted to him as a reliable partner this beautiful life and cosmos, in order to profit from it, while allowing others to do the same. He never meant us to become victims of avidity, of selfish possession. Stewardship and good management of resources, of potentials, of all blessings, so that we move towards a sharing, more brotherly, more human world.

Contemporary scientists and thinkers, proud of the culture that the next generation will inherit, forget that our heritage for them is much wider than paintings, electronics, monuments and buildings. It is the spiritual side, the values that all these convey. If, during this technological era, so much progress is made in many directions, we must pass to another field for success; not in order to destroy the first one, admittedly remaining so important, but to complete it, to elevate it, to integrate it to a conception of the world where man as the most valuable creature of God will be the very centre. The most grave pollutions threatening us are not only those devastating our forests, affecting our rivers and seas, but mainly those which pollute man's sacred nature, deteriorating the most valuable assets we ever had - those values which constitute the moral and spiritual everlasting grandeur of man.

Creativity is a most distinguished characteristic of man. While animals behave always as they have done in bygone days - the birds building their nests exactly as in the past - only man is an inventing creature. Sophocles, the tragic Greek, underlined this potential due to human wisdom and, above all, inspiration by using the key term, μηχανη - mechane. His statement is very important for the advancement of technology and science: We produce arts which nobody could believe "ουδεις δυναται πιστευσαι" (Antigone, v. 332). Thus is explained the restless spirit of man, seeking always the better, the higher, the more perfect, going on and looking to a limitless progress.

Monotheistic religions, therefore, must unite their efforts to stop the progressive implantation of a materialistic totalitarianism which tries to de-spiritualise and de-humanise more and more of our contemporaries. In this respect heavy is the task of educators and teachers. If our present society is dominated by egoism, violence and permissiveness, little by little it risks reaching the stage of desert, where love and dignity are totally absent. Our respective religions facing such threats are not permitted to ignore each other, and even worse, are mutually confronting each other in a deplorable sterile way by antagonistic arguments, obsessed by past historical conflicts.

For a better understanding of each other and our common tasks, it is imperative to find converging views on vital issues. Such an attitude is more constructive than always going back, recalling unjust misbehaviours of the past. This will promote more fraternal relations, starting from what is uniting in the most profound and sacred matters. Often, we suffer from an amnesia of the eternal transcending our religions. Whether we like it or not, we are condemned to a common future. If we start from now to plant trees for future forests, our children will not ask whether these had been planted by Christian, Jewish or Moslem hands. What matters, above all, is to find a green rather than an eroded arid land. If someone is very near to drowning, it is of no importance who will save him. What counts mostly is to be taken out of the water in the quickest possible way.

Religion as such has to face a common unhealthy attitude among our people, namely selfishness. This is already manifested in a passionate over-production, over-consumption, while being blinded with the idea "God does not exist" or "He does not care". This egoism hinders us from realising what has been said by the Prophet Isaiah preaching in the Kingdom of Judah between 760 and 687 B.C. and correcting the then arrogant society: "Yes, O Lord, You are our Father: we are the clay, and you are our potter; we are all the work of your hand. Be not exceedingly angry, O Lord, and remember not iniquity for ever ..." (64, 8-9). We creatures ignore and disrespect our Creator.

Responsible Parenthood

Sexuality or the procreation faculty in marital relationship in all religions is one of the most important ethical issues to be examined but equally a most decisive one for human happiness or degradation. Much of the spiritual equilibrium depends on a right approach to it. Nobody would claim that sexuality is just one of the many bodily functions without further repercussions. Any excessive approach to it may create incurable traumas, obsessions, and psycho-somatic consequences. Behind the act itself a whole mystery of inner disorder is hidden for the simple reason that this act is a product of inner conflicts, where the heart plays a great role, and because the whole affective world is involved, before and after the act.

Let us take celibacy. This is not contempt of carnal and fleshly powers as such. We are not enemies of the human body since sexuality is part of our life. Simply, there are different ways, positive or negative, to live and express it. If by sexuality we mean to take the other partner as an object for our own selfish pleasure or appetite, and after having enjoyed it to let it go, sexuality becomes negative and harmful. But there is equally another way of approach - positive, constructive and liberating.

It must be added, to clarify a point in this inquiry, that the main objective of sexuality is not only procreation, as may be assumed. Mainly, it offers the possibility of having a full affective balanced life by both husband and wife, receiving and mutually giving. Procreation then comes as a kind of consecration of sexuality, before God and men, in terms of an honest exchange of two free beings declaring mutual love. Their experience from now on will not be restricted to enjoyment only, but it will cover several interrelated areas: spiritual, psychological and carnal.

Properly working together, they will offer a new life in the full sense. They will transmit this life which already they project themselves, harvesting an immense joy. Sexuality, therefore, will allow them to realise potentialities of life through their deep love.

This means that sexuality has a most responsible function. That equally means that it needs to be disciplined, and not to be expressed in unrestricted, endless desires. As such it may be most damaging. There may occur perversive attitudes to our own body, to the other man's or to the woman's body. Uncontrolled desires inevitably seek satisfaction without being scrupulous and extend in all the most obscure directions:

homosexuality, bisexuality, abnormal acts, etc. The main problem lies within the heart where all possibilities are envisaged and the game is played. We must be extremely cautious and watchful to see what is happening in the interior of ourselves.

If one is honest, one should have an immense respect for the other, whoever it may be. If love is the supreme virtue, we must also make clear what we mean by that "love". St. Augustine said: "Love, and then do whatever you want", *Ama et fac quod vis* (Tractatus 7,8: 1 Letter St. John), assuming that nothing would contradict true love. If we really believe in human dignity, if we hold to a transcendence in life and that while here on earth life has another finality than simply to rot in the cave, this conviction must be illustrated in our way of life and behaviour. This is the best way for challenging the world. Some naive people often speak of a society. Such a change will be the result of each one's own change, through the example one gives in one's own place and in one's daily relationships.

From this vast and many-sided question we limit ourselves to the Church's attitude. Our primary concern will be to present the Orthodox viewpoint by referring to Patristic sources and to the relevant pronouncements of the Councils of the undivided Church, these being the two sources which usually guide our priests in the hearing of confessions and in pastoral care. It is impossible to consider a subject such as the present one in isolation; it must be viewed in its relation to the teaching of the Fathers in a wider spectrum: namely of self-discipline in regard to sexual desires, on the essential sacredness of the body and its functions, and on those moral responsibilities, conditions and disciplinary restrictions which govern sexual intercourse within marriage.

An Overall Patristic View

The *Didache* already states clearly: "You shall not kill a child in embryo" (ου φονευσεις τεκvvov εν φθορα - 2,2). Athenagoras similarly remarks: "All those who prevent childbearing become responsible before God". He considers as murderers those using drugs to exterminate embryos from women's wombs (τας τοις αμβλωθριδιοις χρωμενας ανφροφονειν - Delegatio 35; *PG* 6, 969).

Tertullian very clearly disapproves of any action that hinders the natural process of the birth of a conceived child, because it is already a full human being (Apolog. 9,8).

In assembling more Canonical evidence, we must bear in mind that the Church wanting to ensure a better world, present and future, took all steps needed to ensure a healthy family life. And the focus on sexual behaviour is seen in the pronouncement of eventual sanctions against those using abortive means. The frequent reference to such poisons, very common in those days, reveals that the society in which Christians were living was still pagan. Thus the local Council of Ancrya (circa 314), states:

Regarding women who become prostitutes and kill their babies (αναιρουσων τα γεννωμενα), and who make it their business to concoct abortives (φθορια ποιειν), the former rule barred them for life from eucharistic communion, and they are left without recourse. But, having found a more philanthropic alternative (φιλανθρωποτερον ευροντες) we have fixed the sentence to ten years ... (Canon 21).

Of high importance are the Canons of St Basil of Caesarea (330-379) writing to his friend Amphilochius to answer questions of a pastoral and moral nature sent to him. Although he seems too rigid, he allows a merciful attitude to women sincerely repentant for having used poisonous plants preventing child-birth:

A woman who aborts deliberately is liable to the crime of a murderess (ηφθειρασα κατ επιτηδευσιν). For her there is involved the question of providing justice for the infant to be born, but also for the woman who has plotted against her own self (εκουσιως φονευουσι καταλογιζονται). The destruction of the embryo constitutes another murder (Canon 2).

In another canon he repeats the same attitude: "those women who bring about a miscarriage by giving drugs for this purpose, and the women who take abortifacient poisons (αμβλωθριδια διδουσαι φαρμακα, φονευτριαι), they too are murderesses" (Canon 8).

In the above 8th Canon, St. Basil treats the thorny issue of voluntary murders, by distinguishing which ones are wilful and which are involuntary murders committed without the concurrence of the will of the person committing them (και αι δεχομεναι τα εμβρυοκτονα δηλητηρια). He is clear by stating that both women and men who concoct certain poisonous draughts and administer them or furnish them to women with the object of killing the infants in their womb, are unquestionably guilty and subject to penitential discipline.

St. Paul's attitude towards continence or intimate matrimonial relationship is exposed very clearly in his letter 1 Cor 7. The background of this letter is well known. Certain Corinthians having heard extremist views of "sexual abstentionism" have sent a letter to Paul asking whether they should abstain from women in general. Paul seizes this opportunity to make a fundamental statement about virginity and marriage, at the same time raising the delicate issue of what to do if one of the partners (πυρουεσθαι),"burned by the desire of the flesh", wants sexual intercourse. We follow here the most penetrating reflections of John Chrysostom, in his synthesis on the text:

In such a critical moment either of the two has to obey the other for the sake of harmony. Rather, this duty and logical compromise become imperative. To insist, unilaterally, upon abstinence and proposing continence, without the other's consent, contradicts the very basis of Paul's instruction: 'defraud you not one another' (v.5).

Now there are women, who, by depriving their husbands of this pleasure, commit more harm than good. By behaving like this, they become responsible for any eventual debauchery in their husbands, thus breaking down everything. Above anything else mutual unity should prevail; much more than that is preferably a mutual concord, because this should remain always the most essential element of their bond. But let us examine more in detail.

Suppose that in a certain case of a given couple of a man and woman, it is the woman who prefers chastity against the will of the man. If he, then, accidentally, commits fornication due to such an attitude, what will be the result? Or, if he, let us suppose, does not fornicate, but badly suffers, on account of this, feeling pain, burning and wrestling, and causes in addition so many annoyances to the wife? What would be then the value or gain of fasting and continence, if their love is broken because of this disagreement? Certainly none! How much railing from this, how many disturbances, quarrels thus turn into sad reality?

If in a given family the husband and wife are quarrelling, then such a home would not differ much from a vessel being dangerously tossed about by the rough sea, because it is similar to what would happen if the master captain was arguing with the pilot. "... And come together again, that Satan tempt you not for your incontinency" (v.5).

Let the husband render unto the wife due benevolence; and likewise also the wife unto her husband. What is the due benevolence all about? That the wife henceforth does not dominate her own body, but with regard to her husband is both his servant and his matron. If you try to be discharged, O woman, of this binding servitude, then you offend towards God. And again, if you want to remain matrimonially alone, provided the husband consents to this, let this be done for a short time only. That is why Paul called this a 'duty', in order to show that nobody is master of his own self, but both are servants of one another. When you see a harlot tempting you, say: my body is not mine alone, but is of my wife ... Husbands should love their wives, the wife should fear her husband (Eph 5,25). Here there is not between them anyone greater or lesser but the authority - εξουσια - is one and the same over both. For what reason? Because the matter here is about continence - σοφροσψνι. On any other matter let the wife, says the husband, have her advantage. But whenever it is a question of continence, not at all. It is a question of equality and neither excels the other.[3]

Deserving special attention is the penetrating remark of one of the Books of the Old Testament with regard to the degree of gravity in a matrimonial relationship not resulting in completed procreation. The ancient law admits that abortion, concerning a complete human embryo, cannot be accepted and therefore is condemned formally. But quite different is the case where the process of formation of the human image is not too advanced. Here a lenient attitude is recommended. Here is the verse of Exodus 21, 22-23:

When men strive together, and hurt a woman with child, so that there is a miscarriage, and yet no harm follows, the one who hurt her shall be fined, according as the woman's husband shall lay upon him; and he shall pay as the judges determine. If any harm follows, then you shall give life for life, eye for eye, tooth for tooth, hand for hand, foot for foot, burn for burn, wound for wound, stripe for stripe.

Not only in those days but even in our days this burning question as to when precisely the embryo is identified remains a mystery. What one can say is that the embryo becomes a person from the moment of its conception. The above text of the Old Testament distinguishes between ανεικονιστον and εξεικονισμενου. In the first case, its accidental death is not punishable but in the second when the embryo is already visible, the offender is liable to penalty.

Around the fourth century, Gregory of Nyssa (died 394), in writing to a certain Hierus, "On the infants and their premature death" (*PG* 46, 161-192), states clearly that the embryo is animated, that is, gets a soul - *anima* - from the moment of conception, while in the West many theories were expressed putting as time of the full formation of embryo after 40 days.

Rejecting radical views that see only an amount of cells, we are reminded by Saint Paul of his firm conviction of being early as in the womb of his mother: "God set me apart before I was born... (Gal. I, 15). The term used here εκ κοιλιας μητρος, signifies that since that time, that is, of conception in the womb of his mother, he was already personhood in the process of developing. This was the deep conviction of the apostle and contemporary genetics converges with such an approach.

Athanasius of Alexandria, referring to the creation of the first human couple, remarks that in reality human life is formed in the mother's womb once both the elements necessary from the married couple come together (αρχην του ειναι λαβοντα εκ γαστρος), becoming extremely difficult at the exact precise time.[4]

The debates were going on as to whether the Church ought to modify the rigid spirit of the penitential discipline concerning such abuses on child-birth. Each Bishop was trying to interpret the relative Canons with certain elasticity. To face this uncertainty, during the autumn of 691 what is known as Trullo or Penthekti Ecumenical Council was convoked, reaffirming all previous formulated disciplinary measures. Our concern is its Canon 91: "As for women who furnish drugs for the purpose of procuring abortion (αμβλωθριδια εμβρυοκτονα), and those who take foetus-killing poisons (και αι δεχομεναι δηλητηρια), they are made subject to the discipline prescribed for murderers (τα του φονεως επιτιμιω)".

Although as a whole the discipline imposed for such offences seems severe, the last canon of the Trullo Council (102) offers more humane guidelines to the spiritual fathers while exercising their ministerial function: to be more lenient, provided signs of sincere repentance are shown. This concession being more charitable, επιεικεια, does not contradict the whole attitude of the Church on sexual offences, but manifests the readiness of the caring pastoral clergy hearing confessions to show the mercy of God. This canon opens a comforting way against any intransigent attitude that would forget that the canons are made for the salvation and spiritual healing of sinners and not the opposite. The Council is very clear by allowing priests to be more charitable avoiding extreme attitudes, ακριβεια.

The imposed discipline or *Epitimia* must not be accepted out of fear of God but out of love for His mercy. The soul's therapy consists of wise treatment reaching as near as possible to the suffering. The true attitude of the healing Church is not to regard penitential discipline as an absolute practice, but rather as an instrument employed to cultivate contrition and true *metanoia*. The ultimate aim of such discipline is to restore a new relationship between God and the penitent, broken by sin. Maximus the Confessor reminds us that what counts above everything else is the rupture of love by our transgression and the reconciliation coming after one's sincere repentance: "Every askesis and hardship, not accompanied by love, become alien to God" (Lib. ascet. 36; *PG* 90, 941).

Throughout the Bible the mystery of the divine judgement for sexual offences oscillates between mercy and justice. Again this couple of attributes emerges from two fundamental notions of the Scripture: love and truth. Both these notions in Hebrew are associated and accompanying each other. Thus *hesed-we'emeth*, exactly as in the known Psalm 85,12. The *hesed* signifies at the same time God's love, His compassion, His sweetness and tenderness towards humanity's miseries. On the other side, *emeth* leads us to the idea of absolute Truth, but also indirectly to the ideas of justice, of judgementand the determination of God's prerogatives as the unique Lord of the universe to apply the demands of the Law.

The reader must not lose sight of the fact that the finality of Mosaic Law is to maintain the chosen people in optimal purity with the accomplishment of the prescribed worship of the covenant. But even such a cult is bound to the miraculous manifestation of God: the *shekina*, this cloud covering the Tent at the moment of its inauguration. It is a sign of Yahweh's presence, but also that such a God who inflicted punishments on Egypt accepts now to choose this people and to live in its midst forever.

The Byzantine wedding or crowning rites, which are considerably influenced by Jewish liturgical customs, include frequent appeals to the procreation of many children. There is no doubt that this is a visible sign of prosperity and faithfulness to the will of God, who commanded people to "increase and multiply on earth the human race". In the Litany sung at the beginning of the ceremony, we pray for the newly married "that they may see with joy their sons and their daughters ...". This repeated encouragement is due to the fact that Israel, surrounded as it was by so many enemies, always needed young people ready and able to defend their unique faith, revealed by Yahweh, against constant threats and numerous enemies. Thus we find an eloquent passage in the Psalms included *in extenso* in the Orthodox service: "Give to them a heritage of the Lord, the fruit of their womb, fair children; and may they see their sons' sons as newly planted olive trees round about their table" (Psalm 127, 3).

While in the West Tertullian and Augustine, basing themselves on Exod 21: 22-25, clearly made a distinction between an already formed embryo with soul and an embryo without a soul, Eastern writers avoided such scrupulosity. Basil of Caesarea states that it is a superficial investigation to try to find out when an embryo is already complete or incomplete. What is known is that once conception has taken place, there begins the process of union of soul and body, thus preparing the human being in its fullness already in the woman's womb. Euthymius Zigabenus (early twelfth century), a Byzantine commentator, referring to Luke 1, 41, sees that in the womb of Elizabeth, the mother of the Virgin Mary, the baby was already conscious and expressed its joy, feeling beforehand the great event to come for the redemption of humanity.

Askesis is Needed

Similarly, Theophylactus of Ochrid, then Bulgaria, (eleventh century) underlines that Elizabeth, when pregnant, felt the joyful movements of her child in a mysterious way. Accordingly, Origen remarks that John the Baptist's mother was fully conscious that the child under preparation was a full human being, composed of body and soul. Anastasius Sinaita, the Abbot (seventh century) admits that once the soul enters the body it remains forever eternal, even if it belongs to the embryo rejected by the mother. It is not lost, but in the last day of resurrection will be convoked by the almighty God. Actually, feeling the movement of the child in the womb is common during the months of pregnancy (Question 91; *PG* 89, 725).

Whatever views may be held on birth-control, continence and abstinence will never be abolished. On the contrary, they will always remain the basic elements in matrimonial relations. In fact, continence raises to a higher level the inner life of the couple. Sexuality is not everything in this bond. Excess of sex may create the disgusting feeling called "post-coital sadness". In fact, beyond sexual pleasure partners expect lasting and not instant tenderness, to allay one another's pain through true love. While sexuality on its own will produce an abysmal void, disappointments, a bitter aftertaste, mutual accusations, feelings of exploitation and eventually defilement. Then matrimony will be degraded, sensuality killing higher aspirations and ideals. Neither of the partners gives true love, but only expects to receive it; therefore, neither receives it.

In reality, people are looking for something more. If there is no chosen periodic continence, sexuality becomes a tyrannising, mechanical performance; and the partners are sooner or later going to get bored. At that point, a couple may start to question the validity of their union and whether they are really in love. If they see sexual interest as the key of the entire relationship, they may think that their love and happiness are over and done for. There is much more in love than the instinct to receive pleasure.

Using different terms, for example the "new celibacy", modern sexologists defend the value of continence and deny that the couple risks losing totally the desire for sex. In fact, one does not lose the sexual desire but only the desire for sexual desire. Such a pause is wisely recommended by the Church Fathers in the various Canonical sources for the benefit of a healthy relationship and for the growth of real love. This mutual respect in deep agape and in only exclusive eros is what brings enjoyment: a kind of surrender in love in which feelings of affection grow deeper, a contact not spoilt by fatigue or boredom. Often a union is considered a "real" one if it reaches the height of orgasm. We forget the value of all the non-sexual relationships rich in affection and the high quality of love that they engender.

Abstinence for a time is not a sign of sexual decline, not a closing-off but an opening-up. The couple finds that a period of such abstinence enables them to experience a greater degree of self-sufficiency and freedom, and at the same time offers a chance to explore new dimensions in relationships. It can be a time to sort out our feelings about a particular relationship without the mask of sex, to allow the deepening of a lover relationship occurring in a wider field.

Habits are repetitive and tend to inhibit growth. Habits, as routine behaviours, have been found to reduce creativity in building up a spiritual life, reduce the expansive nature of love and hinder its growth. A lessening of sexual activity may be indicative not of defeat and failure of virility or a sign of perversion, but of the canalization of hidden potentialities to other areas of joy with common consent. Once a couple is united in commitment to each other for mutual growth, marriage becomes an ideal avenue for further spiritual development. The two unite, forming a base of strength and a broad channel of energy through which society may be enriched. From this commitment, marriage becomes a medium of service to each partner from the other and from both to the Christian family and the wider world. Growth in self-emptying and out-flowing love from an increasingly fuller heart is the sign of spiritual ascension.

It becomes clear that the defence of the rights of the child to be born is considered a crime - an outside intervention for interrupting and killing. However severe may seem to be such penitential discipline, it reflects the clear warning of God's word, as expressed by the Psalmist appealing for respect of life: "Truly you have formed my innermost being. You knitted me in my mother's womb. I give thanks that I am fearfully, wonderfully made. Wonderful are your works" (Psalm 139, 13-14).

Evidently, there can be no pronouncement on harming unborn children without reference to interrelated issues. The human being remains a complex creature, and the Church regards all these sexual and matrimonial problems in a holistic way, without disregarding the bodily needs at the expense of the spirit, or vice versa. In order to maintain a sound, healthy and balanced couple, it is necessary to harmonize all needs in their just dimension. In this respect, the pastoral assistance is of immeasurable importance.

Yet, the so widespread individualistic approach to sex problems for exclusive personal gratification betrays a lack of responsibility, as if sex concerns only oneself; sex is a great threat if it is solely based on egoistic criteria. For many contemporaries, sexuality, foetus conception and procreation belong properly to the sphere of decisions exclusively of the individual or the married couple. They claim that everybody is free to use sex as he wishes, since it is his own business.

Man, nevertheless, is called upon by God to assume responsibility over his body. The meaning of human sexuality goes beyond its purely biological aspect. Men and women are summoned to integrate the sexual dimension into their lives in a joyful and reconciling manner. Here, some might say that the number of children is the sole responsibility of the parents. Thus, the old problem of πολυπαιδια comes up again. God's providence is believed to be operative through the grace-sustained free choice of mother and father. Contraceptives for such people are important in the life process, prompted by the people's responsibility for the future. They think that the parents' responsibility includes the authority, in an emergency case, to interrupt pregnancy.[5]

Even worse is the imposition, especially by legislation, of family planning. It is a symptom of ultimate selfishness, where people claim total control not only over their property but over their bodies. It is a kind of *reductio ad absurdum* of the individualism that our permissive society has generated. What has been lost is a sense of wonder before life itself and the hidden forces operative within it. While a theologian does not wish to reduce significant moral standards to the level of diverse social conditions alone, he must recognise that the conditions of modern life have produced a changed outlook on traditional issues such as birth-control, extramarital sex, divorce, etc.

Furthermore, it is not enough to speak about "responsibility" in a vague way. The question remains, to whom is one responsible? Is he answerable only to himself, so that every man is his own moral authority? Or are there, conversely, moral "laws" or standards, built into human life itself? Does "this is wrong" mean merely "I do not like it", or is it a statement about something real, irrespective of our likes and dislikes, to which all are under obligation? Is there an "objective" morality? It is on social grounds that the traditional claim is now meeting strong resistance, and the whole ideal of moral responsibility is notoriously under criticism. Our forefathers knew no such doubts. They believed that there is a Church discipline, higher than any earthling, to which all human authority is answerable and by which all will be judged; that conviction, fundamental to the Bible, has been the basis of Church life. It is now widely written off as the echo of an arbitrary, authoritarian ethic incompatible with our adult status

The Christian Conscience *versus* Individualism

For the Christian, it is impossible to exercise judgementwithout reference to a scale of moral values, which also include suspension of judgements where the whole truth is not to be known, and the possibility of delaying judgement until more facts have come to light. But he is also entitled to await illumination from within, before making a choice or refusal.

While Christianity values highly the role of conscience in moral life, it does not affirm that it is an absolute. The true Christian only follows his conscience after having submitted it to God, to Christ and to His Church for direction. While a sincere conscience is always to be respected, yet for it to be considered the supreme moral value, it has to be in line with the Divine conscience.

Such thorny problems as those of marital love and procreation, for example, need to be viewed in the light of man's fall and redemption, if they are to be satisfactorily assessed. The universal reality of the redemption has to be seized upon by Christians and lived out in their lives, both for their own sakes and for others'.

Here they are faced with a great mission: that of proving that the ideals of Christianity can be achieved. Their humility will spur them on to work and study harder than most, especially in the application of scientific, medical and sociological discoveries to the Church's doctrine on society, with practical results. They will have sufficient faith and hope to hang on through the difficult moments of their personal and collective lives according to the directives of the Church, which in its maternal solicitude may well be strict. (The upbringing of children of broken marriages comes under this heading.) They will have sufficient simplicity of soul not to equate or confuse the "new morality" with new Christian solutions, since moral shortcomings (the gravity of which only God can judge) can never be condoned, though they can be forgiven. While showing great understanding and sympathy for those who have collapsed under the weight of their difficulties, they must beware of a false charity, leading them to propose comfortable compromises for others which they could not allow to themselves.

As everybody knows, these are not easy times. Yet there is one contemporary ill which can and should be openly denounced: that of an "aphrodisiac" atmosphere, encouraged by opportunist commercialism, which excites and perverts all instinctive desires beyond control, instead of disciplining them and ennobling them. It is not only the salvation of souls that is here at stake, but the very health and equilibrium of the human being, the human race.

There is a very real danger that the selfish pursuit of happiness in the search for a long-promised Utopia will run counter to the basic laws of nature itself. Even Christianity, with its message of spiritual regeneration, has its roots in a careful assessment of the requirements for a normal, healthy human life. To impart equilibrium, one needs to make whole the nature of man, not to oppose its natural laws. Through the ages the Church, with its strict morality, acts to preserve mankind, not to destroy it; its action is not as paradoxical as it seems for it stands behind those same values with which men have tried to supplant it. Indeed it is not possible to evolve sound moral criteria without falling back on the Church's eternal teaching concerning ethical truth. Those Christians who find unswerving moral witness difficult to practise in this day and age may take comfort from the certainty that the Church's teaching will once again prevail, since it alone is the true guardian of essential human values and because it remains true to its ideal of the Perfect Man - Christ.

One more explanation is needed here. While the promptings of conscience are important, another consideration is even more relevant to our inquiry. That is the fact that a Christian is above all an "ecclesial being". He is a member of the eucharistic community, the Christian family. Whatever he does may have repercussions upon the others too.

Therefore, he must bear in mind the link which unites all members. Our responsibilities go beyond narrow limits; it has short or long-term consequences upon the whole Christian family, for its spiritual health and growth in Christ.

Excessive confidence in one's conscience may cause one to absolutise one's personal self-relying views rather than rely on an impartial Christian consensus. This explains why there are disciplinary canons formulated by Ecumenical Councils, considering personal views inadequate and subjective, and intervening by underlying the voice of the wider body of the Church of Christ. This is not to ignore human liberty, but to show that in a community such as the Church, each member has to respect certain norms guiding daily behaviour, and especially vital issues influencing the whole body.

If in the old covenant mortal sins were penalised with heavy punishment, in the new covenant prevails the "grace, the mercy and God's love". These attributes of God are clearly indicated in the office of forgiveness of sins, by which the confessor in charge of hearing confessions and consequently proposing the corresponding healing steps, *epitimia*, refers to a merciful God who wants none to perish. A penitential discipline on sexual transgressions is an agency for good as long as it is exercised for a remedial, reforming purpose, to strengthen, to restore. If the penitential acts, that is *epitimia*, are employed not pastorally but penally, not to strengthen the weak, the fallen, not as a therapeutic means but expiatory of God's wrath, then the penitential rules, however carefully formulated, lose their main function, becoming an instrument rather of legalism which dragoons the many into purely outward advance. Thus, it breaks the very heart of the spiritual genius who needs freedom and interior purification.

What in many periods of Church history resulted from such legalistic penitential practice is a wholly wrong attitude towards ethical principles. Less and less are those thinking of them as means to secure inner conversion from grave offences and the energy of service which retains and attests conversions to God. More and more they become mere conditions of membership in the body of Christ where external conformity is to be rewarded with assured salvation.

Attention is concentrated upon law rather than upon life: penitential actions become more important than motives; obedience takes the place of intimate personal communion with God as the mainspring of the Christian life; outward submission rather than inward spontaneity is not what is expected of the penitent. Thus, as far as ill-informed Christians are concerned, we often see as the result of these developments an immediate deterioration of moral standards, with a widespread dominance of hypocrisy and a purely formalist observance.

But if we go deeper, we shall discover the whole mystery and dimension of God's immense love in seeking the return of His most precious and loved fallen creature, so well formulated in the absolution prayer: "I do not want the death of a sinner but rather that he may live and turn from the wickedness which he has committed and lived, and then even unto seventy times seven, sins ought to be forgiven."

Family Life Needs Renewal

In dealing with the Future Generations topic we cannot escape from including all that concerns a healthy family in the heart of which most future generations are born and educated. The family consists of the intermediate bond linking one generation to the other. Our care towards future generations is reflected in the principles and values animating family life. The quality of life of future generations will much depend on the quality of family life of present generations.

Speaking of issues touching the family, one cannot avoid the issue of procreation so central to matrimonial relationships. We all know that not only in the Christian camp, but even in the Old Testament and among non-Christian faiths, sterility was seen as a serious handicap, a deficiency, while the begetting of children was seen as the normal way before God and society as a whole. On such ground appear many Pro-Life groups fighting the daily mass murders of helpless and innocent human beings: the unborn human fetuses.

It is time to investigate the genetic research and practices, the laboratory murders, the right to live based on moral and legal ramifications, and the disastrous broken bond: namely abortion as the natural way to kill one's body and spirit. Christian theology has much to say on the continuing crime against the unborn.

Marriage is considered as the answer to many human needs: the need for affection, for protection, for fulfilment, plus the constant need to love and be loved. However when the intimacy we look for in marriages becomes overcharged with a whole lot of false expectations and unrealistic dreams, couples start feeling cheated. When what we anticipate is not returned, disillusionment creeps in; the unrealistic demands that we put on the relationship block any expression of true feelings and the relationship starts to dwindle.

This implies that, though man and woman need an intimate relationship, neither one really possesses the full capacity to share life with the other. Each wants to receive something from the other while unable to give it of oneself. Trying desperately to keep harmony, to avoid conflicts and to appease one another, marriage becomes a state of co-existence rather than an adventure open to all that is human.

Another manifestation of the confusion is in the meaning of the word "sexuality". In our age there is increasing uncertainty as to just what it means to be a man, and just what it means to be a woman. In the midst of this uncertainty and confusion, with the basic state of dehumanization, many seek the "blueprints" which our society offers, the "blueprints" of masculinity and femininity and follow them with a seriousness and thoroughness worthy of the greatest thermonuclear scientist.

This search, it seems to me, accounts for the uncanny popularity of *Playboy* magazine. This magazine presents the total blueprint (or image) of what it means to be a man, plus the means for its attainment. The image involves such items as sports cars, clothes, jazz music and hi-fi. Since being a male necessitates some sort of relationship to females, that formula is presented with skill and detachment. Sex must be contained at all costs within the entertainment-recreation area. Don't get serious. The symbol of this formula is the playmate of the month, who is rather like a toy, a "leisure accessory", to be put away after play time. *Playboy*, together with other sensational literature, really feeds on the presence of a repressed fear of involvement with women. I think that the male identity crisis has at its roots a deep-set fear of sex, a fear that is uncomfortably combined with fascination. Magazines such as *Playboy* are essentially anti-sexual. They feed on the fear of intimacy on a personal involvement level.

Conclusion

To conclude let me make some suggestions towards a "new" basis for perspective and behaviour. First, we need to recover and nurture the Christian image of humankind. We need to "get back to the Bible ...not for ethical absolutes, but for the fullest measure of our humanity". Holy Scripture is "our story, holding up to us who and what we really are. And it is very clear about this identity: we are made in the image of God" ... and "fallen". This is to say, first of all, that our creation is good. Soul and body as a unity are good.

Furthermore, "made in the image of God" assumes that each one of us is a responsible decision-maker. Our greatness emerges from our freedom to choose, to exercise our responsibility for our own lives, for the other person, as well as for the created order of things. "Made in the image of God" assumes that each of us is created to be with the other and to be for the other. "It is not good for man to be alone." To be fully human necessitates "mutuality" and interrelatedness. It means exposing oneself to the risk of personal encounter.

The fullest measure of our humanity wisely takes into account the fact that we are "fallen". This is to say that each of us is capable of magnificent self-deception about his or her own behaviour. We can believe without the shadow of a doubt that "the grass is greener on the other side of the street". We can delude ourselves into thinking that whatever disappointments there may be in our marriage (or in any other corner of our lives) they are completely someone else's responsibility. Here I'm reminded of the old cliché, sometimes expressed in the sophisticated variations, "My wife doesn't understand me".

To grasp the full significance of our "fallen" condition is to comprehend how naturally inclined each of us is to control the other person (even by becoming helpless and passive), to dominate the other (even in the name of love), and to misuse our powers in such a way that we treat persons as objects. Self-interest is as difficult to submerge as is a large beach ball in a swimming pool; it keeps returning to the surface.

Secondly, towards a "new" basis for perspective and behaviour, we need to risk some communication with one another about the present state of things: husbands with wives, parents with children, friend with friend. We who are poorly adjusted to things as they are, we who are not bound to this age, we who find ourselves somewhere in between the fading tradition with its specific absolutes and a complete relativism that permits anything - will something as immediate become the means towards reflection and appraisal with one another? Or will we have to keep our thoughts completely to ourselves after we have read it? Perhaps even tucking it away out of the reach of our teenagers? Are we really that unsure of ourselves? Are we really that bound to this age - to "let sleeping dogs lie"? As Dr Kreuzer, a character in Graham Greene's play *The Potting Shed*, observed, "You were clever at keeping them asleep, but sometimes they wake up your children."

By means of such communication and conversation, as risky, as halting as it may be, we could take one step towards establishing sex much more as a part of life. We could begin to view sex as a fact of creation - not to be idealized, yet not to be scorned at or feared; not to be humanized, yet not to be absolutised. By such "conversation" we could begin to assert a human transcendence over sex, even to the point of laughing at it from time to time. Laughter does not mean a snicker, which implies contempt. Nor does it mean a giggle, which implies embarrassment. Laughter is a natural and graceful way of asserting our humanity over that impersonal yet necessary force. Nowadays, the subject of sex is often treated with an earnestness and seriousness bordering on the lugubrious. Nowadays we do not have many writers like the late James Thurber, who once entitled a book *Is Sex Necessary?*

The gradual recovery of the true image of man, along with the recovery of perspective about the meaning and purpose of sex would contribute an immeasurable amount towards our becoming "salt" to an unflavoured, sometimes vapid, often graceless society.

In concluding we advocate the Patristic thought: that the emphasis in such a controversial issue as the anti-contraception argument is not "how many" children and how to see the core of family happiness etc., but rather how to improve the quality. Thus John Chrysostom puts the emphasis on the quality of parents and of the children rather than on the size and the number. He attacks the unworthy, arguing for the few but good, quoting Eccles 16,3 and commenting:

ouc orate, oti euteknia meta oligotekniaV beltiwn, h polupaidia meta kakopaidiaV ... For me, what counts mostly are the saintly people. In a war one saint alone can win more than one hundred thousand people. Thus Joshua of Nave succeeded on the battlefield, while the others did nothing. Is it not better to have one healthy sheep than many sick ones? Do you not see that a few well-educated children are preferable to many unrighteous ones?[6]

Notes

1. Omran, A. R. (1992). *Family Planning in the Legacy of Islam*, London, Routledge.

2. Lavelle, L. (1939). *L'Erreur de Narcisse*, Paris: p.18.

3. Hom. 19, 1-2 in I Cor; *PG* 61, 152-153.

4. *De exemplo ex natura Hominis allato*: *PG* 26, 1233.

5. See John Chrysostom's penetrating reflections: *Hom: 83 on the Acts: PG* 60, 74-75.

6. *Hom. 83 on the Acts: PG* 60, 74-75.

9

The Earth Belongs to All Generations: Moral Challenges of Sustainable Development

EMMANUEL AGIUS

The history of the Church's social teaching is characterized by a continuous effort to defend the weak members of society from those socio-political and economic forces which, in some way or another, threaten their fundamental human rights. The body of "social wisdom" on socio-economic, political and cultural matters, which has developed in a rich fashion especially during the last one hundred years, spells out the Church's deep concern for "the joys and hopes, the sorrows and anxieties, of ... those who are poor or in any way oppressed."[1]

Christian social teaching is by no means a fixed set of tightly developed doctrine. Rather, it is a collection of key themes which evolved in response to the challenges of the day. One may conclude that modern Christian social thought is characterised by three distinct perspectives. During the pre-conciliar era, the main concern of the Church was how to resolve the conflict between advantaged and disadvantaged individuals or classes. Many workers and their families became poor, vulnerable and powerless as a result of the socio-economic and political structures created by the industrial revolution. Both Liberalism, as expressed in selfish capitalism, and Collectivism, as manifested in the theory of Socialism, were strongly attacked because they hindered the full and authentic development of the worker.

During the conciliar and early post-conciliar era, Christian social thought shifted towards an outlook that was more international or global. This shift was the result of the awareness of the interdependence and interconnectedness of all reality. The conflict between the developed and developing countries caused by the world economic order was the main concern of the Church during the 1960s and 1970s. In a shrinking world, everything is affected and everyone is responsible. It became unrealistic to speak simply of progress, without taking very seriously into account the limitations of natural and human resources, the ecological crises, the dangerous consequences of modern technology and the ever growing difference in the standard of living between the rich and the poor countries. The pattern of development as it took shape after the industrial revolution has deprived whole nations of achieving an adequate standard of living. The Church pleaded for a new international economic order that does justice to the so-called underdeveloped nations, which were powerless and vulnerable in a political and economic structure that advantaged and protected the already developed countries.

Since the early 1980s, the Church's global outlook has evolved to an intergenerational perspective. Without abandoning her concern for the integral development of the individual and her defence of the right of every poor country to development, the Church became more sensitive to the social problems resulting from the conflict of interests between advantaged and disadvantaged generations. During the last few decades, it has become evident that solidarity must be shown not only with poor individuals or nations but also with unborn generations, who are also poor and powerless in the face of today's technological power and short-sighted political and economic planning and decisions. The Church's "preferential option for the poor"incorporates nowadays unborn generations, who are disadvantaged and powerless with respect to present people since they are voiceless, "downstream" in time and vulnerable to the long-term consequences of our actions.

This paper focuses on the last feature of social thought, namely, the Church's concern for protecting and preserving the planet earth which is ours and the future generations' common home. The first section shows that towards the late 1970s the Church, like the rest of the international community, became gradually more conscious and conscientious of our moral responsibility towards generations yet to be born. Then, I argue that the Church's central arguments about our ecological responsibility towards unborn generations can be traced back to patristic social teaching. Early Christian theologians insisted that earthly goods belong to all generations. It is interesting to note that contemporary social teaching grounds our moral responsibility to unborn generations on this patristic theological assumption. In the last section, I argue that the Church's support for the concept of "sustainable development" is a corollary of the Christian belief in the universal destination of created goods.

Solidarity with Future Generations

In post-conciliar years, the social teaching of the Church has been characterised by an increasing sense of solidarity with unborn generations. This was the result of a further development in environmental awareness which came about in the late 1960s. At that time it became increasingly evident that nothing exists in isolation. Everything affects everything else. Advances in technology and the pattern of development adopted by industrialised countries can have serious negative consequences not only on the global community but also on generations yet to be born. Many began to realise that current political and socio-economic decisions can create future risks and burdens. In recent years, this social problem has become for the Church one of the most urgent "signs of our times" which demands immediate attention and action. In fact, many recent papal documents and speeches draw more and more the attention of all men and women of good will to examine their conscience on how they are using and sharing the goods of the earth and on their moral obligations to unborn generations.

The 1971 Synod of Bishops had already observed that "men are beginning to grasp a new and more radical dimension of unity; for they perceive that the resources, as well as the precious treasures of air and water - without which there cannot be life - and the small delicate biosphere of the whole complex of all life on earth, are not infinite, but on the contrary must be saved and preserved as a unique patrimony belonging to all mankind."[2] The Synod questioned "what right the rich nations have to keep up their claim to increase their own material demands, if the consequence is either that others remain in misery or that the danger of destroying the very physical foundation of life on earth is precipitated. Those who are already rich are bound to accept a less material way of life, with less waste, in order to avoid the destruction of the heritage which they are obliged by absolute justice to share with all other members of the human race."[3]

In his message to the 1972 Stockholm Conference, Pope Paul VI insisted that "no one can take possession in an absolute and specific way of the environment, which is not a *res nullius* - something not belonging to anyone - but a *res omnium* - the patrimony of mankind; consequently those possessing it - privately and publicly - must use it in a way that rebounds to everyone's real advantage."[4] Then, the Pope continued that "our generation must energetically accept the challenge of going beyond particular, immediate objectives in order to prepare a hospitable earth for future generations."[5]

The future generations issue was again mentioned in *Octogesima Adveniens* (1971). Pope Paul VI remarked that "man is suddenly aware that by an ill-considered exploitation of nature he risks destroying it and becoming in turn the victim of his own degradation. Not only is the material environment becoming a permanent menace ... but the human framework is no longer under man's control, thus creating an environment for tomorrow which may well be intolerable. This is a wide-ranging social problem which concerns the entire human family."[6]

Pope Paul VI's message for the occasion of the 1977 World Day of the Environment focused specifically on our responsibility to pass on a healthy environment to future generations. The Pope appealed "for a universal sense of solidarity in which each person and every nation plays its proper and interdependent role to ensure an ecologically sound environment for people today, as well as for future generations ... It is our earnest prayer ... that all people everywhere ... commit themselves to a fraternal sharing and protection of good environment, the common patrimony of mankind."[7]

The future generations issue came more and more to the foreground of Pope John Paul II's social documents and speeches. He made several direct allusions to unborn generations in order to remind the present generation of its responsibility to be "the guardian of the earth".[8] In 1981, Pope John Paul II reminded the participants in a study week on energy and humanity that energy is a universal good that God has put at the service of all humanity, whatever part of the world they may belong to. He insisted that we must think also of the men of the future. It is a duty of justice and charity to make a resolute and persevering effort to husband energy resources and respect nature, not only so that humanity as a whole today may benefit, but also the generations to come. We are bound in solidarity to the generations to come.[9]

On 7 October 1983, Pope John Paul II received in audience a group of participants in the International Congress of Science and Technology against Hunger in the World. His whole speech was an exhortation to study ways and means to feed the population of this generation and generations yet to come. "Science and technology," he said, "must attack the problem on different fronts in order to arrive at solutions which are both adequate for the present and will meet the demands of the future."[10]

Our responsibilities towards future generations were mentioned once more in Pope John Paul II's address in 1985 to the United Nations Centre for the Environment, in Nairobi. He remarked that

it is a requirement of our human dignity, and therefore a serious responsibility, to exercise dominion over creation in such a way that it truly serves the human family. Exploitation of the riches of nature must take place according to criteria that take into account not only the immediate needs of the people but also the needs of future generations. In this way, the stewardship over nature, entrusted by God to men, will not be guided by short-sightedness or selfish pursuit; rather, it will take into account the fact that created goods are directed to the good of all humanity. The use of natural resources must aim at serving the integral development of present and future generations.[11]

In November 1987, Pope John Paul II addressed a group of scientists who were attending a study week on the protection of the environment. He remarked that inadequate farming systems in many countries and the need for energy have continued to create very serious inroads into forest resources. He pointed out that "adverse effects on the environment can be corrected in the causes that produce them only by teaching people a new and respectful attitude towards the environment, an attitude that ensures the rational use of the natural resources which have to be preserved and passed on for the use of future generations."[12]

To the participants in a Symposium on the Environment, held in Rome in December 1989, Pope John Paul II remarked

our generation has been blessed by having inherited from the industry of past generations the great wealth of material and spiritual goods which stand at the foundation of our society and its programme. Universal solidarity now demands that we consider it our grave duty to safeguard that inheritance for all our brothers and sisters and to assure that each and every member of the human family may enjoy its benefits.[13]

It is "within this broad perspective," the Pope continued, that "man bears a grave responsibility for wisely managing the environment."[14]

In his address to the diplomatic corps accredited to Madagascar, Pope John Paul II said that the international community should create the juridical and technical means to guarantee the protection of the environment and to prevent abuses inspired by what must be acknowledged as selfishness. He then added that "Christian faith believes that God made man the master of the earth. That means that he is responsible for it, that he is more the steward than the discretionary owner. He must pass it on, living and fruitful, to the coming generations."[15]

With his 1990 World Peace Day Message, Pope John Paul II wanted to insist to the world community that the ecological crisis cannot be tackled adequately without seriously considering the "future generations issue". He urged the need of fostering a new sense of intergenerational solidarity. Political and socio-economic decisions and planning must give attention to what the earth and its atmosphere are telling us, "namely, that there is an order in the universe which must be respected, and that the human person, endowed with the capacity of choosing freely, has a grave responsibility to preserve this order for the wellbeing of future generations."[16] Indiscriminate application of the advances in science and technology "has led to the painful realization that we cannot interfere in one area of the ecosystem without paying due attention both to the consequences of such interference in other areas and to the wellbeing of future generations".[17] Thus, the far-reaching effects of technology point to the urgent need of a deeper sense of responsibility for generations yet to be born.

In a speech delivered in 1990, Pope John Paul II appealed for the protection of tropical forests. He observed that greedy development is threatening these forests. He lamented that the rate at which these forests are being destroyed or altered is depleting their biodiversity so quickly that many species may never be catalogued or studied for their possible value to human beings. Then, he said that "it is possible ... that the indiscriminate destruction of tropical forests is going to prevent future generations from benefiting from the riches of these ecosystems in Asia, Africa and Latin America. Should the concept of development in which profit is predominant continue to disrupt the lives of the native populations which inhabit these forests?"[18]

Both *Sollicitudo Rei Socialis* (1987) and *Centesimus Annus* (1991) specifically refer to our responsibilities towards unborn generations. The 1987 social encyclical speaks about the limitations imposed by the Creator on man's freedom to make use of the natural resources of the earth. This limitation is symbolically expressed by the prohibition not "to eat of the fruit of the tree". The Pope interpreted these words as a moral law not to abuse of the resources of the earth which are common to all humankind. Then, the encyclical continues that "the usage of natural resources as if they were inexhaustible, with absolute dominion, seriously endangers their availability not only for the present generation but also for generations to come."[19]

Centesimus Annus focuses on three current problems. The first concerns the unjust distribution of resources between the industrialised countries and developing countries. The second problem concerns the unjust distribution of resources within each country. The third current interest on the topic of the purpose of resources concerns the responsibility we have for creation and future generations.[20] Pope John Paul II wrote that, in his desire to have and enjoy more rather than to be and to grow, man consumes the resources of the earth in an excessive and disordered way. Man thinks that he can make an arbitrary use of the earth, as though it did not have its own requisites and a proper God-given purpose. In all this, one notes the poverty or narrowness of man's outlook. Then, he continued to say that "humanity today must be conscious of its duties and obligations towards future generations."[21]

The Universal Purpose of Created Things

The import of recent Christian social teaching on our responsibilities towards future generations cannot be fully comprehended unless it is situated in the Church's traditional doctrine on the universal destination of created things. This belief, which underpins our ecological duties towards unborn generations, can be traced back to the heritage of patristic social teaching. Strictly speaking, this teaching has biblical roots. In fact, the Bible reminds us that the earth is God's gift to all generations.[22] It is indeed remarkable that today's sense of global and intergenerational solidarity had already been developed extensively by the early Christian theologians.

In the tradition of the Church, there are two main tenets with reference to the resources of the world. The first is that by nature, *all* earthly resources have a universal destination, that is, they are intended for the good of humankind as a whole.[23] God has given the fruits of the earth to sustain the entire human family, without excluding or favouring anyone. Since material goods of the earth are the common patrimony of all humankind, both present and future generations have the right not to be excluded from access to the earth's resources. The earth is given as a gift from God for the nurture and fulfilment of all, not for the benefit of a few or of one particular generation. This implies that everyone has an inherent right to use the resources of the earth. Since the right of usage is primary in character, it ranks among fundamental human rights.

The second is that some modes of appropriation are allowable and, in certain cases, required, to a limited extent. Since patristic times, the concept of the right to private property was discussed within the context of the universal right to use the resources of the earth. Property is seen as the institutional actualization of man's fundamental right to use the material goods of the earth. Property should always be administered for the benefit of all. Though the right of property is important, the universal right to usage is prior to and conditions the right to private property. Since private property is a means to an end, it must always remain subordinate to its proper end, namely the universal right of usage.

According to the social teachings of the Fathers, ownership of material goods is not possession but stewardship. All creation is made available by God to all humankind and the rich are essentially its stewards. Those who have should imitate God's beneficence and generosity in sharing their material goods with others. It is only due to sin and greed that earthly goods have been drawn into the present oppressive state of affairs in which there are such differences between the rich and the poor.[24] The early Fathers of the Church harshly attacked the idea of ownership as an exclusive and unlimited right of disposing of material goods. They attempted to develop an ethical perspective which aimed at safeguarding those who were being deprived of their fundamental right to use the resources of the earth.

In one of his homilies, Clement of Alexandria (c.150-216) proposes two guiding principles for the use and possession of earthly goods: *autarkeia* and *koinonia*. The first ethical principle, namely *autarkeia*, suggests that every possession is for the sake of self-sufficiency. *Autarkeia* denotes a standard of living that enables one to live a life consonant with human dignity. Beyond the limits of *autarkeia*, the holding of goods makes no sense in the patristic view. But the purpose of possessing earthly goods is also to attain *koinonia*, the equal fellowship that abolishes the differentiation between the few rich who live in luxury and the "many who labour in poverty". According to Clement of Alexandria, the ethical principle of *koinonia* should remind christians of everyone's right to share or participate in earthly goods:

It is God himself who has brought our race to a *koinonia*, by sharing Himself, first of all, and by sending His Word (*Logos*) to all alike, and by making all things for all. Therefore everything is in common, and the rich should not grasp a greater share. The expression, then, 'I own something and I have more than enough; why should I not enjoy it?' is not worthy of a human nor does it indicate any community feeling. The other expression does, however: 'I have something, why should I not share it with those in need?' Such a one is perfect, and fulfils the command: 'Thou shalt love thy neighbour as thyself'.[25]

One of the most important texts on social matters written by Cyprian (c.200-258), bishop of Carthage, is *On Works and Almsgiving*. Cyprian wrote: "For whatever belongs to God is for the common use of all, nor is anyone excluded from his benefits and gifts, nor is the human race prevented from equally enjoying God's goodness and generosity."[26] Another early Christian Father who affirmed that God entrusted the earth to all humanity was Lactantius (250-317), who was called "the Christian Cicero" on account of the elegance of his style. In his writing on *The Divine Institutes* we find that "God has given the land for the common use of all men, so that all may enjoy the goods it produces in common, and not in order that someone with grasping and raging greed may claim everything for himself, while another may be deprived of the things the earth produces for all."[27]

Moreover, Ambrose (c. 337-397), bishop of Milan, wrote that "God has ordered all things to be produced, so that there should be food in common for all, and that the earth should be a kind of common possession for all. Nature, therefore, has produced a common right to all, but greed has made it a right for a few."[28] Ambrose insisted that all things of the earth are created for the use of all human beings. All human beings have a natural right to make use of them. The right to private property is not unconditional, exclusive and absolute, but essentially limited. There is a strict duty of justice, and not merely of charity, to share these goods with others. In his writing *On Naboth*, Ambrose commented as follows: "When giving to the poor you are not giving him what is yours; rather you are paying back to him what is his. Indeed what is common to all and has been given to all to make use of, you have usurped for yourself alone. The earth belongs to all, and not only the rich." [29]

In one of his writings, Ambrose referred also to "injuries done to nature". What are these "injuries" which Ambrose spoke about? He said that a few rich are trying to keep the earth for themselves so that, in consequence, "few are they who do not use what belongs to all than those who do."

St. John Chrysostom (c. 347-407) had also insisted that God created the earth for the common use and benefit of all humankind so that all should receive from it what they require. Everyone has therefore an equal right to use the resources of the earth. He explained the universal destination of the earth's resources as follows:

Mark the wise dispensation of God ... He has made certain things common, such as the sun, air, earth, and the water, the sky and the sea ... Their benefits are dispensed equally to all brethren ... And mark, that concerning things that remain in common there is no contention but all is peaceable. But when one attempts to possess oneself of anything, to make it one's own, then contention is introduced, as if nature herself were indignant. [30]

The Moral Challenge of Sustainable Development

Development, both as an ideology and as a project, was the dream of many Western countries in the post-World War II era. Development policies adopted by many governments were built around the notion of ever-increasing "growth", which meant the production of more and more goods. But it also involved the using-up of more and more resources of the earth. People everywhere have been led to expect that "development" will increase the amount of goods available to them, and that there is no foreseeable limit to this kind of growth. This utopia caused immense harm to both present and future generations.

The Church did not remain indifferent to the negative consequences resulting from the pattern of development adopted by government leaders and their advisers. On the contrary, Churches have taken a critical stand on the myth of development. Since the late 1960s the issue of "development" has come to feature more prominently on the social agenda of the Catholic Church and the World Council of Churches.

During the last few decades, the Churches have become receptive to the emerging ethical principle of sustainable development. The international community has become increasingly aware that a new development path is required, one that sustains human progress not just in a few places for a few years, but for the entire planet into the distant future. Past experience has shown that development processes taking place at the expense of others, today or in the future, through inequity or through environmental degradation, should be referred to not as "development" but as "exploitation". It was this newly awakened environmental awareness that led to the concept of "sustainable development" or "development without destruction" which has now become the goal not just for the developing nations, but for industrial ones as well. The crux of this new concept of development is the belief that in the long term, the future of life on earth depends on caring for and conserving the environment - the natural resources of the planet, its land, air, water, biodiversity, forests and other life-supporting systems.

The concept of sustainable development lies at the heart of *Our Common Future*, the 1987 Report of the World Commission on Environment and Development (the Brundtland Report), and of the 1992 Earth Summit's *Agenda 21*, which is a global plan of action for the 21st century. These two documents define sustainable development as meeting the needs of the present without compromising the ability of future generations to meet their own needs.

It is this concept of development which came to feature more and more prominently in the Churches' social teaching. Both the World Council of Churches and the Catholic Church began to insist that a morally acceptable model of human development should incorporate a basic value: it needs to be sustainable from an ecological point of view, so that it respects the rights of future generations to a fair share of the resources of the earth. This means that development should express genuine respect for the earth itself and be based on partnership with nature rather than exploitation.

It is interesting to note that the Churches' arguments in favour of a pattern of development that respects the needs of the individual, the international community and unborn generations are based on the belief about the "universal destination of created things". God destined the earth and all it contains for all peoples, so that created things would be shared fairly by all humankind, present and future.[31] The right of present and future generations to full development is a corollary of the universal destination of creation.[32] Sustainable development is part of justice that recognises that God's gifts belong not only to us who are living but also to those who will come after us.[33]

The Churches' social documents insist that development which fails to respect this central Christian principle leads to the degradation of individuals, peoples, unborn generations and the environment itself. Progress and development can be achieved only through a process which guarantees the sharing of the earth's benefits by all, including generations to come. There is no development without the integral development of the individual. There is no development without the common development of humankind.

Though first mentioned by Pius XIII, the theme of "development" became prominent in the social teaching of John XXIII, whose writings reflect the widespread belief that each individual country, and the world as a whole, can "grow" out of poverty. Prior to this time, justice was primarily a matter of ensuring the proper distribution of existing wealth and resources. During the 1950s development was seen in terms of the production of increased resources which could be used to overcome poverty and to ensure that those who had little would catch up with those who had more. The ideology of growth has been seductive because it offered a potential solution for poverty without requiring the moral challenge of sharing.

This optimistic view of development was adapted by Pope John XXIII in his encyclical *Mater et Magistra* (1961). He insisted that the wealthy countries should assist the poor ones to overcome poverty by becoming "developed". He interpreted his contemporary world situation as a suitable time to facilitate a wider distribution of ownership. He thought that it was an opportune time because an increasing number of countries were experiencing rapid economic development. Pope John accepted the common assumption that rapid economic growth offers the easiest way to overcome the problem of the unequal distribution of wealth. Economic growth could be achieved by importing both Western capital and Western skills and technology.

The weakness of Pope John XXIII's solution to his contemporary social problems was his uncritical acceptance of the whole model of development that was being exported from the West. In a world of limited resources, it is unrealistic to expect that all countries can attain such a degree of growth. The belief that the best way to solve social problems is to speed up economic growth is detrimental to the needs of unborn generations because it encourages the exploitation and destruction of the environment. The positive aspect of his teaching was to move the topic of international development cooperation towards the centre of the social justice agenda. Pope John called for active solidarity among the nations - and especially between the rich and the poor. In this way he paved the way for the great encyclical *Populorum Progressio* issued by his successor.

The notion of development is central to Vatican II's document *The Church in the Modern World*. In fact, it functions as an organising principle for the whole treatment of socio-economic problems. *Gaudium et Spes* challenged the concept of development defined in exclusively economic terms. The Council Fathers had in mind a notion of a balanced development - one where economic values are not the only consideration but are linked to other fundamental human values such as freedom, dignity and participation. They were concerned not just about material welfare but also about the requirements of "intellectual, moral, spiritual and religious life". Furthermore, they saw development at the service of all peoples, all groups and every race. So the process of development should not be controlled by a minority of peoples or nations; the largest possible number of nations and peoples should have a share in its direction.

Gaudium et Spes has also pointed out that authentic development means a more equitable distribution of resources, including land,[34] a better sharing of fruits of economic activity among the nations,[35] as well as taking account of the needs of future generations:

Those responsible for investment and the planning of the economy ... must keep these objectives in mind; they must show themselves aware of their serious obligation, on the one hand, to see to it that the necessities for living a decent life are available, and, on the other hand, to provide for the future and strike a rightful balance between the needs of present-day consumption, individual and collective, and the requirements of investment for future generations.[36]

Though the Council Fathers envisaged that our moral responsibility must take heed of the needs of generations yet to be born, they were however uncritical of the Western pattern of development which had created burdens to posterity. They also failed to understand that this type of development could not be applied all over the world. The ecological costs were so high because the earth's resources could not sustain it. Furthermore, development in the West was at least partly dependent on underdevelopment in other parts of the world.

During the late 1960s and 1970s, when the environmental issue emerged as a major international concern, both the Catholic Church and the World Council of Churches reviewed their social teaching on development in the light of the emerging concept of sustainable development. The setting-up of joint commissions and committees to search for new approaches to international affairs was the result the Churches' critical attitude to the Western pattern of development.[37] As a follow-up to these initiatives, the Churches pledged to make their contribution towards a just, participatory and sustainable development. A number of reports issued by these joint commissions and committees highlight the importance of a "new economics" which does not threaten the life of future generations and the preservation of God's creation.

The issue of development has dominated the social teaching of Paul VI. His encyclical *Populorum Progressio* (1967) represents a remarkable advance on previous Church teaching about human development. He did not take the current conception of economic development as a starting-point and then modify it. Instead, he laid down certain basic standards by which we can measure to what extent any changes brought about in society deserve to be called authentic human development. In other words, what *Populorum Progressio* gives is a framework or anticipation of the "shape" of genuine human development. Pope Paul's social encyclical on the development of peoples does not give a privileged place to economic dimension of human development, any more than to the cultural, psychological, political, ecological, or religious dimensions. Rather, it challenges christians to take full account of the non-economic elements. The subject of development as a process which involves more than economic growth was discussed also in the 1975 Nairobi Assembly of the WCC.

In *Populorum Progressio*, Pope Paul VI insists that what is in question is the development "of each person and of the whole person".[38] He starts from the obligation of each person to attain self-fulfilment.[39] But development is not a purely self-centred affair. Each of us is part of a community and a civilisation which has its own history. So we are bound together in solidarity. Thus, just as each of us has benefited from the efforts of others in the community and of those who have gone before us, so each of us has to take account of the welfare of others in the community and of those who will come after us:

each man is a member of society. He is part of the whole of mankind. It is not just certain individuals, but all men who are called to this fullness of development. ... We have inherited from past generations, and we have benefited from the work of our contemporaries; for this reason we have obligations towards all, and we cannot refuse to interest ourselves in those who will come after us to enlarge the human family. The reality of human solidarity, which is a benefit for us, also imposes a duty.[40]

Pope Paul VI's vision on social solidarity with all humankind provides a basis for integrating personal development with community development, for reconciling national development with global development and for balancing international development with intergenerational development. In other words, development must be reconciled with ecological restraint. Moreover, the encyclical states that individuals and peoples should be enabled to have the prime responsibility for their own development.

The 1971 Synod of Bishops, which offers a reflection on "the mission of the People of God to further justice in the world", affirms the right of all peoples to development. One of the most significant points in the final document, "Justice in the World", is the emphasis on structural injustice at the international level. According to "Justice in the World" there is one issue which lies at the heart of the structural injustice of today's world, namely, the lack of participation by people in determining their own destiny. The Synod document does not hesitate to say that the conditions left by the colonial domination of the past may evolve into a "new form of colonialism in which the developing nations will be the victims of the interplay of international economic forces."[41] The outspoken links of past imperialism with present structural injustices in the international economic order are much stronger than the position adopted by Paul VI about colonialism and neo-colonialism in *Populorum Progressio* (7, 52, 57). The liberation of poor countries could be attained only through development. The document criticises the myth of development adopted by Western countries because of its high environmental costs. The Western pattern of development has exploited not only people but also the resources of the earth. The exploitation of the earth's resources, which are the common heritage of all, is an indirect exploitation of other people, living now or in the future.

The issue of a just, participatory and sustainable society was one of the main themes discussed in a conference on "Faith, Science and the Future" convened in 1979 by the WCC. The final document states that sustainability is a condition of social justice. The massive squandering of the world's resources by the industrialised countries is causing both global and intergenerational inequality. The norms of sustainability must encompass the concerns of the developing and developed societies as well as the interests of unborn generations.[42]

In the Vancouver Assembly held in 1983, social and economic justice (including the sustainability of creation) became a central theme to the ecumenical understanding of development. The documents of the WCC continued to re-affirm the ecumenical conviction that human development includes social justice, people's participation and qualified economic growth for the benefit of posterity. Moreover, at the Canberra Assembly held in February 1991, it was observed that "humankind has failed to distinguish between growth and development. While advocating 'sustainable development' many people and groups in fact have found themselves promoting 'growth.' ... Growth for growth's sake is increase in size without control, without limit, in disregard for the system that sustains it. ... As Christians we also emphasise our obligations towards future generations ..."[43]

The main purpose behind Pope John Paul II's encyclical *Sollecitudo Rei Socialis* (1987) is to meet the need for "a fuller and more nuanced concept of development" in continuity with that of *Populorum Progressio*. Like his predecessor, John Paul II understands development to cover all aspects of human life. His emphasis, like that of *Populorum Progressio*, is on "being more" rather than "having more". In the light of this perspective, he speaks out not only against the underdevelopment of the poor countries but also against what he calls "superdevelopment" existing side-by-side with the miseries of underdevelopment.

Development includes an economic and social component. But the Pope insists that development cannot be assessed simply in terms of such economic and social indicators. To limit development to its economic aspect, he says, leads to the subordination of the human person to "the demands of economic planning and selfish profit". One must take account of cultural aspects such as literacy and education, and of political aspects such as respect for human rights and human initiatives.

John Paul II's notion of solidarity is at the very heart of his understanding of development. He emphasises strongly that genuine development must be understood in terms of solidarity.[44] Pope Paul VI's account of development begins with self-fulfilment. He then extends it outward by including among the criteria of genuine development an increased concern for others and a desire to cooperate with others for the common good.[45] John Paul II developed this further, offering his teaching on solidarity as a strong bridge to span the gap that might arise between personal fulfilment and concern for others.

Briefly, Pope John Paul develops the following argument: first he spells out the fact of interdependence. Interdependence must be transformed into solidarity, based upon the principle that the goods of creation are meant for all.[46] Secondly, solidarity is presented as a moral response to the fact of interdependence. Thirdly, such acts of solidarity spring from the virtue of solidarity. As a virtue, solidarity is not just a feeling but "a firm and persevering determination to commit oneself to the common good".[47] Fourthly, the virtue of solidarity transforms the interpersonal relationships of individuals with the people around them. It causes the more powerful people to feel for those who are weak and makes them ready to share what they have with them. Fifthly, the virtue of solidarity is exercised also by whole nations in their relationships with other nations. Nations, like people, are linked in a system which makes them dependent on each other. Within an international system, the powerful and wealthy nations are morally bound to assist underdeveloped countries.

Moreover, 'human solidarity' should not be divorced from 'ecological solidarity'. Though the Pope does not use this phrase, he speaks of "a greater realisation of the limits of available resources and of the need to respect the integrity and cycles of nature."[48] Finally, the present generation must show solidarity with future generations. The encyclical points out that "natural resources are limited; some are not renewable. Using them as if they were inexhaustible, with absolute domain, seriously endangers their availability not only for present generations but above all for generations to come."[49]

To the participants at the twenty-fifth General Assembly of the United Nations Food and Agriculture Organization, held on 16 November, 1989, Pope John Paul II spoke about the relationship between sustainable development and ecology. He said that the protection of the natural environment has become a new and integral aspect of the development issue. The concern for ecology, seen in connection with the process of development and in particular the requirement of production, demands primarily that in every economic enterprise there should be a rational and calculated use of resources. Moreover "it has become increasingly evident that an indiscriminate use of available natural goods, with harm to the primary sources of energy and resources and to the natural environment in general, entails a serious moral responsibility. Not only the present but also future generations are affected by such actions." [50]

He insisted to the participants at the FAO meeting that we have to operate beyond narrow national self-interest and a sectarian defence of prosperity of particular groups and individuals. "It is increasingly evident," the Pope continued, "that development policies demand a genuine international cooperation which is carried out in accord with decisions made jointly and within the context of a universal vision, and which considers the good of the human family in both the present and future generations." [51]

Moreover, in his 1993 message for Lent, Pope John Paul II called all people of good will to detach themselves from superfluous goods and to live in an ever more active solidarity and in an ever wider fellowship:

it is quite clear to everyone that uncontrolled industrial development and the use of technologies which disrupt the balance of nature have caused serious damage to the environment and caused grave disasters. We are running the risk of leaving, as our heritage to future generations, the tragedy of thirst and desertification in many parts of the world. [52]

At the European Ecumenical Assembly "Peace with Justice for the Whole Creation" held in Basel (15-21 May 1989), all Churches agreed that they are committed to an ecumenical process for justice, peace and the integrity of creation. After referring to the threats to justice, peace and the environment, the assembly declared that "humanity has to preserve and promote the integrity of creation in obedience to God, for the good of future generations." [53] In its list of basic affirmations, commitments, recommendations and future perspectives, the assembly considered it as vitally urgent that the resources of this earth are to be shared with the coming generations and future life. [54] The Churches promised to commit themselves to a new life-style. They also urged that "every economic development has to be submitted to the criteria of social sustainability, international sustainability, sustainability for the environment and sustainability through generations." [55]

Concluding Remark

The focal theme of this paper is the Churches' contribution to environmental issues, particularly on our moral responsibility to bequeath to unborn generations a world worth living in. The Catholic Church and the World Council of Churches support environmentally sustainable economic policies in order to reduce current stress on natural systems and at the same time to safeguard natural resources for the future of humankind. This stand was the result of a gradual change in the Churches' perspective on development. The world community was awakened to the awareness that unless we act today, generations yet unborn will have to bear the cost of our irresponsible actions and decisions. It is unethical to make progress at the expense of posterity. The Churches, as a leading moral force in the contemporary world, are not only contributing to today's ecological awareness, but are also promoting plans of action that protect the planet earth which is ours and the future generations' common home.

The ecological issue is directly linked to justice for the poor. The goods of the earth, which in the divine plan should be a common heritage, often risk becoming the monopoly of a few who often spoil them and, sometimes, destroy them, thereby creating a loss for all humanity. Unborn generations, like the contemporary poor of the earth, offer a special test to our solidarity. The option for the poor embedded in Sacred Scripture and the Churches' social teaching inspires us to foster trans-spatial and trans-temporal solidarity. The concept of sustainable development challenges all men of good will to work for global and intergenerational solidarity.

May all Christian Churches continue to foster dialogue and collaboration with other religious communities so that all men of good will continue to be inspired to build an equitable and sustainable future in which all generations can share in the resources of the earth created by God for the benefit of all humankind.

Notes

1. Vatican II, *The Church in the Modern World, (Gaudium et Spes)*: par. 1.

2. 'Justice in the World', p. 696 in Flannery, A. (ed.) (1982), *Vatican Council II. More Post Conciliar Documents*, vol.II, Collegeville, Liturgical Press.

3. *Ibid.*: p. 709.

4. Pope Paul VI (1972). 'Man's Stewardship of his Environment', p. 102 in *The Pope Speaks* 17.

5. *Ibid.*: p. 101.

6. *Octogesima Adveniens* (hereafter *OA*), par. 21.

7. Pope Paul VI (1987). 'Give Future Generations a Healthy Environment' (message on the occasion of the Fifth World Day of the Environment, 5 June 1977), pp. 468-469 in *Paths to Peace*, Brookfield Liturgical Publications. In his message to H.E. Dr Kurt Waldheim, the then Secretary-General of the United Nations, on the occasion of the Special Session of the General Assembly, Paul VI stated: "Through the good will of all, the riches of this world must serve the true benefit of all - as they were indeed destined by the Creator who, in his bountiful providence, has put them at the disposal of the whole of mankind", *ibid.*: p. 216.

8. Pope John Paul II (1988). 'Towards a True Ecology', (an address of Pope John Paul II to representatives of science, art and journalism), pp. 324-5 in *The Pope Speaks* 33 (June 26). In his first encyclical *Redemptor Hominis* (1979): par. 15, Pope John Paul II has also encouraged all of us to be the 'guardian' rather than the 'exploiter' or 'destroyer' of his natural environment.

9. Pope John Paul II (1981). 'A Universal Good in the Service of All Men', *Osservatore Romano* (hereafter cited as *OR*) (19 January): p. 16.

10. Pope John Paul II (1983). 'Survival of Millions: the Solemn Duty of All Mankind', *OR* (24 October): p. 11.

11. Pope John Paul II (1987). 'Environmental Programmes to Ensure Food and Settlement are Concrete Ways for Further Peace', p. 55 in *Paths to Peace*, see note 7 above.

12. Pope John Paul II (1987). 'Teach a new and respectful attitude towards the environment which will ensure the preservation of natural resources', *OR* 47 (23 November): p. 3.

13. Pope John Paul II (1990). 'The Exploitation of the Environment', *OR* 8 (January): p. 10.

14. *Idem.*

15. Pope John Paul II (1989). 'The Needs of the Less Favoured Nations and the Poverty of So Many Human Beings is an Appeal for International Cooperation', *OR* 21 (22 May): p. 3.

16. Pope John Paul II (1989). 'Peace with God the Creator, Peace with All of Creation', *OR* (18-26 December): p. 3.

17. *Ibid.*, p. 2.

18. Pope John Paul II (1990). 'Saving Tropical Forests', pp. 371-372 in *The Pope Speaks*, vol. 35.

19. *Sollecitudo Rei Socialis* (hereafter *SRS*), par. 34.

20. Pope John Paul II (1991). 'Social and Political Problems are the Responsibility of the Whole Church', (Discourse commemorating the centenary of the promulgation of *Rerum Novarum)*, pp. 4-5 in *The Pope Speaks*, vol. 37.

21. *Centesimus Annus* (hereafter *CA*): par. 37.

22. Genesis 1,1-31; 17,7-8: "I will maintain my Covenant between Me and you, and your offspring to come, as an everlasting covenant throughout the ages, to be God to you and to your offspring to come. I give the land you sojourn in to you and to your offspring to come, all the land of Canaan, as an everlasting possession. I will be your God."

23. It is interesting to note that the Koran also announces to all humankind that "all wealth, all things, belong to God" and thus to all members of the human community.

24. Troeltsch, E. (1960). *The Social Teaching of the Christian Churches*, vol. I, New York, Harper & Brothers: p. 116.

25. As quoted by Avila, C. (1983). *Ownership: Early Christian Teaching*, London, Sheed and Ward: p. 37.

26. As quoted by Phan, P. (1984). *Social Thought. Messages of the Church*, vol. 20, Wilmington, Delaware: p. 91.

27. As quoted by Phan, P., see note 26 above: p. 95.

28. *De Off.* 1, 132.

29. As quoted by Phan, P., see note 26 above: p. 173.

30. As quoted by Avila, C., see note 25 above: p. 95.

31. *Gaudium et Spes* (hereafter *GS*) 69, *Populorum Progressio* (hereafter *PP*) 22, *SRS* 7, 42, and the Final Document of the European Assembly *Peace with Justice for the Whole Creation*, (15-21 May 1989), Basel: par. 33.

32. Pope John Paul II (1993). 'Nations Need an Environmental Ethic', *OR* 44 (3 November): p. 4.

33. Albrecht, P. (1980). *Faith and Science in an Unjust World,* Report of the World Council of Churches' Conference on Faith, Science and the Future, vol. II, Geneva, World Council of Churches: pp. 159-160.

34. *GS*: pars. 71, 87.

35. *GS*: pars. 69, 70, 85-7.

36. *GS*: par. 70.

37. In 1968, the WCC and the Pontifical Commission for Justice and Peace established jointly "The Committee on Society, Development and Peace" (SOPEPAX). Since the Uppsala Assembly (1968), Churches all over the world have taken many initiatives to participate in the development process. Then, in 1970, the World Council of Churches set up the Commission on the Churches' Participation Development (CCPD). Its function was to provide a forum for discussion of the meaning of development and the Churches' role in it. Many prevailing assumptions about development were challenged.

38. *PP*: par. 14.

39. *PP*: pars. 15-16.

40. *PP*: par. 17.

41. 'Justice in the World', see note 2 above: par. 16.

42. Albrecht, P. (1980). *Faith and Science in an Unjust World*, see note 33 above: p. 130.

43. Kinnanon, M. (ed.) (1991). *Signs of Spirit* Official Report, Geneva, World Council of Churches: pp. 64-65.

44. *SRS*: par. 33.

45. *PP*: par. 21.

46. *SRS*: par. 39.

47. *SRS*: par. 38.

48. *SRS*: par. 26.

49. *SRS*: par. 34.

50. Pope John Paul II (1990). 'Aid to Debtor: Respect the Environment', p. 146 in *The Pope Speaks*, vol. 35.

51. *Ibid.*, p. 146.

52. Pope John Paul II (1993). 'Remember the Thirsty', *OR* 7 (17 February): p. 2.

53. *Peace with Justice* (1989). The Official Documents of the European Ecumenical Assembly, Basel (15-21 May), Geneva, World Council of Churches: p. 43.

54. *Ibid.*, p. 54.

55. *Ibid.*, p. 55.

10

Envisioning a Curriculum
for Future Generations

RONALD GALLAGHER

In recent years, much has happened in the West Bank, suggesting that Palestinians might begin to think about and plan a concrete and stable life for the future. The agreements made in Oslo and signed in Washington and Cairo seem to portend the possibilities for peace. Indeed, there is a great need for a life approaching normalcy, autonomy, freedom of movement, economic stability, education, improvement in health conditions and freedom of religion. Conditions of occupation have made even the envisioning of such possibilities a futile exercise, forcing people to concentrate on the necessities for day-to-day survival and safety, rather than to engage in the luxury of future planning. Yet, a true, just and lasting peace must be forged from the hope of a positive vision for the future generations. The Justice and Peace Commission of the Jerusalem Latin Patriarchate, commenting on the Washington agreement, called this process "Wagering on Hope":

In spite of its inevitable ambiguities, it remains a first step -the first step of a long process, whose path should lead to a just, comprehensive and definitive peace in the region. Among the desirable, the possible and the acceptable, we have chosen the acceptable, in the hope that what is now acceptable - strengthened by growing mutual trust - can evolve toward that which is possible and even toward that which is desirable.[1]

Perspectives of the Present

A university can and should play a positive role in the process of creating a stable society, characterized by peaceful, tolerant and respectful relations among neighbours. To do so its curriculum must be guided by an ethical as well as educational vision. The current political and societal changes warrant such a new vision, for the sake of all who live in the Holy Land. Bethlehem University is a case in point. For the past several years, the faculty has discussed curricular change in an attempt to redefine the qualities and attributes its graduates should possess. Such an effort can have far-reaching consequences, certainly into the future generations of the society it serves. In order for this to happen, the proposals for curricular change must arise out of a wide rather than narrow view of the role of the educated person in society. At the heart of the educational vision must be a vision of the human person. This must be the starting point.

For the De La Salle Brothers, who have managed the University since its founding, the common statement of their mission derives from the vision of their founder, St Jean Baptiste de La Salle. In his writings, he continually refers to the Brother/Teacher as minister, one whose goal it is to procure the salvation of his students. The students confided to his care are to be considered as the children of God, and the teacher as God's minister to them. Clearly, the philosophy of education developed by De la Salle is a student-centred one, in which the teacher/educator is a minister and representative of God, and the full human and spiritual development of the student is the primary objective.

A recent publication from the Vatican, entitled *The Presence of the Church in the University and in University Culture,* amplifies this most important point about the centrality of the development of the human person:

Within the University, the Church's pastoral action, in its rich complexity, has in the first place a subjective aspect: the evangelization of people. From this point of view, the Church enters into dialogue with real people: man and women, professors, students, staff, and, through them, with the cultural trends that characterize this milieu. But one cannot forget the objective aspect: the dialogue between faith and the different disciplines of knowledge. In the context of the University, the appearance of new cultural trends is, indeed, closely linked to the great questions concerning humanity: the value of the human person, the meaning of human existence and action, and especially conscience and freedom. At this level, Catholic intellectuals should give priority to promoting a renewed and vital synthesis between faith and culture.[2]

In addition to the ethical and theological imperatives which must necessarily propel any programmes and activities setting forth the mission of an institution like a Christian university, there must also be a concrete and realistic analysis of its cultural, political, economic and human environment. Planning for future generations begins with the movement from response to present realities towards the creation of future possibilities. This sort of analysis plays a vital part in the structuring of a curriculum *qua* response to the needs of society and the individual.

Let me place these thoughts in a practical framework. In the past several years, the process of curriculum revision has moved on a number of different tracks, with concurrent activities moving the revision both internally and externally. On the one hand, there has been a regular conversation amongst the various faculties, a conversation whose purpose is to identify the qualities of the graduate, with a view to forming the educated, concerned Palestinian citizen of the future. On the other hand, various departments, individual researchers and external agencies (eg. UNESCO, Save the Children Fund, *Médécins sans* Frontières, University College Dublin, and many others, more than 30 in the case of Bethlehem University) have been compiling regular research about health needs (birth rates and conditions, care for handicapped, health care training) environmental concerns (agriculture, water), business environment, human rights, educational conditions, religious issues, emigration and other issues.

The thrust of these activities has been primarily twofold: to identify the most pressing needs of the present and to construct programmes and strategies to address these needs. In one sense one should consider such activities normal in the life of an active university, and rightfully so. But we have a saying at Bethlehem University, that "the normal is impossible". It's our way of reflecting on the difficulty of carrying on academic life under occupation. It is a marvel to me we can do any planning at all. Equally impressive, on the positive side, is the dedication of the students and faculty; they place an extraordinarily high value on education and have willingly put themselves in dangerous situations in order to procure the education we offer. Despite the dangers and disruptions, people want dearly to continue; this fact alone gives one hope that the students and faculty of this generation truly want to create a better life for themselves and for the students of future generations.

Curricular Goals

In developing a paper describing the characteristics of the graduates, the faculty kept a number of important goals in mind. The most fundamental of these is to produce an educated person who has reached a level of linguistic competence, has been exposed to important cultural, religious values, knows about his or her own history, is capable of making ethical choices and moral decisions and has been challenged to develop leadership qualities. This is not an exhaustive list, but it gives a good idea of the general education and rather broad skills thought to

be essential to a general education. Above this formulation stands the
overarching set of goals of the university. These include the vision of
developing the skills and experiences which will foster the social,
cultural, political and economic development of a people. The University
expects to prepare students to support the educational, economic, health
care, social service, natural resources and communication structures of
society. In short, the University expects that its programmes will have
an immediate as well as long-term impact on the Palestinian society.
Behind this goal lies another, which is even more far-reaching in its
implications. Because of the unique combination of factors which
brought the University into existence and continues to foster its
development, a special goal of the University is to provide the
opportunity for Palestinians (Christians and Muslims) of diverse
backgounds to meet, study and work together at their common tasks of
teaching and learning and, thereby, foster and model cooperation and
mutual support in a pluralistic setting. This goal underlines the
importance of dialogue as essential to the life of the University, and by
implication, to the future society.

In an address to the graduates of 1993, many of whom had spent
more than seven years completing their degrees due to the interruption
of the Intifada, the Patriarch of Jerusalem, His Beatitude Michel
Sabbah, spoke eloquently about the importance of dialogue:

This university is, in an inseparable way, a Christian Palestinian university. It
is the expression of the will of the universal Church, and particularly of the local
Church, and of all its faithful. It is a Christian endeavour sharing in all the
national efforts, and contributing to the development and growth of the
Palestinian people ... Among its constructive elements is to be a school of
dialogue. It teaches the Christian how to be a brother to his Moslem brother,
and it teaches the Moslem how to be a brother to his Christian brother.
Brotherhood is achieved when every one understands the other, his hopes,
sufferings and ambitions. All of these, from the national point of view are the
same, and from the religious point of view are different. True brotherhood
consists in each one accepting the other, differences included, and in seeing in
this acceptance an enrichment and a source of growth.[3]

The two aspects of the goals, then, which are most important in the light
of the future are, put simply, development and dialogue. I would like to
look at each of these in some detail, outlining the most cogent areas
where each must occur, as well as paying some attention to the very real
obstacles to the future of each.

In the area of curricular development for the future, I would like to
comment on three areas: health care, education and science. These are
not the only areas where future planning is being done, but they provide
good examples of areas of great need.

Health Care

Health care education has perhaps seen the most expansion since the founding of the University. Qualified health professionals are in great demand in the Palestinian society, in part due to the large population living in refugee camps, and in part due to the very uneven distribution of proper health care facilities in the West Bank and Gaza. The Faculty of Nursing annually produces graduates with a B.Sc. in nursing, all of whom become employed in local hospitals and clinics. In addition, the University has established a Physiotherapy programme (1987) and a Midwifery programme (1991). The latter is the first midwifery training programme in the West Bank. An occupational therapy programme is currently in the planning stages.

This expansion of programmes took place as the result of a survey of health care needs which indicated several areas of urgent need. The recommendations of this survey indicated a need for response in two areas: "First, there is a great need for the upgrading or enhancement of provisions in many areas. Second, a programme of education, aimed at raising the level of health awareness of the community, should be developed."[4] The particular recommendations of the survey are responses both to immediate needs and attempts to address long-range needs of the society. Among the immediate needs were cited the urgent need for a programme of training of midwives, due to the high incidence of stillbirths and the problems and handicaps encountered at delivery. Allied to this was the alarming number of vacant staff nurse positions in surrounding hospitals.

The creation of the midwifery programme is a good example of the sort of international cooperation needed to secure a more stable future. Initial trainers for the midwifery students came from Denmark and Scotland. Funding for the programme came from the Norwegian Government, the Norwegian Nurses Association and the Knights of Malta. At the end of a five-year period, the goal is not only to have produced 50 trained midwives, but to have turned the programme over to local leadership for the training and upgrading of midwives and practical nurses. A long-term goal envisions the strengthening of health care education in the entire population, through qualified midwives who regularly visit homes, not only as nurses but as teachers of hygiene and proper health care practice.

Education

The issue of education for future generations comprises changes and expansion of the present school curriculum. With the change to autonomy, some curriculum revision is underway already. Our own education department has begun to look at ways of strengthening the elementary and pre-school education programmes, as well as offering programmes for upgrading the skills of teachers. But if the educational enterprise at any level of society is to survive, there must be peace and stability. Any change in curriculum must also be accompanied by efforts to create peace. How can this be done? How can one move from a situation of conflict, anger and oppression to one of peaceful relations and cooperation?

One education professor has proposed that "Education for Peace" means that the individual must learn to "transform the evil effects of conflict into forces of change promoting the growth and development of the individual and his or her community". This process has several requirements. First, "recognition of the other" and second, "recognizing that making peace requires a radical change in set attitudes".[5] In the context of the Israeli/Palestinian conflict, the process of re-education involves three important components: challenging stereotypes, especially those which dehumanize others; forgiving but not forgetting the past, implying mutual recognition of wrong done to the other; and recognizing that anger is legitimate, so that each party can move on to communication and eventually a letting-go of the anger and breaking the cycle of violence.

A new curriculum, from the elementary level through university levels, would then address itself to a broad understanding of the region. Such study might include views of the history of all the peoples in the region, a study of the Jewish, Christian and Islamic religious traditions in an attempt to promote ecumenism and understanding, a study of the various cultures of the region, as well as the geology and geography of the region. This is certainly not exhaustive, but meant only to be a sampling of the sort of topics which should be considered. One hopes that this kind of curriculum would promote the dialogue necessary for peaceful coexistence. Subjects which teach the skills necessary for competent and full human development, as well as environmental development would of course be part of such a curriculum.

Science

Preparation of a science curriculum for future generations begins with a response to present needs as well as long-term ones. A recent UNESCO study of higher education needs in the West Bank and Gaza cites an urgent need to expand the science and technology programmes to include industrial manufacturing, industrial management, quality control of goods and services, water technology and water management, civil engineering and construction, food industry and technology, electronic engineering, computer science, information system management and environmental quality and conservation.[6]

Creating a self-sufficient society through the sort of programmes suggested here is an essential first step in planning for future generations. A second step will require regional scientific cooperation in areas such as water technology and management, environmental protection, geological and archaeological research and agricultural research and planning, to name a few areas.

International groups, such as UNESCO, will be indispensable in gathering together various international donor groups and participants in the cooperative ventures to come not only in the areas of science, but in other fields in higher education. Some of these might include teacher training, nursing, medical studies, tourism management and related areas including archaeology and heritage preservation technology.

This, then, is a very brief survey of some of the future planning at the university level. But what about the obstacles? What might stand in the way as a deterrent? A first obstacle might well be the factional divisions which currently exist in the Palestinian society. A refusal of factions to cooperate in the building of a societal infrastructure will certainly cause a kind of paralysis, if not outright violence and civil strife. Universities are particularly vulnerable to factionalism, as they have often been the stage for political expression in the recent past. A predominance in control by any one faction, whether it be Hamas, Fateh, the PFLP, or any of the numerous others, might well defeat the cooperation of others in the society.

A second obstacle might be the tendency towards dependence on external assistance, towards becoming a sort of an international welfare state. Economic self-sufficiency as well as political self-determination are important not only for the universities, but for the whole of the Palestinian people and society, now and certainly for the future.

A third might be that mentioned previously, the refusal to forgive the other for previous wrong, whether that one is internal to the society (an opposing faction) or external, the opponents in the Israeli/Palestinian conflict. The lack of reconciliation would prevent the very important dialogue which is fundamental to building a stable future for coming generations.

A fourth and major obstacle might be the lack of resolution of regional religious issues. This is the Jerusalem question, in its far-reaching political and religious ramifications. Can the three religious traditions share the Holy Land and holy places in a way that respects both internal religious differences and the differences in the three different traditions?

A fifth obstacle, particular to the Christian perspective on planning for future generations, is the problem of emigration. This brings us back to the initial founding purpose of Bethlehem University which I mentioned at the beginning of this paper. Having come full circle then, I would like to close with a comment on emigration by Patriarch Michel Sabbah, which speaks directly of the necessity to plan for future generations: "The Church of Jerusalem demands much from its children to build this world so as to become the world of love and peace. The children of the earth are those who build it. So if its children desert it, who will be the builder?"[7]

Notes

1. Justice and Peace Commission - Latin Patriarchate of Jerusalem, October 1993, p. 2.

2. Laghi, P., Pironio, E. and Poupard, P. (1994). *The Presence of the Church in the University and in University Culture"*, Vatican City, Vatican Press: p. 13.

3. Sabbah, M. (1993). Inaugurating Speech at Bethlehem University (10 July).

4. 'Overview of the Results of the Bethlehem University Community Studies and Socio-Economic Survey' (1990), *Bethlehem University Journal*, vol. 9: p. 67.

5. Sfier, J. (1994). 'Education for Peace: The Palestinian Challenge', excerpts from an unpublished manuscript, Bethlehem University, Education Department.

6. *Higher Education in the West Bank and Gaza Strip* (1994). A report of a UNESCO Mission on Higher Education to the West Bank and the Gaza Strip (4-14 January 1994), Paris: p. 21.

7. Sabbah, M. (1992). 'The Position of the Church in Regard to Emigration in Our Palestinian Society', *Al-Liqua Journal,* vol.2 (December): p. 13.

11

The Inter-Faith Dialogue at the Cairo Conference

MANFRED KULESSA

The World Declaration on Our Responsibilities towards Future Generations[1] was a result of the effort in preparation for and in support of the Rio Conference (UNCED). This gathering was the first of a series of international conferences, all dealing with the same issue of sustainable development, each from a different perspective: environment, human rights, population; it was followed the next year by broader social issues at the Copenhagen summit, and by the conference on women in Beijing.

All these meetings are part of a secular effort to carve out a secular world consensus, to express a world ethos, and to try to formulate global action programmes accordingly. In my understanding, there is a clear connection between them and the topic of our discussion. We can recognize, as the prime mover in all this international activity, something like the new categoric imperative which was so clearly stated by Hans Jonas: our actions should be in line with the permanence of truly human life on earth.[2]

We know that very often this is not the case with most of us. We live in contradictions which we know we should reduce. We contribute to the destruction of true human life on earth, and a good deal of other life as well. We feel that we are in the wrong way, and we try to find a way out of this dilemma. Even politicians are starting to call for more coherence and consistency in matters of sustainable development.

The question is, then: What can the world religions contribute to this effort? Perhaps, in the population issue it is more obvious than in other fields, because here we are confronted with a number of serious ethical questions. That may explain why representatives of different religious traditions and experiences were so actively involved in the population debate, before and during the Cairo event. There are, of course, different motives for doing so:

- some are eager to present their views because they are convinced of their message being in line with the well-being of humankind and with the demands of the categoric imperative;
- some may want to show that the Holy See is not the only voice and authority speaking on behalf of religion;
- some use the occasion to look for common heritage and spiritual experience across the boundaries of their religious circles;
- some want to demonstrate that religion is not only putting up barriers and obstacles in the way of reasonable solutions, but is indeed able to offer advice and encouragement, setting people free to take responsible decisions.

The last argument does not remain without serious challenge: not only did we hear some critical voices from the feminist camp assembled at the "Women's Caucus". Gro Harlem Brundtland, the respected Prime Minister of Norway and former Chairperson of the famous World Commission on Environment and Development usually called after her name, presented us with such a challenge when she addressed the Cairo meeting and said: "Traditional religious and cultural obstacles can be overcome by economic and social development with the enhancement of human resources." She then mentioned the examples of Thailand for Buddhism, Indonesia for Islam, and Italy for Catholicism. Unfortunately, we found no opportunity to take this matter up in discussion with Mrs. Brundtland, though she did pay a visit to the NGO Forum, as we were told. Perhaps, someone else did. I am sure the debate will go on.

Whatever we decide and do today in the area of population and development will certainly be of great concern to future generations as they are the population of the future. We notice again that we have a major responsibility for these coming generations.

Population: A Recurring Theme

The population theme itself is not a modern invention of the Malthusian era or of the demographers of our time and age. It found many expressions in an old myth which is part of the heritage of all religions, from the nature religions to the monotheistic ones. In the Mahabharata version of this story, Mother Earth is crying to Heaven, complaining of the growing multitude of human beings. She fears coming to the end of her carrying capacity. Then, in reply, the powers in heaven prescribe a limit to human life: Death becomes the destiny of men and women. The population theme is, indeed, a matter of life and death.[3]

The same story is reflected in our biblical tradition. It is true that we usually only remember Genesis 1,28 when we talk of population topics. There, humankind is asked to multiply and to subdue the earth and all creation. However, in Genesis 6, 1-4, we also find a clear link between such multiplication and the limitation of human life as God's decision. Thus, natural death was recognized as a fact of human destiny, after mankind had already experienced violent death from human hands (Genesis 4).

Of course, there are not only these basic ancient myths that religions have in common when population topics are being discussed, as we found out in the many inter-faith conferences and seminars that took place in preparation for the Cairo Conference. Most important was the common belief in the sanctity of life which was shared by all, though it had a much wider meaning for some, especially for the Buddhists, than for others. At the same time, we also noted some differences in teachings and ethical consequences among the religious traditions presented, though usually less than expected, apart from some fundamentalist quarters. Such fundamentalist views, which appeared rather marginal in the dialogue, were of course not limited to just one religion. The Southern Baptist participants presented us with the perfect example of a dogmatically closed position.

Perhaps, I should explain that I do respect dogma. We are in need of criteria and norms. However, we also know how dangerous it is to narrow our vision when human dignity is at stake. Let me give you three examples from the Cairo debate:

- We all believe in the value of family life, and we cherish the image of the holy family. However, when faced with the reality that there are societies in which the vast majority of families are of the single-parent type, we cannot close our eyes to this reality in a self-righteous manner. Instead, we have to look for the appropriate advice and support for people in that situation.
- Nobody of serious opinion likes or advocates abortion. However, an estimated number of about 150,000 abortions are being performed every day, most of them not "lege artis", i.e. unsafe. As a serious problem, such a threat to women's health has to be addressed. The best solution would be to create a situation which would exclude unwanted pregnancies. In the case of adolescents, this would require proper education and access to means of contraception.
- Children are surely a blessing of God. However, we owe them their right to a full life in dignity.

In Germany, both the main Churches appointed study groups who produced major statements on the population issue which were then published: the first by the Catholic Bishops in December 1993, the second by the Evangelical Church in Germany in June 1994.[4]

The common messages were mainly four:

i) There will be less people through less poverty. It is necessary to fight poverty, not the poor. Family planning programmes should go hand in hand with those combating poverty.

ii) An ecological re-orientation in the industrialized countries is required to protect and preserve the natural resources that form the very basis of human life.

iii) A new gender relationship is advocated, as women and their social status are seen playing the decisive role.

iv) It is necessary to advocate a responsible and humane population policy. This is also a task of the Churches.

The Catholic statement received wide attention, particularly in the international discussion, as it not only stressed responsible parenthood, but also the freedom of responsible choices that mothers and parents have to make. Obviously, there were also some differences between the two statements. Just to mention a major example: the Protestants could not see a distinction, in ethical terms, between "natural" and "artificial" methods of contraception.

Both the German Churches also decided to participate in the national preparations for the International Conference on Population and Development (ICPD). Two of us were nominated to serve on the national commission and later also as members of the German ICPD delegation. Together with other competent NGOs, we organized a public hearing on population issues in Bonn in June 1994.

The close involvement of the government and NGO groups in preparation for this international meeting provided us with a new educational experience. There were, however, also a few points of disagreement, notably in the field of migration. Recalling that Jesus, according to our biblical legend, had been born homeless and later became a refugee in Egypt, where his family found asylum when they faced persecution from their king at home, and finally told us that we would encounter him again in the homeless, distressed and destitute, we could not see a national consensus in the way our government was formulating its non-immigration policy. Though we agreed to disagree on this issue, it turned out that even this debate helped us to find a better way of conducting serious discussions on the national level.

As for the Conference itself, we had written to the chairperson of the NGO Forum to be organized at Cairo, suggesting that:

a) a regular caucus meeting of religiously motivated and interested participants be convened;

b) an inter-faith dialogue programme be conducted and publicly announced during the Conference.

These suggestions were accepted.

A Rewarding Experience

As we found out, such gatherings do not have much chance of success unless someone accepts the burden of management and organization. The interreligious caucus met several times, but did not move beyond the stage of mutual introduction.

The inter-faith dialogue, in contrast, had been entrusted to the World Conference on Religion and Peace, which had been active in its preparation, organising a pre-meeting in Switzerland, assembling a reader of relevant documentation before the Conference, and inviting competent speakers to start the dialogue.[5]

Thus, we did have, in spite of occasional elements of chaos in between, a series of meaningful and highly educational meetings. It started off with a presentation of Islamic teachings, offered by three professors of Al Azhar University. For this event, we had been allocated a room with one hundred seats. About five hundred participants showed up. In other words, the room was packed with people of good standing. After the presentation, a number of Muslim women took the floor, demanding equal time for reporting on their views and findings. Thus, a further major meeting was already secured.

During the following days and throughout the Cairo Conference, we listened to Christian voices of different traditions, and we heard speakers from Judaism, Buddhism, Hinduism, Bah'ai and others, including natural religions and indigenous peoples from different parts of the earth. In all this, the spirit of tolerance prevailed, with a few marginal exceptions. This was indeed a very rewarding experience for all of us. At the same time, we also learned that, instead of having each religion presented separately, the dialogue character could have been brought out more forcefully if we had organised the meetings by topics, asking an interreligious panel to address a given theme or a number of clearly defined questions. Perhaps this approach could be tried out at future conferences.

As we soon found out, ours was not the only gathering concentrating on interreligious encounter and exchange. The World Council of Churches was there with a sizeable delegation, offering a statement at the plenary session, though not a common position of its member

Churches. The Parkridge Center of Chicago, the Catholics for Free Choice, Professor Dan Maguire and his group, the Temple of Understanding and many other congregations were busy calling for meetings and discussions. As it turned out, the inter-faith community was by far the most active movement at the NGO Forum, in which about five thousand persons participated, and second only in efficiency and organizational strength to the *Women's Caucus* which served as the focal point for women's policy concerns.

Towards International Understanding

The results of ICPD are known. The agreed programme of action represents a major step in terms of a global consensus in the fields of reproductive health and the empowerment of women. Now, everything will depend on consequences in follow-up action.

At the same time, the Conference was also a typical child of our times. Its deliberations and recommendations concentrated mainly on the responsibility of the individual and of the family whose rights and freedom governments should respect and serve. It was probably still too early to face what I would call the "Chinese question", namely the responsibility of community and state for limiting population growth. Vittorio Hösle, a young German philosopher, argues that we should prepare ourselves to face that question sooner or later. He thinks that governments can be ethically justified and compelled to limit family size by force of law if there is no other way of avoiding disaster and fights for survival, and if the regime is applied to all in a just manner. Perhaps, future population conferences in ten or twenty years will have to deal with this question.[6]

It is also possible that they may consider this a far-fetched concept as we do right now. Let me, then, return to the topic of my contribution and to the main message I wanted to set out: our experience in inter-faith dialogues at this international conference in Cairo was rather encouraging. With a little improvement in interaction and organization, this approach could become an important part of the process of international understanding and common awareness-building. After all, we cannot leave the globalization effort to the financial markets and CNN alone. Perhaps, caucus and dialogue could become regular features at secular international events of this nature.

If there is no peace without peaceful dialogue among religions, we better get together to give proper shape to that dialogue so that future generations will not blame us for missing this opportunity in our time on earth. At the same time, we recognize the task to sharpen the conscience of those holding power, and to help them to avoid issuing statements of consequenceless perfection. In other words, the religious communities can and should assist the international organizations and debates to become more meaningful for the life of present and future generations. After all, such international conferences are no longer just diplomatic meetings providing opportunities to well-dressed envoys to exchange in style the instructions of their governments. They have become world events, and they deal with the effort to formulate secular world ethics.

Notes

1. This Declaration was unanimously approved by all participants of the International Conference on *Our Responsibilities towards Future Generations* held in Malta in April 1992, by the Future Generations Programme of the Foundation for International Studies, University of Malta.

2. Jonas, H. (1984). *Das Prinzip Verantwortung*, Frankfurt/M.

3. Gensichen, H. W. (1991). 'Bevölkerungswachstum und Religionen', p. 75 in Mensen, B., *Die Zukunft der Menschheit als Gegenwartsaufgabe*, Steyler Verlag-Nettetal; Schwarzbaum, H. (1957), 'The Overcrowded Earth', *Numen* 4 : p. 59.

4. *Bevölkerungswachstum und Entwicklungsförderung - Ein kirch - licher Beitrag zur Diskussion, Herausgeber: Sekretariat der Deutschen Bischofskonferenz*, December 1993. *Wieviele Menschen trägt die Erde? - Ethische Überlegungen zum Wachstum der Weltbevölkerung, eine Studie der Kammer der EKD für Kirchlichen Entwicklungsdienst, EKD Texte 49*, Hannover 1994 (both studies are also available in English).

5. *Religion, Population and Development: Multi-Religious Contributions*, (NGO Forum '94, World Conference on Religion and Peace), New York, United Nations.

6. Hösle, V. (1994). 'Moralische Mittel und Ziele der Weltbevölkerungspolitik', *epd-Entwicklungspolitik* 9.

12

The Churches' Response to the
Population Problem

GEORGE GRIMA

There is hardly any other problem which has brought up more thorny and complex issues for the future of humankind than the population problem. The expression "population explosion", which was fairly popular during the Cold War period, was very significant at the time when the attention of the world was fixed on the fast growing arsenal of nuclear weapons. The fact that the population was increasing at a very rapid rate, expected to rise to over 6,000 million by the end of the present century, was something with which the individual countries and the international community had to reckon. The threat to the future of humankind did not lie only in that a nuclear war could break out at any time but also in that a growing population was like a very powerful bomb which had to be defused as quickly as possible, for it was exploding without being noticed. Like the arms race, population growth rightly became a global issue which could be adequately solved only through international cooperation.

The Christian Churches realized progressively the impact of world population growth on present and future generations. They were not the first institutions to consider this problem. In fact, they entered the scene as soon as the international community began to study it and to make people conscious of its serious implications. The international community continued to take the lead in the field with the last three conferences organized by the United Nations in Bucharest (1974), Mexico City (1984) and Cairo (1994) specifically to formulate and agree on a common plan of action. The Churches, wisely enough, participated in the debate and the Catholic Church played a direct part in all the three conferences.

The response of the Christian Churches, therefore, was elicited by opinions that were circulating outside their own circles and, in a way, conditioned by an agenda which somebody else had drafted. It illustrates a point which Vatican II made in the Constitution on *The Church in the Modern World*, namely, that the Church (one may speak also of the Churches) is to take part, along with humankind, in the search for new and better forms of life in the world.[1] The Churches can only be co-responsible with other religious institutions and with the rest of humankind for the creation of a more human world.

It is not my intention here and now to make a historical survey or a detailed comparative study of the way in which the Christian Churches have tried to deal with the population problem in recent years. In this paper, I shall be examining only the positions of the Catholic Church[2] and the World Council of Churches,[3] which incorporates Churches with somewhat different traditions. I shall be focusing on the dimensions of the response of the Catholic Church and the WCC to the population problem.

The Churches' response includes three main dimensions: (i) the hermeneutical, which concerns the interpretation of the situation, (ii) the confessional, which consists in a more or less elaborated statement or definition of religious beliefs and ethical convictions and (iii) the strategic dimension, which deals with the implementation of the Churches' response: their relation with their own faithful, with the public, particularly governments, and with the international community.

The Hermeneutical Dimension

The way in which individuals, groups and institutions respond to situations depends on how they interpret them. Naturally, the more complex a situation is the more difficult is its interpretation, because there may be so many factors and variables involved that only a very rough picture may be possible. This is exactly the case with the population problem. Its scope and complexity are impossible to determine in an exact way.

The Churches are not experts in demography, although they obviously need to know what experts in the field are saying. At first, studies in population growth were not given any significant importance by the Catholic Church and by the World Council of Churches. Pope John XXIII could dismiss the population problem quite simply and conveniently by saying that the statistical information about the rate of growth of the world population and its impact on the available resources was inconclusive.[4] Vatican II paid more attention to population studies and even recommended the setting-up of appropriate centres for the promotion of such studies in universities.[5] More recent documents which the Holy See has produced mainly through the Pontifical Council for the family prove the increasing importance which the Catholic Church has been attaching to a scientific approach to the subject and an objective picture of the real situation.[6] The same is true of the World Council of Churches. The vast and serious proportions which the problem was already taking in the 1950s were at first noted only in a general way. In the World Assembly at Uppsala in 1967 the population problem still did not receive extensive treatment but the message conveyed in and through the current figures was taken. They confirmed that as the world population would have doubled by the end of the century, "food supplies would have to be doubled; twice as many habitations must be built as have been built during man's entire history".[7] As one can see from subsequent documents, the scientific aspect of the population problem was duly taken into account by commissions of the World Council of Churches working on the subject.[8]

The problem with statistics, however, is well known. They may reflect only certain aspects of the reality being considered and the conclusions, based upon them, can have, at most, only a relative, though valid, significance. Both the Catholic Church and the World Council of Churches took the current interpretations of the population problem in a constructive and, at the same time, critical way.

In their view, the link which the international community was making between population and development was justified, for the population which individual countries and the world could have in ten, twenty, thirty years time should be able to have a truly human life. The kind of life it would have depends, in a considerable measure, on decisions taken now on the family, national, regional and international levels.

The Catholic Church[9] and the World Council of Churches[10] found many positive points in the three Action Plans which the last three United Nations' Population Conferences approved. Greater participation on the part of traditionally disadvantaged sectors of the population, like women, old people, immigrants and refugees, access to better health services, protection of the family as a basic unit of society - subjects which the international community had been bringing up for systematic study and coordinated action - have been very well received by the Christian Churches.

It has been argued, however, that the link between population and development has not been brought out adequately in international debates and action plans. The Catholic Church, in particular, hammered out this point practically in all its interventions on the subject. It protested against the one-sided view in which the population problem was being approached in international fora. Rather than seeing the problem in the context of a broad concept of development, as one should expect, the United Nations has been in reality looking mainly at the demographic aspect, as if the problem were one of numbers.

The concept of development has also to be critically considered. On this point both the Catholic Church and the World Council of Churches have been constantly insisting. The Catholic Church criticised the concept of development implied in the Action Plans of the last three World Population Conferences for being understood in predominantly economic and quantitative terms and, especially in the case of the Cairo Conference, in terms of an individualistic style of life. The World Council of Churches also called for a revision of the concept of development, because it was too restrictive and biased in favour of the economic aspects. To avoid misunderstanding it recommended[11] the expression "quality of life" in place of the term "development", which term, in the mind of many people, including those who draft and approve international documents, has a strongly economic connotation.

The Christian Churches depended on the current interpretations of the population problem but they were also critical of those interpretations. They realized, like the rest, the critical stage through which humankind had been passing in the course of this century, with the significant drop in mortality at birth, infancy, childhood and adolescence and, accordingly, with a longer span of life for an increasing number of people, and the crisis which would be confronting humankind in the near future, unless appropriate decisions were taken now. As communities having a religious tradition, they had to respond to the situation in accordance with the faith they professed. Faith opens up a perspective for interpreting human situations. It provides new insight and motivation. By itself, it cannot and it is actually not meant to solve human problems. The solution to these problems has to be found through dialogue and cooperation with others and it is never definitive, because new aspects of the same problem are always emerging, along with new issues. In their interventions on social problems, the Churches often note that they are participating in discussions on those problems and trying to contribute to their solution as religious institutions. What does this mean?

The Confessional Dimension

In the documents of the Catholic Church and the World Council of Churches on population one finds references to the Christian doctrine of the creation of man and woman in God's image to justify the Churches' stand in favour of the dignity and rights of the human being or insistence on the human responsibility to intervene in an appropriate manner in critical situations; to the Christian doctrine of sin to explain the persisting tendency towards individual and group egoism in human relationships and to the Christian doctrine of redemption to stress once more the dignity of every man and woman and their vocation to share in God's own life.

But underlying the doctrine of creation, sin and redemption one finds in the Christian tradition the view of God as a Reality that is coming and is already present, although always in a hidden form. This idea of God and His coming Kingdom, which, in my opinion, very much helps the Christian community to interpret any critical situation, like that created by the population problem, has not been consistently used by the Catholic Church and by the World Council of Churches except in a fragmentary fashion. It has been adopted by Vatican II in the Constitution on "The Church in the Modern World" as a theological framework for a deeper and a broader understanding of the "crisis of growth", as the Council said, through which humanity was passing at the time.[12]

It is important, I think, to point out that the specific contribution which the Christian Churches have been trying to make, on the basis of the Christian faith, lies precisely in their attempt to place the "crisis" brought about in recent years by a rapid population growth in the context of hope. Hope enables one to look at crises as opportunities for growth, as a challenge to accept the new in a joyful spirit.

From a religious viewpoint, it is very significant that both the Catholic Church and the Council of Churches reacted against the "fear" that was being spread by several population projections. Fear may dictate the adoption of morally objectionable or doubtful measures especially when it is triggered by the threat of individual or collective extinction. It is no wonder that a "lifeboat ethics" has been applied as one possible way of dealing with the population problem.[13] This is the ethics to be followed in "life or death" cases, such as the case of the four persons on one boat who discover that they would all drown, unless one of them is thrown into the sea. The Catholic Church in particular has been constantly preoccupied about the adoption or promotion of population policies which are the product of fear rather than a realistic and, at the same time, hopeful account of the actual situation. As Paul VI beautifully put it in the concluding paragraph of his message to the Bucharest Population Conference, what is needed is to combine a sense of realism with a spirit of hope.

Interpreted in the light of God's coming Kingdom, the population crisis implies the reaffirmation of certain values. Both the Catholic Church and the World Council of Churches stressed that one should reaffirm that the population problem is not about numbers but about people. People are human beings having their own individual dignity and rights. Marriage should continue to be regarded as the institution which provides the right kind of context for a fully human expression of sexual love and as the basis of the family. The value of the family needs also to be reaffirmed, being the basic unit of society and the best type of environment for the transmission of human life as well as the upbringing of children. The family constitutes a bridge between generations: the young, the adult and the old generation. Solidarity is a value which has to be re-affirmed, particularly in our own times, when the world has become one in the sense that all people and nations have become dependent on each other and global problems, like those of population and development, can be solved only through international cooperation.

Responding to the population problem with faith in God and His coming Kingdom means, therefore, choosing not to do violence to anyone, not to destroy institutions like marriage and the family which are basic for the stability and proper functioning of any human society, not to deprive the other of his or her due share in the available resources. Such choice can be nourished by the hope that the future would be better for all when those values which have sustained human communities in the past are not destroyed in our attempt to cope with a situation before which we may feel afraid and our survival is thought to be at stake.

Values need to be reaffirmed in situations where they are threatened. On the basis of Faith in God's coming Kingdom the Catholic Church and the World Council of Churches could take very seriously, as I have already noted, the critique of current population policies which disregard, very often in subtle ways, those values which the present generation is expected to pass on to future generations.

Reaffirmation, as used in this context, is different from re-assertion. One may re-assert one's views independently of what the other side is saying. Reaffirmation is an exercise that takes the other side and what it is saying and doing into account. It listens to the other and tries to discern what is actually being said and done behind appearances. There is, of course, always the danger in this sort of exercise that one starts to suspect things which are not intended or implied. For this reason, the Christian Churches as critics of population policies, are required by the same faith which they profess to examine themselves and submit their own analyses to continual criticism.

The Catholic Church, much more that the World Council of Churches, went through very detailed analysis of the action plan submitted for the consideration and approval by the United Nations in each of its last three conferences on population. It pointed out the lack of clarity and, therefore, ambiguity in the language used. This was especially the case, it argued, with respect to the sections dealing with marriage and the family as well as with reproductive health, a concept which was introduced for the first time in the Cairo Action Plan.

Let me take the right to life. Reaffirming this basic right required, according to the Catholic Church, a close and critical reading of such texts as those speaking on reproductive rights and reproductive health. It was observed[14] that these two terms, which appeared more than 100 times in the Cairo Draft Final Document, were quoted from working documents of the World Health Organization without even having been approved by WHO itself or by other international assemblies. Through this very subtle procedure, the Vatican delegation argued, rights which had never been sanctioned nor recognized by the international community were advanced, even though they were in conflict with and in violation of basic human rights like the right to life. In fact, the extension of the concept of reproductive health in the above-mentioned document to include "the right to have access to methods of fertility regulation which are safe, efficacious, accessible and acceptable" would include the right to abortion, for in the definition of WHO the phrase "fertility regulation" includes abortion.

Reaffirming the right to life required, according to the Catholic Church, a critical examination of the new language about human rights which may in reality amount to the violation of such a right.

An alternative way of reaffirming the right to life in the context of current debates on the population problem is found in two documents of the World Council of Churches. One document notes that the majority of Protestant Churches tend to broaden the therapeutic reasons for abortion.[15]

The reason is not stated but evidently it is that the human condition may give rise to situations of conflict of rights and duties and, while heroic decisions are not to be excluded particularly in view of the radical demands of the Gospel, some form of compromise may have to be found in conflictual situations. But in justifying abortion for therapeutic reasons only, Protestant Churches are limiting the scope for abortion by excluding, for example, that it may be lawfully performed as a means of birth control. The other more recent document[16] states that "the unjust treatment and systematic exploitation of women make legal recourse to safe, voluntary abortion a moral imperative".[17] Abortion is here seen as something which ideally should not be performed and legalized but, considering situations of injustice and systematic violence against women, it may be a morally acceptable option. This view is, of course, disputable - after all it appears in a discussion or working paper of one of the commissions of the World Council of Churches. In fact, one may ask whether legal recourse to safe abortion may actually divert attention from the real issue, namely, the progressive elimination of the causes of abortion, particularly those linked to situations of injustice towards and exploitation of woman. Nevertheless, what is being claimed is again that the affirmation of the right to life involves taking the dark and tragic side of the human situation into account, while abortion purely as a means of birth control is rejected.

I have taken the right to life as an example to show how the re-affirmation of this right has been interpreted by the Christian Churches in their response to the population problem. Divergence in interpretation should not conceal a common Christian belief, namely that life is a gift given by God which we are called upon to welcome in joy and not to terminate to keep population figures down. Differences of views on abortion and other issues may have kept the Catholic Church from approaching the World Council of Churches to make a common front against certain trends in population policies today. One cannot expect that differences in the teaching of the Christian Churches on such delicate issues can be altogether eliminated. But it may be possible to reach a consensus at least on certain matters and make a joint effort in the interest of humankind.

Solidarity is also a value that the Churches have been trying to reaffirm in connection with current discussions on the population problem. In this problem or crisis one can hear God's judgment condemning imperialist tendencies and an international order based on domination by the stronger and wealthier. Both the Catholic Church and the World Council of Churches took the side of the poorer section of the world's population and attacked policies linking international aid with the acceptance of objectionable methods of birth control and aiming at placing the blame on the developing countries. They also stressed the obligation of developed countries to try to consume less, given that they are actually using most of the energy, consuming most of the products and availing themselves of most of the services being provided.

In religious terms, one may say that population growth involves a crisis calling for conversion or a turning away from certain modes of thinking and behaving to allow God's Kingdom - a Kingdom of truth, justice, freedom and love - to manifest itself, albeit in a fragmentary manner, in our midst.

Besides the hermeneutical and the confessional, there is the strategic dimension to be considered.

The Strategic Dimension

Let me take first the communication of the Churches with their faithful. The Catholic Church produced fairly elaborate documents[18] to help episcopal conferences and Catholic organizations to be correctly informed about population trends throughout the world, attitudes towards demographic realities and ethical principles that can enlighten and guide discussions and pastoral action on the problem. The strategic importance of these documents lies in that they can explain the Church's viewpoint on the problem and, through the various episcopal conferences, ensure "a joint action that will be as complete and as efficacious as possible".[19] In this sense, they serve as an instrument for the mobilization of action at local and regional levels hopefully involving as many of the faithful as possible, so that the line pursued by the central organ of the Church's administration namely, the Holy See, may have a fairly strong backing from the Catholic community.

The Catholic approach cannot be described as one coming from the base to the top. It has been dominantly one from top to base. As a matter of fact, while the Catholic Church has been taking the preparations for the last three world population conferences very seriously, among other things, by communicating the views of the Holy See to its member Churches, to my knowledge, local Churches as a general rule did not participate in the formulation of the stand which the Holy See actually held in international fora.

The World Council of Churches seems to have been favouring a much less centralized and unified approach. Its first major report, written on the occasion of the Third World Population Conference, was intended as a help for the Churches in every country to become better informed and more deeply concerned "so that they may make a timely and relevant contribution to the national and global search for socially responsible policies".[20] The approach is one that stresses initiative from below and participation from the base. In fact, this type of approach may be required in view of the different convictions which the member Churches have on certain issues such as contraception and abortion on which the majority of Protestant Churches do not share the same views as the Eastern Orthodox ones.[21]

But why should the Christian Churches try to elaborate a common viewpoint on global issues? This is quite a significant and relevant question to raise, as one Commission of the World Council of Churches has recently done,[22] at a time of increasing fragmentation when talking about programmatic concepts of development and systems, whether of the right or of the left or of some other kind, has become anachronistic. The reconstruction of the basic fabric of social life is possible only if one moves close to the *base* and starts "again from the everyday lives of people, their struggles and their hopes, their powerlessness and their inherent strategies for life in community".[23] "The new challenge", in fact, "is to develop new ways of recognizing diversity while affirming relatedness (catholicity)".[24] Our concept of theology itself has to change from one (with a capital T) which presumes to offer the true answers to questions about ultimate meaning, to one which provides "space" for the emergence of different theologies reflecting the aspirations and struggles of real men and women.

The emphasis of the World Council of Churches on the need for the individual Churches to discuss global issues on the local level where they assume concrete form and call for quite specific commitment is a very positive one. It is a healthy complement to the Catholic approach which, though following a "top-down" model, certainly does not exclude the responsibility of the local Churches to study global issues, as that of population, from the perspective of their own cultural tradition. Surely, how to reconcile global demands and the call and commitment to unity with the diversity of local needs remains a problem for which there is no easy and simple answer.

The strategy which the Catholic Church and the World Council of Churches have adopted in their relations with States and international organizations, particularly the United Nations, is a complex topic on which only some very general observations can be made in this context. Indeed, I wish to restrict myself to the Catholic Church as I am not familiar enough with the activities of the World Council of Churches in this field.

In its interventions on population issues the Catholic Church followed basically the same pattern, with some very telling differences in the case of the Cairo Conference. The Vatican participated in the preparatory meetings of the last three UN population conferences and, of course, in the conferences themselves. Some time before the conferences began, the Pope addressed a message to the Secretary-General of the respective conference in which he expressed his reaction to the proposals being advanced and identified briefly both the positive and negative points which the Catholic Church felt the need to make. On the occasion of the last conference, John Paul II also wrote a letter to Heads of State showing his concern about the individualistic philosophy behind the Draft Final Action Plan and the harmful consequences of this philosophy on the right to life as well as on marriage and the family. This move on the part of the Holy See was certainly suggested by the big pressure which it was anticipating from certain quarters in favour of certain trends. Anyway, the papal messages contained, in a nutshell, the position which the Vatican delegation later maintained in discussions during the three conferences.

It is not possible here to review, not even in a general way, the points which the Vatican delegations at the population conferences raised and the "compromise" which was reached on certain issues.[25] Something, however, should be said regarding the premises on which they generally argued and the sources they often used to back their views. Religious considerations featured very little, often at the beginning. One cannot simply say that they argued on the basis of premises derived from reason, because the reasoning of men and women in and outside the Churches occurs within specific cultural traditions. The Catholic Church, like the other Churches, has inherited a tradition in which certain values are believed to be basic for the proper functioning of society.[26] Its challenging task when arguing in secular fora in favour of marriage and the family, to mention one example, is to find out suitable passages that enable it to make its stand meaningful and possibly acceptable. Correctly enough, the Holy See sought to make fruitful use, where possible, of relevant international documents to substantiate its claims. References to past documents of the United Nations were made, for example, to show that what was being proposed (e.g. on the family or abortion) marked a step backward on earlier pronouncements.[27]

Another significant element in the Catholic strategy to promote its views on population policies is the role played by episcopal conferences.[28] In what direction these conferences moved and what influence they succeeded in exercising on governments regarding population policies are again too broad a subject to deal with in this paper. One may say only that they can certainly contribute positively to the development of policies that would correspond to the needs of their own country or region and join forces with representatives of other Christian Churches and other religions. Joint action has been taken by Churches and other religious bodies in several countries on various social issues, including the population issue.[29]

Episcopal conferences, as it is fairly well known, intervened very prominently, apparently as part of the Vatican's strategy to get the support it needed from as many States as possible at the Cairo conference. In fact, public statements were issued to show the concern of the local Churches on those points which John Paul II had already underlined and to appeal to their respective governments to take a truly responsible stand on the matter.[30]

The fundamental question confronting the Catholic Church (and other Churches) when arguing on population policies on national and international levels concerns the role of the State in contemporary societies. On the one hand, the modern State assumed increasingly greater power in development policies, particularly in the economic domain. Hence, its interest in the number of people for whom food, housing, suitable health care services and jobs have to be found. This is, in itself, a positive thing. But as increase in production and in the generation of work is a painstaking and long process, which is itself subject to various conditions on which even the State can have very limited control, if any at all, States have generally a particular interest in checking population growth. For this reason, their tendency is to intervene in the domain of human procreation.

On the other hand, in contemporary societies, where the right to self-determination has established itself firmly, talk about the responsibility of the State to protect values such as life from the moment of conception, marriage and the family has become problematic. The tendency of certain modern States is to intervene less and less for the purpose of providing the necessary protection, through law and education, to such values.

In its interventions on population policies the Catholic Church and, to a lesser extent, the World Council of Churches insisted on the limits of the competence of public authorities *vis-a-vis* population planning. Vatican II acknowledges that "government officials have rights and duties with regard to the population problems of their own nation, for instance, in the matter of social legislation as it affects families, of migration to cities, of information relative to the condition and needs of the nation".[31] But the inalienable right to marry and beget children should be equally recognized and so "the question of how many children should be born belongs to the honest judgment of parents".[32]

In view of the present-day awareness of the value of freedom, insistence on parental freedom in matters related to family planning may be acceptable to many and may, therefore, be effective in the formulation of population policies which take the legitimate rights of parents into account. How acceptable and effective is the Catholic insistence on the responsibility of public authorities to protect life (e.g. from the moment of conception), marriage and the family is another matter. The Catholic Church has been arguing that it is not fair for public policies to promote "a life-style typical of certain fringes within developed societies, societies which are materially rich and secularized".[33] How marginal are the vision and style of life reflected in Action Plans proposed for the approval of World Population Conferences in contemporary society is surely open to question. But the dispute on this point has very serious repercussions on our responsibility towards future generations because the kind of life they will have depends largely on the kind of life we shall be transmitting to them.

Notes

1. The Church in the Modern World (*Gaudium et Spes,* hereafter referred to as *GS*), Vatican II Documents: par.1.

2. For a brief but quite comprehensive survey of Catholic teaching on the population issues see the document entitled 'Ethical and Pastoral Dimensions of Population Trends' (1994), Vatican City, Pontifical Council for the Family: part III, ch.1.

3. On the World Council of Churches (WCC) and Population Issues

see Albrecht, P. (1991), 'Population Explosion' in the *Dictionary of the Ecumenical Movement*.

4. *Mater et Magistra*: par. 188.

5. *The Church in the Modern World*: par. 87.

6. Cf. 'The World Population Year and Conference' (1974), Vatican City, Committee for the Family; 'Ethical and Pastoral Dimensions of Population Trends' (1994), see note 2 above.

7. As quoted in Appendix I to Document No.C.6 of the Committee on Programme Unit III, WCC (1994). To be referred to as WCC Working Paper on Population and Development.

8. *Population Policy, Social Justice and the Quality of Life* (1973). A Report from the WCC. To be referred to as WCC Report on Population.

9. For the Catholic reaction to 1) the proposals of the 1974 conference on Population and Development see Paul VI (1974), 'Message to Antonio Carrillo-Flores, Secretary General of the World Conference on Population', Bucharest, and Rafael Salas, Executive Director of the United Nations Fund for Population Activities (UNFPA), *Osservatore Romano* (hereafter *OR*) (30 March); Statement by Gagnon, E. (1974), Head of Holy See Delegation to Conference, *OR* (5 September); Press Conference by the Holy See Delegation in Bucharest, *OR* (19 September). For a review of the Holy See participation, see Lombardi, F. (1974), 'Bucharest 1974: Il Piano d'Azione Mondiale della Popolazione", *Civiltà Cattolica* 11 (hereafter *Civ.Catt.*): pp. 181-202.

For the Catholic reaction to the proposals of the 1984 Conference see John Paul II (1984), 'Message to Rafael Salas, the Secretary General of the World Conference on Population', Mexico City, reproduced in *Population Perspectives: Statement by World Leaders UNFFPA* (1984), New York: pp. 175-178; Statement by Schotte, J., Head of Holy See Delegation (1984), *OR* 30 (August). For a review of the Holy See participation, see Rulli, G. (1984), 'La Conferenza sulla Popolazione nella Citta' del Messico', *Civ.Catt.*11: pp. 183-195.

For the Catholic reaction to the proposal of the 1994 conference see John Paul II (1994), 'Message to Mrs Nafis Sadik, General Secretary of World Conference on Population', Cairo, *OR* (23 March); John Paul II (1994). 'Letter to Heads of State', *OR* (20 April); statement by Martino, R. R., Head of the Holy See Delegation (1994), *OR* (14 September); Joaquin Navarro-Vals, J., Head of the Vatican Press office (1994), 'Press Statement in Cairo', *Origins* 24(14): pp. 245-248.

10. For WCC reaction to the 1974 Conference see WCC Report on Population (1973) and to the 1994 Conference see WCC Working Paper on Population and Development (1994). See also *Contact* 135 (February), WCC, and WCC's intervention at the Cairo Conference through the Commission of the Churches on international affairs.

11. Cf. WCC Working Paper on Population and Development (1994).

12. *GS* : pars. 4-10.

13. Cf. Gustafson, J. (1984), *Ethics from a Theocentric Perspective,* vol. II, Chicago and London: p. 225.

14. Press statement in Cairo by Joaquin Navarro-Vals, see note 9 above.

15. *WCC Report on Population* (1973), see note 8 above.

16. WCC Working Paper on Population and Development (1994), see note 7 above. See, however, the intervention of the WCC at the Cairo Conference for a more nuanced position on the subject of abortion.

17. *Ibid.*: p.5.

18. See note 6 above.

19. 'The World Population Year and Conference', see note 6 above: par. 4.

20. WCC Report on Population (1973), see note 8 above: p. 1.

21. *Ibid.*: p. 3.

22. Unit III Commission on "Justice, Peace and Creation", Working Paper on Population and Development (1994), see note 7 above.

23. *Ibid.*: p.2.

24. *Ibid.*

25. A case in point is the compromise which the Holy See delegation was prepared to reach on the matter of contraceptives at the last preparatory meeting of the Cairo conference. It stated that it would not delay the negotiations with continued debate on this issue "as soon as appropriate language is inserted in the text to the effect that abortion will not be promoted as a means of family planning". Cf. J. Navarro-Vals, see note 9 above: p. 246.

26. Finnis, J. (1991). *Moral Absolutes. Tradition, Revision and Truth,* Washington: ch.1.

27. See references made in support of stronger protection for the family by Gagnon, E. in his statement to the Bucharest Conference to the pronouncements of the *Universal Declaration of Human Rights* and the *UN Declaration on Social Progress and Development.* Regarding abortion it was pointed out that the *Cairo Draft Final Document* modified substantially the position taken in the Mexico City Conference.

28. Documents by episcopal conferences on population issues include: Statements by US Bishops, Latin American Bishops, Federation of Catholic Bishops' conferences of Oceana, Latin American Episcopal Council and Presidents of the Latin American Episcopal conferences' on the Cairo conference. These are all reproduced in *Catholic International* 5(10) (1994). The Canada's Bishops' statement on Cairo conferences is reproduced in *Origins*14 (1994). A Commission of the Catholic Bishops of Germany has also published a document entitled *Population Growth and Promotion of Development* (1993).

29. As an example, see the Joint statement made by Cheema, M. A.,

president of the American Muslim Council and Archbishop Keeler, W., president of the National Conference of Catholic Bishops on the Cairo conference (1994), *Origins*15: pp. 250-252.

30. See note 28 above.

31. *GS*: par. 87.

32. *Ibid*.

33. John Paul II's Letter to Heads of State on the occasion of the Cairo Conference.

13

Jesus' Reconciliatory Mission: An Effective Call to Unity

JOSEPH CALLEJA

Christ's salvific and redemptive mission is to be understood in the light of humanity's spiritual condition especially against an Old Testament perspective.[1] We have to view Christ's ministry and self-sacrifice as being the initiative that provides the remedy to humanity's sinful condition. Thus, we are invited by Paul, especially in some of his epistles, to examine humankind's condition beforehand simply to place Jesus' mission within the correct perspective.[2] Various Old Testament references throw sufficient light on our experience of sin and on the immediate effects of sin. Although several Old Testament quotations speak in terms of humankind's spiritual condition, still, we are going to refer mainly to what is actually stated in Genesis 1-11.[3] That section of the Bible sheds light on the condition of every human being. In the first two chapters we are told that God has created (and is responsible for) man and woman and the world they live in. There is an evident equilibrium based mainly on the obvious relationship that existed between God and humanity. Humankind lived in good terms with the whole world, its natural habitat. It is when we think in terms of such equilibrium that we understand the evil effects of humanity's sin.[4]

When humanity detached itself completely from God's sovereign rule and dominion through its sinful rebellion, it did this at the cost of its healthy interests and relationships. Human beings tried to assume and usurp what was not their own, what strictly belonged to God; for all this, humanity had to suffer the evil consequences of its insubordination. Once humankind refused to acknowledge God's rights, nature itself failed to submit itself to humankind's legitimate control.[5] Humanity lost not only God's friendship but also the possibility of a peaceful living. Conflicts started within small groups, within the family between male and female partners. Man and woman, therefore, had to earn their own living by means of their unstinting efforts. The role of the female partner was not without its difficulties, especially during child-birth. Both male and female felt an impellent urge for each other and yet each tried to take advantage of the other partner. Such divisions were but the reflection of other conflicts on a larger scale: conflicts within the same nation and within different ethnic groups. Human beings soon came to experience that conflicts were brought about by their insubordination to the order willed and created by God himself.[6]

Something definitely went wrong to the extent that man and woman experience disruption even within their inner selves; we yearn for unity simply because we are more than aware of the ill-effects of division. One could say that history is but the record of such a state of turmoil and disruption. We yearn for peace and a peaceful living which always seems to be the object of our wishful thinking. We long for that peaceful state that must have been ours, but, for some reason or other, has been forfeited and seems to be irremediably irrecuperable. Against such a perspective, Paul invites us to envisage the full meaning of Christ's self-offer. Our endeavours give way to the concrete proposals that are derived from Christ's altruistic mission, whereby humanity at large has been taught and helped to obtain peace and unity.

Christ: The Reconciliation of Humankind with God

Against such a realistic perspective, we have to examine the meaning behind Christ's self-offer in the light of Paul's teaching. We have already stated that the immediate effect of sin is one's inevitable detachment from God. Jesus redresses the evil brought about by our sin through his Paschal mystery. Some of the quotations speak in terms of Christ's mission and the reconciliation that now exists between God and us. We make some comments as we go along: "It was God who reconciled us to himself through Christ and gave us the work of handing on this reconciliation. In other words, God in Christ was reconciling the world to himself not holding man's faults against them, and he has entrusted to us the news that they are reconciled" (2 Cor 5,18-19).

It is always God who takes such initiatives and who guarantees our reconciliation.[7] Then, such initiatives always take place through Christ (or in him). Christ has been instrumental in bringing about a change in the relationship between God and humanity. In very concrete language, reconciliation means inevitably the forgiveness of one's own sins: they are no longer held on account. Reconciliation concerns every individual person and humanity at large, the world as a whole. All receive the full benefit of God's forgiveness and indeed no one is excluded. Such a situation necessitates both the activity of propagation as well as faith on the recipient's part.

"When we were reconciled to God by the death of His Son, we were still enemies; now that we have been reconciled surely we may count on being saved by the life of his Son?" (Rom 5,10). The text stresses more or less the same aspects mentioned in the previous quotation. Still, various other points that are also mentioned are worth noticing. It is stated in very explicit terms that reconciliation has taken place through "the death of the Son".[8] It is not by the death of someone whom we do not know but rather through the death of the Son in particular. Reconciliation brings about the union between God and those who formerly were his enemies because of their sin/sins. The new state guarantees salvation vouchsafed by "the life of his Son". Through Christ's altruistic self-offer, we have been granted a special pardon of our sins; in this case, it is clear that God's pardon brings about life in us and that is precisely what reconciliation is.

In the introductory hymn of the letter to the Colossians, it is stated that reconciliation involves "all things" and takes place not only "through Christ", but also "for Christ". The hymn takes up and explains what has been just stated. The phrase "all things" is taken up once again when the author refers to "everything in heaven and everything on earth" (v. 20): the created order is at his complete dependence and benefits from his concrete and realistic "death on the cross". It is this death that has brought about the "peace", that peaceful co-existence in the whole of creation. No reference is made to the theme of sin, the only cause of division and misunderstanding. The approach is rather positive, even if what is being stated necessarily implies the correction in that order of things that has been thwarted through sin. In the hymn as a whole, Christ is both "the image of the unseen God" and "the first-born of all creation" and these two phrases provide the key to the right understanding of Christ's role.[9]

To bring this section to a conclusion we have to speak in terms of reunion between God and humanity and this through Christ's self-offer and death. Christ has to resolve, through the mystery of the cross, the problems caused by our personal sins.

Christ: The Reconciliation among Human Beings

We have already stated that the estrangement from God is inevitably the cause of so much division among brethren. The only remedy to such an evil effect is reconciliation with God, brought about by Christ himself. We are always aware of such divisions both when they occur within one's own family and also when they occur among different nations. Against such a situation, we experience an inner longing for peace and unity and, at the same time, all this seems to be an unrealistic utopia, the object of our wishful thinking. The irony of it all comes to surface when we recall the fact that religion has often been made to serve a negative purpose: to foment various divisions and create prejudice among different ethnic groups. Nothing more than peace is being looked for by individuals, groups and nations but all these are well aware that more often than not, such a precious value is completely out of our reach. Various theological trajectories within New Testament writings have nourished the hope that all forms of reunion are possible only in Christ, and this in spite of the many attempts that proved to be unsuccessful and futile. Without a doubt, Christ and his teachings provide the solution to man's divisive inner tendencies. It is precisely this basic conviction that invites us to examine the reasons why religions have been so often abused as to become the cause of division rather than of peace and unity among all men no matter the differences that there may be.

Against an Old Testament perspective, we have to speak of the neat distinction between Jews and Gentiles: the Jews considered themselves the rightful heirs of the covenant and therefore as "God's chosen people". Such a privileged position was so exclusively theirs to the extent that all Gentiles, all the non-Jews, did not benefit from the same divine prerogatives simply because they happened to belong to other ethnic groups. Such distinctions led not only to an obvious separation between the two groups but also to open antagonism between the chosen few and the condemned majority. An imaginary wall was constructed to make the existing difference all the more evident: the Jews opposed to the Gentiles. It is against these affirmations that we have to understand the meaning of Ephesians 2,11-22.

"For he (Christ) is the peace between us, and has made the two into one and broken down the barrier which used to keep them apart, actually destroying in his own person, the hostility caused by the rules and decrees of the Law" (Eph 2,14).[10] Christ is referred to as the "peace" that effectively brings about the unity of the two seriously opposed parties.[11] In Christ, both Jews and Gentiles are given an equal opportunity, they are on an equal footing. The Gentiles will no longer be termed "the uncircumcised", nor will they be considered second- or third-class citizens within the "new Israel". The author of this letter speaks of their former state as "those excluded from the membership of Israel" and "as aliens with no part in the covenants with their Promise". It is by describing this state of things, this reality, that the writer wants to highlight the effect of Jesus' self-offer on the cross. Jesus destroyed all hostility to the extent that he "created one single new man in himself out of the two groups" (v. 15). Indeed, the two have been absorbed in

Christ, the Risen Lord. This stage of complete union and fusion has been achieved through Christ and it has become so through our insertion in him by means of our baptism. Jews and Gentiles have been reconciled with God through Christ's intervention. It is in this context that the author speaks of Jews and Gentiles as being "part of a building" of which Christ is indeed the cornerstone. This building is "the one holy temple in the Lord", "the house where God lives" (v. 22).[12]

We have a similar passage in the letter to the Colossians wherein the author speaks of the pagans' former state and their present situation in Christ. Pagans were both foreigners and enemies. One can easily think in terms of enmity between Jews and Gentiles but then what about the word "foreigners"? This word makes sense when we speak of "citizens", people who belong to one ethnic group and live within their own territory: others may live very close but still distinguish themselves from the actual citizens. It is said in very clear terms that the Gentiles were considered not only as foreigners but also as sinners who had to be made "holy, pure, and blameless" through Jesus' self-sacrifice and death (v. 22).[13] This new situation has become a possibility for all those who believe in the Gospel message that has been proposed to them. Although such unity has been entirely the achievement of Christ himself, it was not all that easy to arrive at such a conviction after a long period of division and conflict especially during the last centuries of the Old Testament period.

It is interesting to note the fact that Paul, the apostle of the Gentiles, avails himself of this reality to arouse a sense of sacred jealousy in the mind and heart of his own people. Paul invites his fellow Jews to remember their election by accepting Christ; they should turn to Christ lest others obtain that salvation to which they have been called right from the very beginning, even before all Gentiles. God's mysterious plan has been fulfilled and revealed through Christ and yet it still remains a mystery that goes well beyond the possibility of our understanding. "It is to make my own people envious of you, and in this way save some of them. Since their rejection meant the reconciliation of the world ..." (Rom 11,14-15). Paul is thinking in terms of Israel's temporary refusal that has opened the way for all Gentiles to form part of the one fold, the one people of God. By recalling their own election, the Jews are invited to accept Christ in faith and thus to benefit in an equal way from the effect of his achievement.[14] Christ's self-offer is equally meaningful to both Jews and Gentiles. The antagonism of the past should no longer obstruct that health-procuring unity that has been achieved in Christ.

By means of the Pauline quotations we have seen that reconciliation has taken place between God and us and among ourselves. Still, Paul insists that this reconciliation assumes a cosmic dimension and this is precisely the aspect we are going to examine in the next stage of our study.

Christ: The Reconciliation of the Whole Cosmos

We have already stated that for Paul we are in need of redemption and that ultimately our redemption is made manifest through our reconciliation with God and among ourselves. There are other texts wherein Paul speaks of the world rather than specifically of the individual human being.[15] One has to examine the term "world" as it occurs in some of the Pauline texts to see whether it stands for man or for some other reality. Here we have no intention of being exhaustive on this highly debatable subject. Paul states that "God in Christ was reconciling the world to himself, not holding men's faults against them ..." (2 Cor 5,19). Once he speaks in terms of humanity and sin, one is led to understand the term "world" as being the whole of humankind without any distinction between Jews and Gentiles.[16] In this key statement, Paul is stating that humanity at large depends on Christ's redemptive mission and that this has been the plan and the initiative of God right from the very beginning. The world stands for the totality of humankind which has been reconciled to God through Christ.

Another text that speaks of Jesus' mission in similar terms and that has already caught our attention states "Since their rejection meant the reconciliation of the world, do you know what their admission will mean?" (Rom 11,15). Since the apostle is speaking of "their rejection", that is, of the Jews who failed to believe in Jesus, the term "world" seems to stand for "the pagans", for those who have accepted the apostle's message and received the one message of salvation, the message that guarantees the salvation of both Jew and Gentile in Christ. Thus, the term "world" includes both groups who believe in Christ and that are equally saved through him.

Then there is another text of great importance in the letter to the Romans. Paul states that "the whole creation is eagerly waiting for God to reveal his sons. It was not for any fault on the part of creation that it was made unable to attain its purpose, it was made so by God; but creation still retains the hope of being freed, like us, from its slavery to decadence, to enjoy the same freedom and glory as the children of God" (Rom 8,19-20). In the first statement, creation becomes God's witness as soon as he takes his initiative in favour of man. We soon recall that salvation is mainly addressed to us; we are the ones who have been invited to make the most out of God's plan of salvation.[17] But then what do we understand by "creation", how is it related to God and how is it going to be freed from its decadence? It is certainly something completely distinct from us and God, and yet dependent on and related to both. But then it looks forward to having that same "freedom and glory" that have been bestowed upon "the children of God".

If this creation is distinct from humankind, then it is important to note that it is being personified and it requires those same divine prerogatives of which we are so much in need. Creation so personified groans "in one great act of giving birth" (v. 22): it is like a mother who is waiting to give birth, to reach that particular moment of "freedom and glory".[18] Paul says that we too groan "as we wait for our bodies to be set free". The point of contact between both realities is indeed the future resurrection of the body. There is an evident link between our human body and the created order around us.[19] We have brought about an evil effect on our environment, which, in turn, has proved to be detrimental to our own well-being. If we benefit from the direct intervention of Christ, creation is equally waiting for that change whereby created order will be at the complete service of humanity. Salvation is the object of hope in that it will be fulfilled in the time-to-come. This phase of reconciliation between creation and humankind depends on Christ and it definitely throws light on the vast proportions and far-reaching effects of Christ's self-offer.

When we study the hymns in Colossians and Ephesians against a Sapiental context, we notice that Christ is not only at the very centre of the whole "cosmos" but also its unique principle of cohesion. In the first part of the hymn in the Letter to Colossians, there is an insistent use of such expressions: "For in Him were created all things in heaven and on earth ..." (v.16), which immediately recalls both the active role of the Old Testament's *dabhar Yahweh* and the personification of Wisdom (Prov. 8,22-31).[20] But then the statement "all things were created through him and for him" not only repeats but also explains the opening words of v. 16. There is a similar statement in v. 20, where it is stated "all things are reconciled through him and for him". Thus, Christ has been responsible for all things both on the level of creation and on the level of reconciliation (redemption). What is being stressed here is not so much the reconciliation between man and the cosmos but that between God and the created order. Peace has been achieved "by his death on the cross". It is rather implied that once peace has been achieved through Christ's initiative, peace reigns supreme in creation as a whole. When everything is under the control of Christ himself, that is indeed the sign that order has been restored between humankind and the cosmos (2,15).[21]

Both humankind and the world it inhabits were created and redeemed by Christ; reconciliation reunites both humanity and the world with God and brings about the necessary peace between humankind and the natural habitat. Christ is the Lord of the whole cosmos and this explains how a new equilibrium has been reached. While the created order offers its service to humankind, we become more conscious than ever before that we should not exploit the resources of the world around us for egoistic purposes. Thus, the ultimate conclusion of the Christian's belief in Christ has to be translated into daily concrete terms of conduct.

We may say then that Paul saw disruption and division as being the ultimate effect of humanity's sinful situation. We constantly live in this form of contradiction: we pretend to live in peace and yet our division and separation from other fellow human beings and from the world around us compromise that reunion necessary to guarantee the dignity of a peaceful living. It is God who in Christ made up for such a situation; it is Christ who brought about reconciliation of humankind with God and with all the created order. Still, we play an important role in the light of Christ's redemptive mission; we are constantly invited to make our own efforts so as to obtain the full benefit of redemption on the subjective and the personal level. It is precisely such a consideration which will be dealt with in the final section of this short essay. What has been achieved in Christ will ultimately reach its complete fulfilment in the future, in the time that has still to come.

Christ's Redemptive Mission: A Present and Future Reality

In an act of obedience and self-offer, Christ died for us and has indeed achieved his goal; he has been truly effective in that he really brought about our salvation. The past event, therefore, is always considered a present reality: the present enjoys the full benefit of that past event and, in a way, the past still lives in our present time.[22] And yet, we are not always aware of the reconciliatory situation in which we all live; we are, however, aware of the divisions, conflicts and wars that are still the cause of so much bloodshed within and among nations.

Thus, on both the subjective and the collective levels there exists enough room for man's participation, for man's acknowledgement of God's own initiatives in his favour.

Paul, at times, speaks as if Christians were already saved, and, at other times, he suggests that they are still waiting to be saved.[23] It is in this context that Paul leaves aside his own interest to be of help to others: "not anxious for my own advantage but for the advantage of everybody else, so that they may be saved" (1 Cor 10,33). Very often, to safeguard one's own interest, one is ready to ignore the well-founded rights of others and this becomes the cause of so many disputes and conflicts. Paul leaves aside his own rights to save others; he follows the example of Jesus, his master, even if this may entail the loss of spiritual gain.[24] Paul himself sets an example of pastoral zeal; he was willing to lose some of his benefits provided others managed to obtain salvation through some of his self-sacrifice. One final quotation perfectly sums up what we have been saying in this final section: "When Scripture says: Those who believe in him will have no cause for shame, it makes no distinction between Jew and Greek: all belong to the same Lord who is rich enough, however many ask his help, for everyone who calls on the name of the Lord will be saved" (Rom 10, 10-13).[25]

This particular statement by Paul recalls to us the conviction of the Church as expressed in the documents of Vatican II, namely that in accepting Christ, we become more human and, therefore, less egoistic, more altruistic.[26] We let go of our own personal interest(s), our egoistic tendencies, and become more convinced that one's own interest will be singled out and protected within the group as a whole. Christ opens up the wealth of one's inner disposition and places such riches at the service of the group as a whole. Thus, Christ not only brings about reconciliation but he also provides the means so that each may overcome his own egoism and achieve unity with the others.

We conclude by referring once again to the first chapters of Genesis. What has been made the point of departure for all our considerations has indeed become the point of convergence for the people of all nations. To come to terms with one's inner self is indeed the sure way towards the unity among both individuals and nations.[27] Such considerations, based on Pauline writings, urgently call for the reunion of belligerent brethren. The more we separate ourselves from our fellow brothers and sisters, the more we become alienated from our true identity and nature. Perhaps in no other historical circumstance are we becoming so much aware that our reconciliation with other fellow human beings has inevitably to bring about the reconciliation with mother nature.

This type of reconcilation entails the correct use of nature and by no means its abuse. The Pauline texts call for that form of reconciliation that is always the guarantee of equilibrium; it is through such equilibrium that we avoid all sorts of exploitation that is ultimately the defeat of our own purpose. It is through that network of relationships, relationships even with nature around us, that we become fully aware of our responsibilities as the prudent guardians of nature and hence, as the ones responsible for the safety of our own destiny.

Notes

1. Gen 6,3; 8,21; Job 4, 17; 14,4; 15,14; Ps 120,3; 143,2: these Old Testament quotations speak in terms of humanity's sinful state.

2. Paul often contrasts the former condition of pagans with their spiritual condition now, as Christians; cf. Gal 4,8-9; 1 Cor 6,11; Col 1, 21-22; 3, 7-8; Eph 2,1-6; 2,11-13; 5,8. Cf. Fitzmyer, J. A. (1970), 'Pauline Anthropology, pp. 818-825 in Brown, R. E. et al. (eds.), *Jerome Biblical Commentary* (henceforth *JBC*), London, G. Chapman.

3. In Gen 1-11 there is an evident contrast between the first two chapters where everything is under God's control and the remaining sections where man and woman cannot have the complete control of the situation because of the evil effects of their own sin. Sin becomes the cause (etiology) of all human misery. Cf. Davies, W. D. (1977), *Paul and Rabbinic Judaism,* London, SPCK: pp. 36-57 where Davies deals with' The Old and the New Humanity: the First and Second Adam'. Also Sanders, E. P. (1987), *Paul and Palestinian Judaism,* Philadelphia, Fortress Press.

4. According to both Priestly (ch.1) and the Jahwistic traditions (ch.2) everything was created to be under humanity's control. Humankind owed its allegiance to God. From ch.3 we know that this situation changes completely because of humanity's disobedient attitude.

5. The whole narrative account creates the impression that the event must have taken place in the remote past (pre-history); still it was handed down from one generation to another because of its paradigmatic value.

6. Gen 3-11 show that all relations depend upon our relationship with God. Disunity exists within us, in our immediate environment, among ourselves and finally among nations.

7. Paul (and other New Testament writers) considers Christ's self-offer as an act of obedience that brings about our own reconciliation, expiation, redemption, liberation and finally justification before God. Cf. Fitzmyer, J. A. (1970), 'The Effects of the Salvation Event', *JBC* , see note 2 above: pp. 814-817. Reconciliation with the rest of creation necessarily presupposes reconciliation with God.

8. Fitzmyer expresses himself thus: "At times Paul views Christ's death as a form of sacrifice that he underwent for men or for the sins of men". Cf. 'Passion, Death, and Resurrection', *JBC*, see note 2 above: p. 815. For the soteriological value of the first Easter cf.: 1 Thes 4,14; Phil 2,9-10; 1 Cor 15,12,17,20-21; 2 Cor 5, 14-15; 13,4; Rom 8,34; 10,9-10.

9. Besides the large number of commentaries on this particular Letter, one may consult also Fuller, R. H. (1965), *The Foundations of New Testament Christology,* London, Collins: pp. 214-16. Also Sabourin, L. (1989), *La Cristologia a Partire da Testi Chiave,* Brescia, Queriniana: pp. 106-09. The two expressions are meant to bring out Jesus' relationship with God and with the rest of creation. It is through his human nature that Jesus makes manifest God who, though invisible, is indeed present: cf. also 3,10; Heb 1,3; 2 Cor 4,4; 1 Cor 11,7). In Rom 8,29 we find both terms ('image' and 'first-born') and in this sequence.

10. Scholars have often discussed the origin and provenance of such terminology. They have often accepted Josephus' suggestion and spoken in terms of the stone partition that separates the outer court of the

Temple from the inner. Cf. Penna, R. (1988). *Lettera agli Efesini*, Bologna, Dehoniane: pp. 141-3. Penna submits other possible interpretations.

11. Penna expresses himself thus: "egli in persona è il costitutivo della nuova pace, il fattore decisivo della coesione e dell'affratellamento fra quanti prima erano divisi, i quali appunto in lui si incontrano e si ritrovano uniti"; *ibid.*: p. 141. The phrase 'our peace' referred to Christ recalls the phrase 'prince of peace' in Isaiah 9,5.

12. The imagery that has to do with 'the building' is found elsewhere in NT writings: cf. also Eph 4,13; Rom 4,13; Rom 15,20; Rev 21,14; 1 Pt 2, 4-5; 1 Cor 3,10ff.

13. The adjectives "holy, pure, and blameless" denote not only the new state of all Gentile believers but also the fact that they now constitute a "sacrificial consecration". Gentiles are now worthy and prepared to participate in the celebration of the sacred mysteries. Gentiles, once they remain faithful to the Gospel, continue to enjoy the benefits of their privileged state.

14. Bornkamm, G. (1975). *Paul*, London, Hodder & Stoughton: p. 151. Bornkamm expresses himself thus: "... to make Israel 'jealous' (Rom 10,19; 11,11) and thus carry her back to her beginnings and to her final salvation".

15. Christ's universal-cosmic role comes to the fore also in the following quotations: Col 1,15-20; Heb 1,1-4; Jn 1,3,10; 1 Cor 8,6 and Eph 1,10.

16. Cf. Furnish, V. R. (1984). *II Corinthians*, Anchor Bible, New York, Doubleday: pp. 333-7.

17. Cf. Kasemann, E. (1982). *Commentary on Romans*, London, SCM press: pp. 232-3.

18. Commentators often speak in terms of Greek philosophers and of the customary comparison between the vernal rebirth of nature and a woman's travail. Paul states that suffering and anxiety are soon followed by a condition of real joy. Cf. Davies, *Paul and Rabbinic Judaism*, note 3 above: pp. 38-9. Also Bornkamm, see note 14 above: p. 225.

19. On the theme of resurrection, cf. Davies, *Paul and Rabbinic Judaism*, note 3 above: pp. 285-320. Man's resurrection becomes a pledge and guarantee in favour of the whole cosmos.

20. In the Old Testament writings, creation was always attributed to the effectiveness of God's Word (cf. Ps 33,6; Wis 9,1) and Wisdom (cf. Prov 8,27-30). But then in the New Testament, especially in Paul, creation has been the work of both Father and Son (1 Cor 8,6): Cf. Sabourin, *Cristologia.*, note 9 above: p. 113.

21. Penna, R. (1991). 'Il Sangue della Riconciliazione Cosmica', pp. 407-410 in *L'Apostolo Paolo, Studi di Esegesi e Teologia* , Milan, Paoline Ed.

22. Traditional Christian Theology has always distinguished between the objective aspect (i.e. salvation as achieved by Christ himself) and the subjective (as is made available to the individual through his openness to the mystery of Christ). The theme of unity has to be dealt with while keeping in mind such distinctions within such a theological perspective.

23. The following Pauline texts speak of Christians as already saved: Rom 8,24; 1 Cor 15,2; 1,18; 2 Cor 2,15; Eph 2,8. Still, in other texts Christians are still to be saved: 1 Cor 5,5; 10,33; Rom 5,9.10; 9,27; 10,9.13. Cf. Fitzmyer, 'Pauline Soteriology', *JBC*, see note 2 above: p. 810.

24. In this text, Paul not only imitates the Master's generous self-offer but also provides the only remedy for all divisions and conflicts. Paul insists that this is always the case with Christian charity.

25. Cf. Kasemann, see note 17 above: pp. 290-2.

26. Here special mention should be made of the two conciliar documents, *Lumen Gentium* and *Gaudium and Spes*: where the Council speaks of the nature of the Church and of the situation in which we find ourselves today.

27. In spite of so many conflicts and wars throughout the whole span of human history, Christianity still speaks in terms of a realistic hope. In Christ it is possible for humankind to achieve the much desired condition of a peaceful living. Each is asked to make one's own contribution no matter how small: this will be the beginning of such an attainment on a higher level which certainly constitutes the legitimate aspiration of us all.

14

Intercultural Dialogue as a Source of the Future

STANISLAV HUBIK

For a long time now much has been spoken and written about the paradigm shift which has been occurring in philosophical, social and religious thinking. Hans Küng even writes about a macro-paradigm shift.[1] I suppose that even judgement on questions connected with the destiny of future generations should respect this paradigm shift. In this context, I would like to offer two theses:

  i) the first shift refers to the overall approach to the question of the future as a whole and the role of religious dialogue in future-related matters;
ii) the second relates to the unquestionable advantages of differentiation within this dialogue.

The first thesis shall be referred to in the following text as the approach *sub specie communicationis et communionis* to which we shall refer in short as *sub specie communicationis*. The second thesis, on the nature of the dialogue, shall be referred to in the following text as 'communicative differentiation', or simply 'differentiation'.[2] However, seeking better ways to the future often leads one to the past, to the foundations of our cultures. The slogan *Back to the Future* does have its own meaning in this regard. The foundations of our cultures refer here to the religious foundations. In this expression, the plural must be stressed; it refers to 'cultures', not to one particular culture. Where there is a plural, there is also plurality, and where there is plurality, there is also differentiation. The search for better ways into the future does not have any other form but that of a permanent communication among its seekers.

  This fact is underestimated to a great extent amongst advocates of the old Euro-American socio-philosophical paradigm. This paradigm is centred around the slightly arrogant idea of "autonomous subject/ consciousness". However, the forthcoming paradigm emphasizes the very pluralistic, differentiating and communicative aspect of this phenomenon.

The Paradigm of Communicative Differentiation

The *sub specie communicationis* approach can be considered as a command of the "post-European time" (J. Patocka), when the "first global revolution" is taking place (A. King, B. Schneider), and humankind is becoming aware that the age of signs it is living in is essentially "the age of theology" (J. Derrida). Nevertheless, the paradox of this time is the discrepancy between the great communicative differentiation of various communities (and *plurality* of their values and thinking/views) on one side, and the demand for global (thus a *single*) solution of fatal problems of humankind on the other side. Where are we to seek the source of this new oneness? Definitely not in the pragmatism of a single doctrine. So where shall we seek a solution?

It was already suggested that the source lies in today's cultural foundations. For instance, the religious systems, the origin of which is in the Mediterranean, are of one shared basis. It can be assumed that this fact may be a good starting point to examine the dialogues leading to the moral restoration of European humanness. It is only necessary to set out on a journey for the quest of *sub specie communicationis* and differentiation. Also, it can be assumed that there is a code preserved in the cultural foundations of Judaism, Christianity and Islam, with the help of which the broken entirety/unity of reason, emotion and will may be unified again - for it is purely the entirety of reason/emotion/will that can become the foundation of a restoration of general morals and the start for new generations.

The paradigm of communication is based on the well-known thesis of paradigm shifts in modern philosophy, which was sufficiently articulated by German authors in the 1970s and 1980s. It can be shortly expressed by the slogan "from the philosophy of self-consciousness to the philosophy of communicative reflection".[3] In the discussions about current crisis and about the future, this thesis is methodologically valuable and heuristically effective, especially for the following two reasons: it draws the attention of philosophy to the non-casual objective structures of meaning, inciting the resignation from material reflection; and it brings to the fore the environment (nature etc.) neither as the object nor as the structure of relationships among various beings, but as the structure of meanings of various beings, originating from their mutual interaction. The usage of the displaced Latin expressions from philosophy and the social sciences may be instructive and may initiate such formulation: our world is both the result and the precondition of the communication among the citizens of a community it is the communion itself. From the angle of the mutuality and communication, the world appears as an association, community, not as an object, a structure. Naturally, 'community' and 'citizen' here have different meanings from those they have in common language: they include all participants of the communion, who co-create the significant world of appurtenance (even if conflicting) by a deed. The world involves not only people, but also other creatures, even those which are, according to the reason of the modern age, not real, but are, nevertheless, real according to the reason of other communities/cultures.

Communio, communitas, communicatio are sources of various types of emotivity and rationality. To answer the question "What is real and what is not real?", as well as the question "What is good and what is bad?", means to listen to a real communication of a real community. In order not to bring this approach to boundless relativism, it is necessary to conduct a dialogue with other communities and thus - on the basis of intercultural communication - let humankind speak with several voices. As M. Bakhtin put it, respect the polyphony of human cultures.

Different cultures and communities could be discussed (Judaism, Christianity, Islam). However, this would not be enough, as merely the differentiation or the cultural diversity would be left. The diversity must be preserved, but not as the target or aim of the restoration, but rather as the bearer and the source of the restoration. The aim is the discovery of the union and the oneness of values which are coded in the foundations of Mediterranean cultures. How could this be achieved?

Redefining Civilization

I would like to suggest a solution which offers convincing arguments both for the power of common foundations and for their usefulness. The Old Testament text convinces us of the ability of old cultures to hold together not only reason, emotion and will (hopelessly divided after Kant's philosophical initiative and, even more, after the coming of industrialism and modern emancipation projects), but also the human person, other living creatures and the Earth (hopelessly divided by modern science and by rationality and emotivity ruled by this type of science). This is what we are missing - a concept of civilization as the unity of men and women, living creatures, and mother Earth, where the human person again is understood as the unity of reason, emotion and will.

It may be clear that this concept leans on the basis of cultural anthropology (relativism) on the one hand, and on Leopold's definition of 'civilization' as community on the other. According to Leopold, civilization is the condition of mutual and mutually dependent cooperation among people and other animals, vegetation and soil, a condition which may be disrupted or upset by the failure of any of these elements.[4] Another concept may lean on Heidegger's view of the problem, which is (as far as the result is concerned) very similar. In connection with Heidegger's speculation over a Heraclitean fragment on speech, Heidegger comments that it is the language which gathers beings "according to community",[5] for it is the language which speaks,[6] not the human being. The language speaks in accordance with the community. There is no actual inclusion of the creatures within the community, as found in Leopold. However, this is not significant - it is the phrase "according to community" which is important. Heidegger's post-theological thinking would probably not object to the explanation accompanying Leopold's vision of the Old Testament verses about the 'citizens' of the natural world, as shown by Hosea 4,1-3:

There is no faithfulness or loyalty,
no knowledge of God in the land.
Swearing, lying, and murder,
and stealing and adultery break out;
bloodshed follows bloodshed.
Therefore the land mourns,
and all who live in it languish;
together with the wild animals
and the birds of the air,
even the fish of the sea are perishing.

In the verses of the Old Testament, it is not only people who are the true citizens of our world, but also other living creatures. Even the land mourns. Certainly, the human person does have a special role, namely that of a protector. However, from the creation account the idea of unity is quite evident.

Not only does the human person mourn, but the whole world mourns, for what seems to be purely human concerns all those who are mutually related by virtue of their communion. The world, the community, the Leopoldean civilization include all elements related by their meaning. There is the beginning of the unproblematical way to expanding the moral to the non-human. What is being discovered today as post-modern and new (for example civilization in the understanding of Aldo Leopold and in the concepts of deep ecology) is one of the essential values shared by all the old Mediterranean cultures.

Moreover, the Heideggerian perspective of the communicative (he says speech/language) basis of the being of all creatures is not at variance with the Old Testament view. In other words, the *sub specie communicationis* approach is in compliance with the ideas of Heidegger, those of late Wittgenstein, Bakhtin, Derrida etc. It shows a certain solution to the modern systematic thinking; the solution being a realistic objective structure of meaning, resulting from communion of a particular community. As shown by the knowledge of many disciplines, many communities produce such a vision of the world where nature and environment, etc., are parts of the community.

This is another approach to the paradigm of communication. In summary, the first approach is a mere acceptance of the paradigmatic shift in modern social and humanistic thinking; the second is accepting the pre-modern concept of community. As indicated in the above discussion, referring to the Old Testament, it is clear what prompts the allegation about the heuristic (and first of all practical) effectiveness and methodological advantageousness of the *sub specie communicationis* in the discussions about religion and the future. This approach gets over (does not change) the insufficiency and the one-sidedness of the objective reflection; it respects the results of activities, or actual communion in a particular community, as significant; and it extends (or returns where it had originally been - at least in the Judeo-Christian tradition) the idea of community in the desirable intentions of "tenable future". Moreover, it is an adequate expression of the cultural logic of the communions in the modern world and provides considerable opportunities for an effective breakthrough in theoretical thinking, and into conservative structures of Euro-American modern intellectual work.

However, there is one more issue to be mentioned in connection with the communicative reversal/upheaval in philosophy. After Lyotard had explained everything, it should be obvious that the world comprises a differentiated field of language games, where no other universal game or meta-narration can be added.[7] This is the world of natural communicative differentiation, for it is the world of cultural differentiation. And vice versa, for communication is as much a cultural creation as culture is a communicative creation. The way ahead to the future must have respect for this fact, and the Euro-American works of philosophy in this field shall most probably change into a world discourse, exceeding greatly the borders of philosophical speculations. However, this would bring a shift towards acknowledgement of pragmatism of various communities and probably also the abandonment of the classical paradigm of truth and untruth in favour of a morally oriented paradigm of truth and understanding.

The principle of communicative differentiation and cultural diversity only stresses the aporetic nature of the work done in mainstream modern discussions about the future (of course there are different approaches originating from it, but merely originating from it). This mainstream is, despite all effort, controlled by the paradigm of objective reflection, which explains why environmental discourse, produced by the mainstream, is predominantly a mere variant type of the "ethnocentric metaphysics of the West", as discussed by Derrida.[8]

In principle, the thinking remains unchanged, and it produces what is culturally and metaphysically programmed namely, a reality broken by the logo-centrism of experts, and an arrogant humanity. It may be true that the globally oriented philosophy and ethics seem to seek a common language for the instrumental pragmatism of the techno-science with greater difficulties. But such an attempt still lacks listening to the real pragmatism of communities. The reflection remains a mere reflection, as spoken about by Kierkegaard. "Reflection is not the evil, but persistence on and fossilization in the reflection are ambiguity and depravity, which initiate a reverse movement by changing these pre-conditions into evasive sophistry."[9] Kierkegaard writes on this subject as if he was reading modern texts: "Everybody knows a lot, and we all know which way to take, and we know many ways which could be taken, but nobody wants to go. If somebody got over the reflection in them, and grew up to a deed, in no time thousands of reflections from outside would stand to resist against them; for today only a suggestion of detailed consideration is eagerly welcomed; the deed, however, is accepted indifferently."[10] There remains nothing but to discuss the future better.

The Environmental Community

Time stands against such a way of thinking. The realization of every time horizon of the modern world's crises resists every paradigmatic objective reflection and initiates a paradigmatic shift. In this respect, the status of a 'citizen' of an environmental community seems to be the vital problem. Modern thinking views this problem through human self-determination, which is the view of interpreting various types of humanism. The *sub specie communicationis* offers even here a different solution: it has already been suggested in the formulation of "the realistic structure of meaning". This formulation states that in the community called "our world", the status of a creature originates neither in self-determination nor in determination, but it originates from meaningful correlation of the creatures in the community. Not from the correlation of the creatures, but from the correlation of the meaning of the creatures. The word 'meaning' can be substituted here by the word 'value'.

It is evident that the communicative approach proposes a sophisticated matrix of relations given by the introduction of the thesis of communicative differentiation, the thesis of cultural diversity, and the thesis of correlation. A range of problems different from the problems found within the paradigm of objective reflection originates in this matrix. The status of these problems is similar to the non-modern and pre-modern views of the world and the place of the human person in it. With the approach founded on communicative differentiation, western philosophy has reached a point from which it looks beyond the borders of modern rationality and also beyond the borders of philosophy itself. The pressure of reality forces philosophy to take into consideration the elements of cultural anthropology, above all the thesis on cultural relativism (its current philosophical opposite is the thesis of communicative differentiation).

Communicative Correlation

The thesis on correlation (or better on total mutual correlation) is included both in Leopold's concept of civilization and in Derrida's concept of difference. Moreover, it is even included in the texts of the Old Testament. Leopold expresses the same view in the language of an environmentalist, whilst Derrida expresses himself in the language of a heretic semiotist: communicative space and communicative event have no centre. Communion in a community lacks 'the beginning', and he who is looking for the beginning will always find an 'amendment'.[11] Leopold talks about a fall of civilization caused by a collapse of one of the participants of civilization, namely community. Such a collapse may occur, to put it positively, after the collapse of one part (for example the human element) of a correlated universe, caused by hypertrophy of 'interests' and 'activities' after one part is proclaimed 'the principle'. Then the question arises: Who or what has the authority to cover disorders in the correlated communication of a community? The first and the correct answer is: the human person as the consciousness and self-confidence of that community.

However, Leopold immediately asks: Which human person? Turning to Derrida, we find out that in his concept of communication there are no privileged places; nor are there in late Wittgenstein (where each language game is simply played, is a proto-phenomenon) or in Heidegger (where language speaks according to *polis*). This means that the first precondition of the restoration is the resignation from a privileged place within the communicative space of the human world. Today, the privileged place is the specific communication of the Euro-American world, based on a particular type of rationality (objective reflection) which deprives other types of communication of meaning and space; for example, those which are regarded as unreasonable and unscientific. The first precondition of the restoration is the denial of the privilege of this particular type of communication on behalf of communicative differentiation and cultural diversity. Here appears the great importance of deconstructive 'reading' of the present attempts of philosophy and ethics: these attempts do not enable resignation from the privileged position of logo-centric thinking and institutionalized events, provided that this is their source, their basis and their frame. For the time being, they are relevant.

It is evident that this discussion imitates the discussions of representative communicative (semiotic) theories. Particularly, the Derrida-Heideggerian concept of 'trace' in language and in 'communication'[12] introduces great opportunities of desirable revision of the problem of determination/self-determination (thus, freedom) not because of reason, but out of a sense of community. This is the question of the day, not because of the recent reasoning, the attribute of which is non-fathoming, but rather because of a time-honoured communion which has been the definite source. Thus, one can assume the *sub specie communication* argumentation as legitimate.

This argumentation evokes a desirable need for the restoration of the psychological feeling of communicative symmetry in the community called 'the world'. This very need for the restoration of the communicative symmetry is closely connected with the thesis on mutual communicative correlation and with the concept of 'trace' founding the meaning/value of a being.

Modern rational thinking produces the asymmetric and communicative approach to the world as dominant. However, there is no other choice on the axis of objective reflection. The asymmetry is not the expression of reciprocal, mutually dialogical or participatory communion. In particular, natural science and emancipation projects of the humanities declared natural creatures unequal within the communication space, where the human person communicates. The logo-centric consequence of this process is well known. It is the exhaustion of nature from quality (Husserl), of meaning other than that of utilitarianism. Nevertheless, there are cultures the thinking and mentality of which have not denied the possibility of symmetric communication in the community of environment. In our culture, this phenomenon has survived on the margins of society and amongst children. The communicative asymmetry was declared the norm, and the idea of symmetric communication was displaced beyond the borders of normal rationality. This perspective is quite close to Foucault's concepts of rationality, internalization and ex-communication.

The viewpoint *sub specie communicationis*, as discussed above, suggests the way forward towards the reconstruction of the communicative symmetry with other creatures of the world and towards the re-union of reason, emotion and will. The logo-centric schizophrenia of reason and emotion is *a sui generis* the disaster of our age.

Communicative Symmetry

Seeking better approaches to tackle the future is necessarily connected to the need for reconstruction of communicative symmetry with 'the whole world'. However, the communicative symmetry must be based on cultural differentiation.

It is not difficult to prove that this communicative symmetry did belong to the old religious foundations of our cultures. Due to our wickedness, "the land mourns, and all who live in it languish; together with the wild animals and the birds of the air, even the fish of the sea are perishing" (Hosea 4,3).

The communicative symmetry, conceding meaning to all beings of infinite 'intertextual' events, is an essential dimension of other religions and cultures (Indian, Chinese, nature cults, etc.). A. Toynbee called this (quite wrongly, though) 'pantheism'. It can be argued, however, that he was interested in this particular aspect of communicative equality of various creatures in the community called the world.

The dialogue among the religions of the Mediterranean - Judaism, Christianity and Islam - can, on a common basis of communicative symmetry pronounced in the Old Testament and the Qur'an, gradually reconstruct the general ethical dimension of human actions with a focus on the future, and the deconstruction of the monologue of modern communication. The monologue of modern communication prefers the logic of one type of rationality and the communication of one cultural type to the possibility of 'irrationality', different types of rationality, and to communication among various cultures. And this is the reason why today we cannot hear that "the land mourns and everything that dwells in it languishes", even though this is the code preserved in the most ancient foundations of our cultures and religions.

Thus, it is appropriate to go back to the origins and reconstruct symmetrical communication as a way forward towards the future.

Notes

1. Apel, K. O. (1973). *Transformation der Philosophie*, Bd. I-II, Frankfurt, Suhrkamp; Böhler, D. (1985). *Rekonstruktive Pragmatik. Von der Bewusstseinsphilosophie zur Kommunikastionsreflexion*, Frankfurt, Suhrkamp; Habermas, J. (1982). *Theorie des Kommunikativen Handelns*, Bd. II, Frankfurt, Suhrkamp: ch. 5; Küng, H. (1990). *Projekt Weltethos*, Munich, R. Piper.

2. I do not deny that the main source of the following notes are the theories connected with the authors stated in note 1 above and also theories of the post-structuralists and post-modernists philosophers.

3. Apel, K. O. (1973). *Transformation der Philosophie.* Bd. I-II, Frankfurt, Suhrkamp; Habermas, J. (1981), *Theorie des Kommunikativen Handelns,* Bd. I/II, Frankfurt, Suhrkamp.

4. Leopold, A. (1933). 'The Conservation Ethic', *Journal of Forestry*: p. 635.

5. Heidegger, M. (1979). 'Heraklit', p. 370 in *Gesamtausgabe* 55, Frankfurt, Klostermann.

6. Heidegger, M. (1985). 'Unterwegs zur Sprache-Die Sprache', pp. 10-11 in *Gesamtausgabe* 12, Frankfurt, Klostermann.

7. Lyotard, J. F. (1987). *The Postmodern Condition: A Report on Knowledge,* Minneapolis, University of Minneapolis Press: chap. 13, 14.

8. Derrida, J. (1976). *Of Grammatology*, Baltimore, John Hopkins University Press: p. 79.

9. Kierkegaard, S. (1969). *Soucasnost,* Prague, Mlada fronta: p. 50.

10. *Ibid.*: pp. 60-61.

11. Derrida, J. (1976). *Of Grammatology,* see note 8 above: p. 304.

12. To the problem of mutual 'tracing' of signs in time and in the present see Heidegger, M. (1977), 'Holzwege-Der Spruch der Anaximander', p. 369 in *Gesamtausgabe* 5, Frankfurt, Klostermann; Derrida, J. (1976), *Of Grammatology*, see note 8 above: pp. 62-65.

15

Listening to the Future

JOSEPH FARRUGIA

Being linguistic animals we human beings turn the sounds of life around us and within us into language and seek the meaning that they may have for us by integrating them with our overall understanding of the world and history.

It is in the nature of the human being not merely to hear but also to listen. Indeed we react to the echoes of the world around us as no other living creature does. The human mind takes us beyond the immediate message which the given sound - or its absence - may hold for our ears or our heart, so that we may perceive its deeper and wider significance. That means that it is not only animal instinct which operates in the human assessment of sound or silence, but also reason and deliberation. Thus the human being may be described as that being endowed with the power to raise any sound, even the most inaudible and the most inarticulate, echoing within our spirit or coming from outside, to the dignity of 'word'.

What is the 'word'? Which is its peculiar dignity? The examination of the issues which these questions raise constitutes the object of reflection of some of the most renowned thinkers of the last two centuries. I will just confine myself to saying that the human word is a deliberate, articulate and comprehensible manifestation and communication of human knowledge, human will and human sentiment. Of course, it is bounded by its inherent limits. Human knowledge, will and sentiment have other means of expression and communication. Nevertheless, within its limits the human word carries out its function fully and indispensably. The human being is essentially qualified by the power of word and language, and begs description not only as the being who listens to the word but, indeed, as the being who pronounces the word, creates it, modifies it, endows it with meaning, communicates it, suppresses it or rejects it.

The sounds of life echoing within us or around us are indeed multiform and multitudinous. Some of them reach us endowed with immediately accessible meaning, that is, as 'words'. Others do not. These, though, we cannot help transforming into 'words' containing and communicating to us messages of life or death, joy or pain, peace or fear. The sounds I am referring to may be inarticulate to the cultured mind or inaudible to the ear but their messages are nevertheless unmistakable to the human soul and heart: messages of suffering, hostility, violence, war, plague, hunger, sickness, misery, confusion, as indeed of joy, serenity, health, fullness, kindness, unity, love and forgiveness. They are sounds, or words, which speak to us of the present, but they also speak of the past and evoke the future.

Now, here is another feature which qualifies the human being. It is preoccupation with the future. We, human beings, are distinct from other living creatures in that we discover ourselves to be occupied not only with the present but also with the future. What remains of the past is really contained in the present. But the present has no hold on the future. The present only constitutes our platform into the future.

But what kind of 'future' am I referring to? To borrow from one of Jurgen Moltmann's Gifford Lectures (p.133), "Like history, the future is equivocal. Most European languages have two possible ways of talking about the future. *Futurum*, or its equivalent, is used for what *will be*; *adventus*, or its cognates, for that which *is coming*." Moltmann goes on to say that "if future is understood in the sense of *futurum*, it means what will be out of past and present." It is that era of history which is yet to be and will eventually no longer be, it is "what will eventually become past". If, on the other hand, we understand future as *adventus*, we refer to "what is coming - what is on the way towards the present", "a 'coming' event" which will make of the *futurum* something more than a mere prolongation and intensification of the present. If we take the future as *adventus* we will be referring to what will confront the present "as something new". While future as *futurum* means the mere extension or prolongation of the present, future as *adventus* involves its transformation which, obviously, cannot take place without the intervention of something or, indeed, someone who is not essentially part of the present and transcends it. It supposes a new creative presence in the world or the renewal of this presence.

Both 'futures' summon the human being's attention. Both 'futures' emit their peculiar signals to communicate to us their respective messages, recommendations and imperatives. Both 'futures' weigh us with the responsibility to live our present in openness not only to our own generation but also to the as yet unborn generations of tomorrow. Both 'futures', thereby, bring us face to face with the ground of our existence and its ultimate fulfilment: God. One has to be a believer in order to say this, a believer in God - a practising Jew, a true Muslim or an authentic Christian.

The fact is that our age differs from that of the past. In our "Western" past, everybody tended to accept *a priori* the existence and meaningfulness of God. The rise of humanism, rationalism and secularism, with the consequent cultural pluralism which emerged in hitherto 'Christian' Europe, has made contemporary faith in God (I prefer it to "theism") that much more ambiguous, insecure and vulnerable.

The consequence of it all is that God has generally diminished as an essential factor in contemporary humanity's estimation of itself. Indeed, speaking of God today has become like speaking of a foreign body, if not indeed an intrusive agent. But with the recession of God, mankind has forfeited what we, who believe in God, perceive as the key to the riddle of our existence, the surest ground of our happiness, the most qualified guardian of our human rights, the root of our special dignity amongst other created beings, the surest prop which sustains us in our kindred weaknesses, and the ultimate realization of our mysterious destiny. Contemporary cultures and pseudo-cultures are submerging the God of Abraham as mediated to Israel by Moses and the prophets, as mediated to the tribes of Arabia by Muhammad's recitation of the Qur'an and as mediated to the Church by Jesus Christ, and with God they are submerging much that pertains to our identity as 'image of God', to the mandate which God entrusted us with in creation and to the divine project that God designed for us in this world and beyond it, in this age and in the future. Nevertheless in a surprising turn of events, it seems that God - to borrow Heinrich Ott's expression - is again becoming *fragwürdig*, questionable or, to be more precise, worth asking about.

Couldn't it be that some people are discovering that without God we have become the poorer: in our identity, in the security of our rights as human beings, in our search for happiness and in the hope of achieving it? What militates against this re-awakening to God's presence is mostly the negative image which those who profess belief in God give of God through their insufficient or contradictory witness. Worse still happens when we attribute to him or associate with Him certain historical, social and interracial evils the sole responsibility for which lies with us, evils like the horrors being perpetrated in the Balkans, the suffering from hunger and illness of the peoples of Western Africa, the bloody conflicts of Northern Ireland and the Middle East, the social injustices of the Americas and so forth.

Future as *Futurum* and *Adventus*

Earlier on, I referred to the two kinds of 'futures' which beckon us. One of them is that future which is the mere prolongation of the present, which pertains to its temporality and vulnerability, which will come about and then will no longer be - merely a next stage in the history of humankind, a stage which will be occupied by generations excluding our own.

One may simply opt to ignore this stage and reject any responsibility for it. I believe that it is not in the nature of a human being to do this, it is not within his choice to do it, and doing it would constitute the shedding of an inherent responsibility. I believe that such is the statement which lies at the origin of our discussion here about caring for future generations. I believe that such also is the view of any true adherent to the Jewish, the Christian or the Islamic religion respectively. These three religions are concerned with the future (understood as *futurum*) and, indeed, interpret their presence in the world, and paticularly in the world of today, as a "prophetic" presence, addressing not only the present and its generation but also the future and its generations.

The three religions perceive humankind as an active agent, together with the Creator and in obedience to Him, in the continuation of the construction, maturation and perfection of creation. With God and subject to Him, they perceive mankind as engaged in the laboured realization of the divine plan for humanity and as a co-author with God of human history. They perceive, moreover, that we, as human beings, are originally and essentially constituted as attentive listeners and accountable servants of the Word of God, which reaches us through his prophets - as a Christian, I will also say, through His only Begotten Son made Man - and echoes in our hearts.

Far from absolving us from responsibility towards future generations, all of this confirms us as bearers of another and weightier responsibility: our responsibility before God, who, as a result, will hold us accountable not only for the manner in which we are behaving *vis-à-vis* the present generations but also for what we are doing or not doing for the benefit or to the damage of the generations which will follow our own.

This means that our present does not only beckon the future as *futurum*, but also as *adventus*, that is as "the coming of something new". Future as *adventus* means future understood as an event, an event which will transform the future understood as *futurum*, which will therefore not be a *futurum* entirely similar to the present but a *futurum* which is holier than the present, that is, happier, kinder, fairer and, in general, nearer to God's original project for humanity.

New Images from the Future

If we were to listen to 'the future' we would hear two kinds of voices. Paradoxically the voices more immediately audible would be the vaguer ones, those of the future as *futurum*. If you try hard enough you would hear them surely.

- You would hear together with me, echoing within us, the vigorous cries of countless new-born babies giving the first evidence of their God-given right to life, irrespective of the circumstances of their conception or fetal health, as against the insecurity in which today they are conceived and born.
- You would discern together with me the serene countenance of numerous people, scared and weakened by physical and other pain but sustained by the kindness of the people near them, as against the emargination to which today many are subjected by indifferent and unmerciful hearts.
- You would visualize together with me the peaceful exchanges among people belonging to differing races, nationalities, religions and cultures, secure in their mutual respect and solidarity, as against the hostility and injustice being meted out today by people who would presume to be higher on some scale than their neighbours.

As you see, it is not only voices which our *futurum* evokes, but also images - images which would substitute those of today, those of the starving peoples of West Africa, the war-scarred races of the countries of ex-Yugoslavia, the abused children of Brazil, the mistreated immigrants of Europe, the forgotten refugees fleeing from cruel regimes, the innocent victims of crime, the millions who have succumbed to the maladies of contemporary societies, the desolation brought about by natural disasters, desertification and environmental degradation. "No more such images of pain, injustice and desolation!" is the call of the future understood as *futurum*, addressed to all, but especially to us who profess to be mindful of God and of his creation.

It is a call which discloses itself as being the resonance of another voice that reaches us from another future, 'the future' understood as *adventus*. This 'other' voice, which actually precedes those sent out by the *futurum*, is less immediately audible to humankind; but, when made accessible, as it has been by God through his chosen messengers, it is the clearer voice and the surer one.

- The Jews heard this voice through the mediation of Abraham and the other patriarchs, the judges, the kings and the prophets; the words this voice pronounced are now recorded in Holy Scripture.

- The Muslims testify to hearing this voice through the angel Gabriel's recitation of God's decrees to Muhammad, God's definitive messenger to humankind; his words are recorded in the Holy Qur'an.
- The Christians profess to this voice of God reaching us, with the most unexpected and extraordinary immediacy, through the very presence of God amongst us in the person of His Son made man: the Word of God Incarnate who revealed to us not merely the salvific decrees of God but His very countenance and image.

The peculiar proclamation of the Christians is that God the Father has humbled himself in His Incarnate Son and in the emission of His Holy Spirit in order to make of our created nature an expression of His love for us, to make of all human generations His 'wider' family, and to make of our world His abode. I wonder if there may be other or greater motivations to convince ourselves - of course I am referring to those of us who are Christians - of our responsibilities before God towards the continued and proper estimation of humanity, the continued and proper care for the lot of all present and still to be born generations, for the continued and proper upkeep of our world as the friendly habitat of all human beings.

16

The Principle of Impartiality

SALVATORE PRIVITERA

This chapter outlines some methodological considerations for a historical and geographical actualisation of the hermeneutic circle emerging from the principle of impartiality according to biblical sources and Christian theology.

The Mystery of Creation

The moral perspective emerging from biblical sources and from theological reflection concerning the history of creation would be more comprehensible if it were conceptualised as the incarnation of eternity or the re-shaping of timeless and spaceless transcendency within human history. From the biblical point of view (given in the prologue of the gospel of St. John, the first chapter of the letter to the Ephesians and from the letter to the Colossians) the mystery of creation presents itself as a preparation, anticipation and pre-figuration of the mystery of the Incarnation: Christ, the Word which was in the beginning and through which the project of creation takes place, is also He who recapitulates in Himself everything; the omega point towards which "all things in heaven and earth" are constantly drawn.

The Dimension of Time

Time is the embryo of eternity. As a fragment of eternity, time could be seen as something coming out of its own cocoon; it is not simply a series of flashes that soon fade away. There is in time something that is not identical with time itself, yet this something may perhaps need to expand over time if it is to reveal itself. What we are considering here is the paradox of time itself, which lives in secret from an eternity.

Through the ages the signs of its atemporal origin always remain visible:

- the past can never be fully grasped since it is not and it has never been in the hands of whoever observes it inorder to interpret it;
- the present ceases to be the present as soon as one takes hold of it in order to interpret it;
- the future is never completely predictable and programmable by whoever tries to foresee and predict what will happen.

This fragmented approach to understanding time within its own horizons takes on a more comprehensive and meaningful dimension when one addresses the question from an atemporal perspective, namely that of transcendental eternity. Although time might appear to us in the first place as a chain of individual occurrences stretching forward and backward into infinity, we are sure that these changing phenomena replacing one another are nevertheless manifestations of something permanent which sustains the changing appearances, bringing them together into a totality, a structured history, that cannot disintegrate into pure individual moments. Something of this can be seen in a growing flower, passing through varying stages from the seed until it finally withers. As such, there is no past, present and future but rather the contingency of a reality that tends to immerse and dissolve itself in the infinity of a boundless ocean which escapes any restrictions that could ever be imposed by time.

The Dimension of Space

Even space, circumscribed and defined by its own boundaries, can never be fully comprehended by the human mind. However it offers an expressive vehicle through which infinite reality manifests itself and acquires historical dimensions. Space provides that medium through which transcendental reality can partially mould itself to become tangible to human experience.

Inspite of its temporal limitations and its apparent disintegration when compared to infinity, space fills the human being with awe and wonder when viewed as the ongoing articulation in human history of an inexhaustible reality that transcends any boundaries.

The paradox that gives new meaning to both time and space is that while both tend to become insignificant when viewed from a transcendental point of view, they are both needed to incarnate eternity in the ever receding horizon of human history. Space and time allow the human person to zoom in on eternity and take a glimpse, here and now, at eternal reality that otherwise remains completely incomprehensible to humankind.

Ethical Consequences

The above articulation hints at the importance of the historical and geographical dimensions in our attempt to understand transcendental infinity through the mutual interaction of the philosophical categories of space and time. The here and now, or temporal location, is an indispensable medium for the eternal to communicate itself from generations to generations.

When personal relationships and human life on earth are contextualised within this perspective, one understands better the need to pay due attention to the historical and geographical reference of our existence. Past, present and future generations acquire equal significance from an eternal point of view, even if they exist at different moments and in different parts of the earth. In other words, generations yet to come have a viable moral standing which present generations must respect and take into consideration in all their actions and decisions. To disregard future generations and simply focus on what influences present generations is an irresponsible way of behaving. As long as humanity longs for the eternal, the future of humankind can never be detached from the present moment. Humankind hopes to survive precisely because of future generations.

The perspective of time and space which emerges from the faith in the mystery of creation inevitably implies the attribution of every fragment of time and space to God's creative will itself. Likewise, the principle of impartiality is grounded in the fact that God continually manifests Himself in human history, and is all the time at work to bring humankind to its fullness, whether past, present or future generations.

The Mystery of Redemption

The mystery of creation is completed and renewed through the mystery of redemption. The prayer included in the eucharistic celebration for the third Christmas Day clearly shows how God has recreated everything through the passion, death and resurrection of Jesus Christ. Through redemption God reorients creation to his original plan: the saving effect constitutes the surpassing and, at the same time, the renewal and completion of the original project of creation.

If the event of creation were to be attributed to the divine wish to incarnate eternity and infinity in human history through the horizons of space and time, the event of redemption would then present itself as the mystery of God's attempt (God, to whom nothing is impossible - Gen 18,14; Jer 32,27; Lc 1,37) to bring back space and time - past, present and future - within the eternal life of His own divine reality. Within this perspective, St. Paul's message in his letter to the Romans (8,19-23) becomes more powerful and meaningful:

Creation itself awaits with eager longing for the revealing of the children of God; for the creation was subjected to futility not of its own will but by the will of the one who subjected it, in hope that the creation itself will be set free from its bondage to decay and will obtain the freedom of the glory of the children of God. We know that the whole creation has been groaning in labour pains until now; and not only the creation, but we ourselves, who have the first fruits of the Spirit, groan inwardly while we wait for adoption, the redemption of our bodies.

The Eschatological Dimension

This 'boundless' perspective so to say, opened up by the mystery of redemption, reaches out to an infinite future full of hope; not so much a future programmed by present generations as a future that gradually takes shape through God's unconditional love and kindness. The future gives time and space for God to renew and recreate the whole of creation and allows humanity to slowly give shape to those desires that bring us closer to God's image and likeness. Within this perspective humankind and all of creation find themselves projected beyond time and space into the boundless reality of God Himself. History is thus transformed into that ever evolving segment of eternity.

Christ's redemptive event is one which has already been realised but at the same time awaits the end of time to redeem the whole of human history, including that which is yet to come. "For in Him all the fullness of God was pleased to dwell and through Him to reconcile to Himself all things whether on earth or in Heaven, making peace by the blood of His cross" (Col 1,19-20). Therefore, Christ's redemption is awaited in time as an eschatological event but at the same time orients the unfolding of human history towards the eternal truth which transcends the horizons of time and space. Within this perspective of the mystery of redemption, the present is always fleeing towards the future and subsists only in relation to the transcendental horizon of time and eternity.

This means that, within the perspective of the mystery of redemption, time can be compared to a river which only exists for its dispersion into the vastness of an eternal ocean within which its historical identity disappears. But in disappearing, the same historical identity will find the most significant fulfilment of its existence.

Ethical Consequences

Obviously, within a similar conceptual horizon there is no distinction whatsoever between who already existed and who still does not exist. Human beings are not taken into consideration with reference to their historical existentiality. Nonetheless, they are singularly taken into consideration for what each one of them is worth in the eyes of God.

Human beings were all chosen "before the foundation of the world, to be holy and blameless before Him" (Ef 1,4) and every single generation is the privileged beneficiary of the promises made by God to Abraham, Isaac and Jacob. If all generations are blessed "in Christ with every spiritual blessing in the heavenly places" (Ef 1,3) by God the Father of our Lord Jesus Christ, why shouldn't present generations show care and responsibility towards posterity? The eschatological dimension allows no room for discrimination that could arise from the fact that future generations do not yet exist, for although ethical responsibilities are historically articulated and implemented, they always remain eschatologically oriented.

The Mystery of God's Holiness

The problem of our moral responsibilities towards future generations will have to be addressed in the light of the extract from the Gospel of St. Matthew (5,43-45) where Christ invites everybody to overcome the Old Testament law of retribution which was based on the principle of partiality, and adopt instead the principle of God's impartiality.

You have heard that it was said, ' You shall love your neighbour and hate your enemy'. But I say to you, love your enemies and pray for those who persecute you, so that you may be children of your Father in heaven; for He makes His sun rise on the evil and on the good, and sends rain on the righteous and unrighteous.

It is interesting to note here that Christ presents the law of love towards the neighbour both as a way of overcoming the prejudiced perspective of the law of retribution and also as an imitation of the love of God the Father. God's love reaches out to everyone without distinction, irrespective of whether they belong to a particular nation or another; whether they exist here and now, or will exist in the future somewhere else. In other words, to take up the principle of impartiality as the basic principle of one's moral life means living with an attitude of benevolence towards all others, placing oneself outside the horizons of time and space, while doing whatever possible for others through love. So, even future generations deserve to be considered as beneficiaries of our love and benevolence.

Anthropological and Theological Reflections

Impartiality as a principle rooted in God's unconditional love is of great relevance to the question of our responsibilities towards future generations.

We should not be concerned only with immediate consequences or benefits, but our reflections and decisions should be framed within an intergenerational context where our love and care is extended to all generations. In this way the principle of impartiality could be seen as consituting an ongoing incarnation of God's holiness in time and space.

God's holiness does not only present itself as a transcendental and absolute example but is also offered as a gift to humanity. And it is this gift of holiness that fills us with courage and hope to strive for a better future, in spite of our imperfections. Ultimately, there is nothing wrong that cannot be corrected by what is right, and the awakening to the fact that human development is a maturation process open to mistakes and improvement sustains our fragile attempts in spite of our shortcomings.

Responsibility would also become vested with a deeper significance that goes beyond the mere legality of the term if we were to see our duties and care for others as a call to holiness and human perfection. All our engagements become a response to the gospel invitation to be perfect as our Father in heaven is perfect. God's holiness becomes a goal transcending time and space that keeps reminding all generations of our true human vocation: to love and care for everyone and the whole of creation. As such, ultimate responsible decisions, which involve human lives in their totality, are truly eternity coming to be in time.

If the event of creation demands that we live morally, the event of redemption makes it possible for us to live our moral responsibilities with hope and great courage. And when our moral responsibilities are lived in faith, hope and love, eternity truly occurs now.

Ethical Responsibility

As receivers of the mystery of creation, it is possible for us to participate in God's absolute perfection through our ethical commitment, which although historically implemented and geographically located, is rooted in eternity. Precisely, God's boundless love and eternal presence are the possibility conditions without which our ethical responsibilities and moral commitments have no solid foundation. God's abundant mercy trickles down from generation to generation; it has no historical or spatial limits. Eschatologically speaking, future generations have already been redeemed through Christ's passion, death and resurrection. This eternal viewpoint grounds our care for future generations in the fact that they are part and parcel of that unity which we call humankind.

The moral duty, therefore, to reflect on the consequences which our interventions and activities could have on future generations and their environment is derived not so much from the appeal which posterity makes to present generations but rather from the moral responsibilities, rooted in the principle of impartiality, which the human beings of today (like those of yesterday and tomorrow) always have towards other human beings. *Tamquam homines non tamquam homini* (Aulio Gellio, *Noctes Atticae*, IX,2). To adopt this eschatological point of view means assuming:

- the mystery of creation as the initial event of the historical and geographical development within which each individual human person and all generations are inserted with equal rights and equal dignity;
- the mystery of redemption as an event which enables human beings of all times, without any distinction whatsoever, to participate in God's own life;
- the principle of impartiality as a basic criterion for establishing a just and responsible relationship with others, and as a fundamental principle which guides every ethical and normative reflection towards the imitation of God's absolute impartiality.

From what has been said above, we can locate our responsibility towards future generations within the following perspective:

- from the point of view of eternity, the past, present and future dimensions of time become a continuum within the diachronic projection of human history; stated otherwise, faced by the responsibility of the *nunc,* past, present and future end up substituting each other in a dialogical reciprocity without any dialectics;
- from the point of view of infinity, the diaspora of generations throughout time does not impinge upon the concept of moral responsibility. There is a transcendental overarching dimension that establishes links between the *nunc*, "what already was" and the "not as yet" of the *hic*; thus giving an eternal foundation to moral responsibilities.
- from the point of view of future generations, the vindication of their rights occurs in a manner which is analogous to the way in which we claim ours with respect to past generations.

The eternal viewpoint of God's holiness and boundless love revealed to us through the Bible and theological reflection unites all people of all generations into one big family that has no spatial or temporal limits. Past, present and future generations become that moving image over time and space that incarnates the eternal. If time is the embryo of eternity, and space the womb of the infinite, together all generations constitute an eternal fellowship among human beings who have been redeemed through the cross and resurrection of Jesus.

17

A Christian Perspective on the North-South Debate

PETER CROSSMAN

I should like to approach the subject of our responsibilities towards future generations from the perspective with which I am most familiar in the course of my activities with the European Ecumenical Organisation for Development, namely the field of North-South relations and development policies. The primary question that immediately comes to my mind is: Why discuss this issue when it is scandalously obvious that we have not even met our responsibilities with regard to present generations?

In choosing the North-South, or "development", perspective focusing on responsibilities to present generations, I intend to look at what lessons we can learn for the future from past and present attempts to achieve justice among contemporary peoples, the "intragenerational" question. In any case I do not so much presume to be able to speak on the problem of the hermeneutics of dialogue or contribute to the debate on ecumenism as assume the ability of people of different faiths to cooperate on an ethical basis.

I should like to begin with a somewhat truncated philosophical or ethical reflection on time and responsibility before looking at some of the major symptoms of our unsustainable world and roughly sketching some elements of analysis and response from Christian perspectives. These reflections will remain insufficient until each of our traditions and communities has carried out a practical assessment of those tasks which, as our Jewish friends have said, although perhaps not completed in our lifetime, are not to be ignored.

Reflections on Time and Responsibility

Although a somewhat speculative exercise, it may be helpful to consider for a moment certain concepts of time which have actually conditioned our perspectives on responsibility and history, thus our view of the future of humanity and the planet.

Time as Extension or 'Mythical Space'

Augustine asked in his Confessions, "What is time?" Like many after him, he noted that as soon as we have observed something or spoken about it, the moment itself to which we refer is already past. Although Augustine was aware that time was qualitatively different from space he concluded that the present was somehow more real than either the future or the past. This viewpoint later coalesced into a very subjective approach to time, measured in terms of one's own experience.

Throughout Western thought, there has been a tendency to compare and therefore confuse time with the spatial dimension, making time another, fourth, category. Time is thus seen as flow, or extension of a spatial value. The observation that all four dimensions must somehow be present in order to measure anything at all in turn fed the Western propensity to objectify and measure time itself. It is no wonder that the mechanical clock became the symbol of enlightenment and a self-sustaining universe.

The result was a twofold distortion of the concept of time for Western culture. First, the present is given an objective, empirical reality at the expense of either past or future. Secondly, time is made to be primarily a subjective phenomenon, to be observed and experienced by the individual at the expense of social history and destiny.

Similar reflections, with less decisive results I feel, could be directed to the differences between linear and cyclical time and their consequences for society and ethics. Having dabbled in the study of "traditional" religions, I would have liked to say that for many their outlook on life is oriented to the past and tradition, since they are determined by the ancestor cult. One realises, however, that the ancestor cult, to a large degree, is a function of lineage and posterity. We are reminded here of the now well-known phrase attributed to Chief Seattle "We do not so much inherit the earth from our ancestors as borrow it from our children."

Responsibility and Knowledge

Philosophers agree that it is difficult to reach the concept of responsibility without passing through the logic of rewards and punishment: one is held responsible for performing or abstaining from actions only where they are respectively prescribed and proscribed by a higher authority as good or evil. What is important here is that responsibility does not originate with the ordinance as such but with the system of foundational values and relations which give them meaning. This is a different question from that of how humankind comes to know the will of God, insofar as all religions of the world accept that the divine speaks in order that humankind hears, and it is evident that for the scriptures hearing means obeying. Therefore the necessity, in Christianity at least, of returning to the Scriptures and their interpretation provided by the Church over the ages to describe what responsibility and which responsibilities pertain to the believer, or better, to the community of the faithful.

We then arrive at a helpful principle of moral theology, developed by Louis Janssens. When deliberating the consequences of an action, that is, its future effects, no action is admissible whose possible evil secondary consequence is disproportionate to the good intended. This is a sufficiently demanding principle in itself, reminding me of Mahatma Gandhi's criterion for any deed at all: picture the face of the poorest person you know and ask if that act will be of any use to him or her. The question of knowledge is critical here, for to the extent that one is innocently unaware of secondary consequences the individual person cannot be held responsible.

However, in dealing with the question of knowledge or ignorance in relation to moral action we stumble on a mine of complications, at least insofar as individual and voluntary acts are concerned. In the post-modern age it is common for scholars to point to the blind spots of modern scientific theory: a prejudice for the material, a preference for the path of least resistance in scientific methods, and the stated, if unlikely, intention to abstract any moral or emotively driven behaviour. These are the factors leading to an unholy alliance of the blind yet totalitarian alliance of the sciences dominating social theory today: economics, sociology and politics. It is this alliance, argues B. Goudzwaard, that not only fails to generate a response to chronic poverty but in fact causes its deepening. Again, we shall see the significance of this observation in a moment.

Responsibility, Rights and Needs

In the context of our theme, reference to responsibility leads directly to a discussion on duties and rights. While each of these terms might receive extensive treatment in either a philosophical or a juridical perspective, I shall have to restrict myself to their significance for the "development" debate. Here one thinks immediately of the range of basic human needs which require fulfilment in order for the individual to become human and for society to become a community. We might use the triad "life, liberty and the pursuit of happiness", whose blatant individuality might somewhat be corrected by the variant "liberté, égalité, fraternité". But these refer only to the classic civil and political rights. The development debate has been forced to look further at both the areas of basic human needs and social and economic rights as well, for we now realise that the political systems based on civil liberties do not necessarily guarantee satisfaction of the other basic rights and needs.

In the development debate at least, a categorisation of needs on the whole supported by universal declarations of rights and the policies of some multilateral organisations is accepted:

- basic needs: primarily these are individual and physical but have profound psychological consequences;
- economic and social needs: these introduce the group or community dimension of human life;
- environmental needs: the conditions for human existence, dependent on planetary sustainability; this category is perhaps considered by some a faddish or artificial extension but it is no coincidence that they are raised at the same time as ethnic rights of a people to its survival and culture, for in both we finally have the racial dimension in mind.

Having come to this point, I wish to clarify the use of the term "sustainable development" in the international agenda, paralleling the remarks already made by Dr Emmanuel Agius. The trajectory of ecological awareness has reflected a perverse yet not unfruitful relation with that of international economic justice. Gut-level public awareness of the real and impending ecological catastrophe has actually clouded the European mind at least with such policies as "do something, just anything, to get those irresponsible Brazilians to stop cutting down those trees".

I cannot help but observe that it is perhaps of more than ironic significance that the multilateral agenda has recently tackled global problems in exactly the reverse order of the corresponding demands presented by developing countries. Fair employment issues, seething since colonial days or rather since the invention of the slave trade and endlessly debated under the concept of "an international division of labour", are only now being forced onto the Social Summit and post-GATT agenda by the competitive position of the NICs, or Asian tigers. Equitable trade issues only recently received an as yet far from adequate response from the industrialised countries which, under the

GATT negotiations concluded in 1993, agreed to cut export subsidies and submit the broader scope of their trade activities to a multilateral system. With the increasing awareness in the industrialised countries of deforestation, global warming and pollution of "international" air and water, Northern governments began to apply blatant pressure on developing states to "save the planet's lungs" and only at the 1992 Rio UNCED conference did the latter realise they had the industrialised countries in a bargaining position.

Ecological issues were "dragged out of the closet" in the early 1960s but did not get beyond the "eco-freak" crowds or anywhere near public debate until after the 1970 Stockholm conference leading to the Brundtland report: *Our Common Future*. This document offered perhaps the first definition of "sustainable development", meaning one which "meets the needs of the present without compromising the abilities of future generations to meet their own needs". This point was guided by the thought that economic growth had to be restricted within ecological limits. The Earth Summit held in Rio de Janeiro in 1992 maintained this definition and set out principles to define the rights of people to develop and their responsibilities to safeguard the common environment. It is perhaps only very recently that the variety of aspects or factors has been understood in public policy debate to be clearly interlinked and to involve the issue of justice, as illustrated in a recent UN report:

Sustainable human development addresses both intragenerational and intergenerational equity enabling all generations, present and future, to make the best use of their potential capabilities. But it is not indifferent to how present opportunities are actually distributed. It would be odd if we were deeply concerned for the well-being of future as of yet unborn generations while ignoring the plight of the poor today. Yet, in truth, neither objective gets the priority it deserves. A major restructuring of the world's income distribution, production and consumption patterns may therefore be a necessary precondition for any viable strategy for sustainable human development.

An acrid debate has arisen as to whether the state of the environment now entitles the global economy to go anywhere but backward. It has consequently broken down into an argument as to who will pay the price, that is, who will forgo any further aspirations to prosperity. The World Bank has been at pains to explain that the terms development and environmental preservation are a false dichotomy. The industrialised countries' claims that developing countries are now the major polluters and that economic progress based on environmentally harmless technology is now possible are both cold-blooded, in view of the increase of poverty, and fool-hardiness.

Meanwhile, guided by their awareness of increasing indebtedness and poverty in the poorest countries and a lack of democracy on both national and multilateral levels, as well as mounting concern about the scarcity and pollution of natural resources, the Churches were already in the 1970s arguing for alternative development models and respect for creation. The World Council of Churches, for example, established programmes such as Justice, Peace and Sustainable Society, the Commission on the Churches' Participation in Development, and, in the 1980s, an agenda including the Integrity of Creation. There soon arose among the Churches a fundamental debate on the limits to economic growth.

It should be noted, however, that with the rise of ecological consciousness, the Christian traditions, in particular, quickly came under fire for having adopted an entirely anthropocentric worldview. According to Lynn White's provocative thesis *The Religious Roots of Our Ecological Crisis* (1967), Christianity explicitly taught the subjugation of the natural order, justifying its despoliation by humankind, based on the now infamous Genesis passage (1,26-31) concluding the first creation narrative. Whether or not the Churches' growing sensitivity to ecological issues is in part a reaction to this criticism, other authors such as Martin Brinkman have shown that this attack is not wholly justified and that historians may just as well search for the rationalistic and materialistic roots of Western civilisation to find the grounds for modern society's abuse of the planet.

Our Common Present

Perhaps, one might still object that I focus on present forms of poverty. I hope to make it clear that the visible face of poverty today is only the tip of tomorrow's iceberg of "unsustainablility". The forms of oppression so evident across our world undermine and compromise the well-being, if not the very lives, of future generations. Furthermore, I will argue, our attempts to respond to poverty and injustice today will determine the ability itself of future generations to choose life, for themselves and the earth, over death. I shall present elements of an analysis of current oppression in a certain but not necessary order.

The Spiral of Poverty

It is perhaps not decisive enough to show the current imbalance of the distribution of economic resources: roughly 80% of the world's people must share only 20% of world income. Indeed, most economists do not accept this point, widely published by the United Nations, as a betrayal of an unsustainable system. The most forceful fact of our time is that, despite slight average economic growth across the world measured in conventional economic terms (GNP), poverty has become endemic in industrialised countries and is clearly on an upward trend in most developing countries. A. Durning has extensively documented what he calls the "downward spiral of poverty" in numerous Third World countries. To use the same sort of indicators, a pattern of increased GNP alongside higher unemployment is now the rule in industrial countries while the poorest Third World countries have seen a sharp average drop of 10% in per capita income over the last ten years: Mexico even registered a 50% drop! The main focus of his analyses is in fact the broad extent and increasingly high rate of environmental degradation occurring in a direct parallel with poverty trends.

Globalization of the Economy

Globalization is not only the catchword of Managing Directors of aggressive transnational corporations, it is deemed the justification and victory of the free market economy. I bring this element in here not only because it inversely (perversely) corresponds to the universality of rights, but primarily because it is the symptom, if not the instrument, of the pervasiveness of the dominant economic ideology.

There is a twist to this perversity linked to the reflection on time described earlier in this chapter. Globalization assumes that time is an extensible dimension. Through globalization, economic ideology pretends that prosperity is offered not only to present generations across the world but to all their progeny. Prosperity will assuredly beget prosperity, it argues, since all of the necessary elements of investment - capital, labour, technology, natural resources - are assumed to produce even growth and distribution. This self-assurance is only reinforced in the missionary exhortation of the World Bank and IMF institutions to the poorest nations that structural adjustment programmes are their only salvation. The failures of successive development decades and the constant revisions of development theories would prove otherwise.

The Grasp of Economic Ideology

The most important recent EU perspective on the future of the European economy, the White Paper on Growth, Competitiveness, Employment, states in a marginal chapter called "Thoughts on a new development model" that the present economic system is characterised by "the underuse of labour and the overuse of natural resources". This well-meaning afterthought is belied by the primary focus of the paper expressed in its title and reflecting an inability to escape the grasp of the dominant economic model.

B. Goudzwaard vividly describes the ideological hold capitalist market theory has on our societies and sums up the impossibility of any self-correction insofar as it "cannot recognise something of value which has no price; and it cannot recognise human needs where there is no buying power". And this is where our morality has fallen short: it has failed to recognise the determination of knowledge by ideological systems and the perversion of our moral insight by our having lost sight of the Way or our capacity to hear (obey) the Word.

Consequences for Future Generations

Here I should like to summarise those levels on which oppression, or exploitation of present generations, have enormous consequences for posterity. When speaking of persons and peoples, one thinks immediately of the physical and psychological damage done to individuals on the one hand, and on the other, the cumulative socio-economic degradation which determines the capacities of the next generations to meet their needs. On the racial, or civilisational, level, we have the appearance and persistence of structures such as economic and political systems as systemic factors of oppression, along with their more subtle aspects, the ideological or cultural paradigms which underlie them.

As ideologies, they not only orient political and economic perspectives on the institutional level but ultimately determine the intellectual, moral and affective space individuals have to work with, whether they be considered controlling or controlled. In this way, dominant ideologies easily perpetuate themselves not only through institutional structures but also through personal behaviours which delimit the range of options or choices the next generation will have. The real challenge, however, is for societies and states to realise a level of community and international equity that allows for more just structures and behavioral models.

Here we turn to elements of the Churches' social teaching which might provide clues to a Christian perspective on future generations. Again, I do not attempt to focus on the most obvious ecological strands of thought but rather on the impact of social teachings on the situation for the poor in our generation.

Elements of Christian Teaching

There are many points of Christian doctrine forming the basis for the social and ethical teachings of the Churches. I will not repeat these but move on to two key concepts which focalise our reflection on responsibility to present and future generations: structures of sin and the option for the poor. These two concepts are based on the perception of interdependence and result in the ethical demand to solidarity. They thus comprise both a critical function in Christian thought as well as a prescriptive function opening up the dimension of responsibility. We shall see that the relation between the two is closely linked in the process of moral understanding itself.

Structures of Sin

These aspects of poverty and oppression find considerable resonance in the innovative yet much maligned notions first of social sin and then later of structures of sin. This later concept was explicitly adopted in the 1988 encyclical *Sollicitudo Rei Socialis*, of which I should like to cite the most relevant passage:

It is important to note therefore that a world which is divided into blocs, sustained by rigid ideologies, and in which instead of interdependence and solidarity, different forms of imperialism hold sway, can only be a world subject to structures of sin. The sum total of the negative factors working against a true awareness of the universal need to further it, gives the impression of creating, in persons and institutions, an obstacle which is difficult to overcome.

The document is careful not to allow the collective structures to take on too active or conscious a nature in order to preserve the individual and voluntary characteristics of an act necessary to maintain the concept of sin. Some might criticise this restriction as reflecting the very Western view of individual identity which the teaching elsewhere identifies as the root of individualism. Despite this limitation, however, the encyclical clearly insists that "one cannot easily gain a profound understanding of the reality that confronts us unless we give a name to the root of the evils which afflict us."

The characteristics of evil social structures are given very firm social and economic explanations by B. Goudzwaard in a recent article on poverty mentioned above. He writes: "It is therefore quite possible that an existing social or economic structure, by the power of its own internal dynamics, at a particular moment can run up against the wall of persistent problems and insurmountable paradoxes. For dynamic evolution cannot be the rule of everything in creation". He goes on to demonstrate as well the epistemological problem involved, for the very structure and orientation of a society creates and maintains 'blind spots' in its scientific method and even 'condemns to silence' the immeasurable, existential and moral dimensions of human life.

I submit that the admission of evil structures automatically introduces the concept of time into the doctrine of sin and the analysis of oppressive human institutions and collective behaviours. It therefore allows for a prophetic and critical look at present society and thus provides for the moral response aimed at breaking the vicious circle of evil, the cycle of violence. Future generations would, thereby, be liberated for their own development.

But let us not dwell on the Church's penchant to intricately describe and condemn sin. There are many grounds in support of the positive exercise of moral responsibility towards future generations. I should like to focus on one of the most productive expressions, although a recent one, for our discussion.

The Preferential Option for the Poor

In all that has been said so far there has been a reflection of the pre-eminence of a concept in Christian tradition of a higher justice due to the weak and oppressed. It is very much rooted in the Old Testament in ways which are certainly better understood by our Jewish friends. That Testament so often cites the injunction to guarantee the rights of the "widow, orphan and sojourner" that the phrase begins to sound like a litany. Perhaps our Jewish friends would allow me sufficient liberty of interpretation to compare, for example, the vulnerable situation of the "sojourner", the *gertoshav* of the modern-day migrant worker.

The notion of "the option for the poor" was more recently developed in the context of Liberation Theology and took on formal expression in the Conference of Latin American Bishops, held in Puebla, Mexico, in 1979, which took to heart the challenge of the integral liberation of the poor. The encyclical *Sollicitudo Rei Socialis* again explicitly adopted and supported this teaching, as follows:

The option or love of preference for the poor ... is an option, or special form of primacy in the exercise of Christian charity, to which the whole tradition of the Church bears witness ... It affects the life of each Christian ... it applies equally to our social responsibilities ... Today, furthermore, given the worldwide dimension which the social question has assumed, this love of preference for the poor, and the decisions which it inspires in us, cannot but embrace the immense multitudes of the hungry, the needy, the homeless, those without medical care and, above all, those without hope of a better future. It is impossible not to take account of these realities. Although this "option" is expressed in terms of individual, and therefore voluntaristic, terms of decision-making, it is treated as an obligation.

Initially developed in Catholic teaching, the notion of the option for the poor was readily taken up in Protestant theology, as the 1992 study document of the World Council of Churches, *Christian Faith and the World Economy Today* shows. It reads: "This 'preferential option for the poor' is thoroughly grounded in Scripture and in the best of subsequent Christian tradition. Any economic policy or system has therefore to be tested from the perspective of how it affects the position of the poor."

What this document suggests is that our very social and economic systems should also be subject to such an ethical criterion.

Yet, there is an even more profound element involved. We note that the dialectic of the two concepts, namely, structures of sin and option for the poor, laid out as we said between the poles of interdependence and solidarity, offer both critical tools of analysis of oppression and signposts for an ethical response. However, an important hermeneutical dynamic is introduced here which fundamentally changes the character of the Christian outlook: the fact that the believer is required to take the stance of the poor before being able to discern the proper course of action. Let me again refer to the WCC document to restate, at some length, this notion:

The over-arching standard for interhuman relationships and behaviour is God's justice to be discovered through a "preferential option for the poor"... Because the struggle for justice by human beings can only be incomplete and partial, continuing self-analysis and self-correction is necessary. One thing is however clear: a true awareness of God's justice must begin with a commitment to listen to the poor, the oppressed and the weak (Jer 22,16) ... the actual experience of the victims of exploitation and oppression is the essential key to discern the powers at work. To make a preferential option for the poor is not only to do something for the poor, but also to enlist with them and create ways through the church and otherwise by which they can be heard so that their struggle for justice will gain strength and momentum. In other words, we cannot know our obligations and responsibilities until we have put ourselves in the correct position to learn what they are, that is, an attitude of hearing obedience.

Conclusion

Instead of recapitulating the above points in conclusion I would like to draw out possible signposts for our future orientation: restraint, evangelism and reconciliation. These require clarification.

Restraint or Self-Limitation

Happily there have already been a number of references in this volume to the necessity of exercising restraint and control with regard to the use of natural resources. It is absolutely critical that we in the industrialised countries reflect on and change our present patterns of production and consumption.

Since the Stockholm and Club of Rome conferences impressed upon us the notion of real boundaries to our economic and demographic expansion, limit continues to be seen as a largely negative concept; an obstacle as long as the future is conceived in terms of economic growth and material prosperity. Limit can, however, be a very liberating notion for us today, as it was for the Hebrews with regard to the sabbatical teachings. It has now been recognised that development must be qualitative: the United Nations and World Bank have set out new criteria for measuring development including health, education, social and security dimensions. The 1992 UNCED conference in Rio explicitly pointed to a wide range of changes needing to be made in terms of lifestyle and consumption.

The WCC study document mentioned above devotes a section to "restraint in the human order" and states: "Just as humanity has more or less developed a sense for a required minimum of consumption to ensure a decent life, so we should be considering where maximum limits may lie, and how those might be implemented." In this context as well, we might refer to the sin of omission as failing to respect and exercise proper stewardship of the earth. The damages already incurred by modern industrial societies threaten the existence itself of both present and future generations.

Evangelization or Mission

While it may be somewhat precarious to introduce the notion of evangelization into an inter-faith discussion, there are good reasons to reinterpret, or give added dimensions to, the functions of evangelization for our own day. Pope John Paul II has, in fact, described three missionary levels. The first, pastoral, is directed primarily at individuals; we might interpret it as the process of spiritual and moral education, a fundamental topic many others have addressed in this volume. A second level is the evangelization of peoples, which we might interpret as an effort to share the liberating good news with groups and peoples who are oppressed with either too little or too much. Thirdly, a challenging new twist has been given to the term: that of mission to the "foreign" structures of our modern world, those systems, ideologies and institutions which alienate peoples and oppress the earth.

Reconciliation with Creation

I suggest this as a further theme of reflection and orientation which englobes many of the concerns expressed here. This theme was discussed at the Second European Ecumenical Assembly, held in Graz Austria, in June 1997. It is to be hoped that the continuing inter-faith dialogue will help us mutually to sharpen our perspectives and ethical commitment to bequeath to future generations a sustainable society and a healthy Earth.

I shall not go into the specific socio-economic, ecological and cultural challenges on our agenda which I would admit are broadly shared with secular society, such as environmental preservation, redistribution of lands, demilitarization, debt reduction, the achievement of participatory and accountable government, and reform of multilateral institutions. I trust it is clear that we have to move far beyond a concept of development founded on material prosperity and economic expansion and a notion of justice based on an individualistic and voluntaristic view of charity.

References

Brinkman, M. (1988). 'The Christian Faith as Environmental Pollution?', *Exchange* 17: p. 51.

Durning, A. B. (1989). 'Poverty and the Environment: Reversing the Downward Spiral', *Worldwatch Paper* 92, Washington D.C..

European Commission (1994). *Growth, Competitiveness, Employment: The Challenges and Ways Forward into the 21st Century*.

Goudzwaard, B. (1989). 'Why Poverty Grows', *One World* (November).

Goudzwaard, B. (1994). 'Who Cares?: Poverty and the Dynamics of Responsibility', (paper presented to the National Conference on Welfare Reform, organised by the Centre for Public Justice, Washington, D.C.).

Opschoor, H. B. (1993). 'Use and Abuse of Creation', *The Ecumenical Movement Tomorrow*, Netherlands, Kampen.

Van Prijs, P. (1986). *Les limites de la Croissance et les Fondements de l' Écologié Politique,* Louvain-la-Neuve, (Rapport CMID 1).

Pope John Paul II (1988). *Sollicitudo Rei Socialis*, Vatican.

Agenda 21: The United Nations Programme of Action from Rio (1992). United Nations Pub.

Human Development Report (1994), New York, United Nations Development Programme.

Our Common Future (1987), London, World Commission on Environment and Development.

Christian Faith and the World Economy Today (1992), Geneva, World Council of Churches.

PART IV

ISLAMIC PERSPECTIVE

18

Environmental Issues in the Qu'ran

ADEL A. MEGAHED

The Qu'ran definitively occupies an important position amongst the great religious books of the world.[1] It must be borne in mind that the Qu'ran plays a greater role among the Muhammadans, in that it not only provides them with the Canon of their faith but also provides them with an intricate system that sustains their civil law and customs.

The Qu'ran 'Recitation', the Holy Scripture of Islam, was delivered orally to the Prophet Muhammad between the years 609 A.D. and 632 A.D. It is divided into one hundred and fourteen Suras, each subdivided into Verses. It has created a new phase for human thought and a fresh type of character. About fourteen centuries ago, it was the first to transform a number of heterogenous desert tribes of the Arabian peninsula into a nation of heroes.

This chapter presents a translation of a number of Verses found in the Holy Qu'ran.[2] They are related and deal with our relationship to the environment. All natural resources existing on the Earth must be used and utilized to benefit humankind as a whole. We are allowed to develop natural resources by every justifiable means as long as all humanity, including unborn generations, can benefit.

The Creation of Humankind

1. "And when thy Lord said to the angels: Lo! I am about to place a viceroy on the Earth" (Surah: The Cow, verse 30).
2. "And He taught Adam all the names" (Surah: The Cow, verse 31).
3. "Eat and drink of that which Allah hath provided, and do not act corruptly, making mischief on the Earth" (The Cow, verse 60).

4. "Surely, we created man of the best stature" (The Fig, verse 4).

5. "We verily have created man in affliction" (The City, verse 4).

6. "Then, we appointed you viceroys on the Earth after them, that we might see how ye behave" (Jonah, verse 14).

7. "He hath created man from a drop of fluid, yet behold! He is an open opponent" (The Bee, verse 4).

8. "We have created you from dust, then from a drop of seed, then from a clot, then from a little lump of flesh shapely and shapeless, that we may make it clear for you" (The Pilgrimage, verse 5).

9. "O mankind, be careful of your duty to your Lord who created you from a single soul and from it created its mate from them twain hath spread abroad a multitude of men and women. Be careful of your duty towards Allah in whom ye claim of one another" (Women, v. 1).

Family Relations in the Qu'ran

1. "And we have commended unto man kindness towards parents. His mother beareth him with pain, and the bearing of him and the weaning of him is thirty months" (Surah 46, verse 15).

2. "And we have enjoined upon man concerning his parents. His mother beareth him in weakness upon weakness and his weaning is in two years. Give thanks unto Me and unto thy parents. Unto Me is the journeying" (Luqman, verse 14).

3. "Thy Lord hath decreed, that ye worship none save Him, and kindness to your parents" (Surah 17, verse 23).

4. "And Allah brought you forth from the wombs of your mothers knowing nothing, and gave you hearing and sight and hearts that haply ye might give thanks" (The Bee, verse 78).

5. "Lo! We created man from a drop of thickened fluid to test him so we give him the sense of hearing, knowing. Lo! We have shown him the way whether he be grateful or disbelieving" (Surah 76, verse 2,3).

Some Social Relations

1. "And hold fast all of you together, to the cable of Allah, and do not separate" (Surah 3, verse 103).

2. "And let there be from you a nation who invites to goodness, and enjoin in the right conduct and forbid indecency. Such are they who are successful" (Surah 5, verse 1).

3. "O ye who believe, fulfil your undertakings" (Surah 5, verse 1).

4. "When ye are greeted with a greeting, greet ye with a better greeting than it, or return it. Lo! Allah taketh count of all things" (Women, verse 86).

5. "And if they incline to peace, incline thou also to it, and trust in Allah. Lo! He is the Heavens, the Knower" (Surah 8, verse 61).

6. "Of knowledge ye have been vouchsafed but little" (Surah 17, verse 85).

7. "O ye who believe! When ye rise up for prayer, wash your faces, and your hands up to the elbows, and lightly rub your hands and wash your feet up to the ankles. And if you are unclean, purify yourselves" (Surah 5, verse 6).

8. "This day good things have been made lawful for you. The food of those who have received the Scripture is lawful for you and your food is lawful for them" (Surah 5, verse 5).

Enjoying Life on Earth

1. "Mankind were one community, and Allah sent Prophets as bearers of good tidings and as warners" (The Cow, verse 213).

2. "O, Mankind! Eat of that which is lawful and wholesome on Earth" (The Cow, verse 168).

3. "Wealth and children are ornaments of life of the world" (The Cave, verse 46).

4. "O company of jinn and men, if you have the power to penetrate regions of the Heavens and the Earth, then penetrate. You will never penetrate them, save with our sanctions" (Surah 55, verse 33).

5. "And if you would count the favour of Allah, you cannot reckon it" (The Bee, verse 18).

Creation of the Earth and Heavens

1. "Lo! The number of months with Allah is twelve months, by Allah's ordinance in the day that He created the Heavens and the Earth" (Repentance, verse 36).

2. "Lo! In the creation of the Heavens and of the Earth and the difference of night and day, and the ships which run upon the sea with that which is of use to men ... are signs [of Allah's sovereignty] for people who have sense" (The Cow, verse 164).

3. "We have built the Heaven with might, and We are those who made the vast extent" (Surah 51, verse 47).

4. "Lo! Nothing on Earth or in the Heavens is hidden from Allah. He it is who fashioneth you in the wombs as pleaseth Him" (Surah 3, verse 5, 6).

5. "Who made all things good which He created, and He began the creation of man from clay" (The Prostration, verse 7).

6. "And we created not the Heaven and the Earth and all that is between them in vain" (Sad, verse 27).

7. "And hath made of service unto you whatsoever is in the Heavens and whatsoever is on the Earth; it is all from Him. Lo! Herein verily are portents for people who reflect" (Crouching, verse 13).

8. "And He it is who hath given independence to the two seas (though they meet); one palatably sweet and the other saltishly bitter, and hath set a forbidding ban between them" (The Criterion, verse 53).

9. "There will be for you on Earth a habitation and provision for a while" (The Heights, verse 24).

10. "Work, not confusion on Earth after the fair ordering, and call on Him in fear and hope" (The Heights, verse 56).

11. "Corruption doth appear on land and sea because of the evil which men's hands have done" (Surah 30, verse 41).

12. "Lo! We have created every thing by measure, and our commandment is but one commandment, as the twinkling of an eye" (The Moon, verse 49, 50).

The Meanings of More Verses

1. "Lo! We offered the trust unto the Heavens and the Earth, and the hills, but they shrank from bearing it and were afraid of it. And man assumed it, he proved a tyrant and a fool!" (The Clans, verse 72).

2. "O my son [of Lockman], establish worship, and enjoin kindness and forbid iniquity" (Lockman, verse 17).

3. "Lo! Allah, with Him in knowledge of the hour. He sendeth down the rain and knoweth that which is in the wombs. No soul knoweth what it will earn tomorrow, and no soul knoweth in what land it will die. Lo! Allah is Knower, Aware" (Lockman, verse 34).

4. "Allah will exalt those who believe amongst you, and those who have knowledge to high ranks. Allah is informed of what you do" (Surah 58, verse 11).

Notes

1. The aim of this paper is to present an English translation of the meanings of some Verses in the Qu'ran. Three different books (English translation) on the meanings of the Qu'ran were consulted: *The Koran*, translated from Arabic by George Sale, London, Frederick Warne, 1825; *The Koran*, translated from Arabic by J.M. Rodwell, London, Everyman's Library, 1909; *The Glorious Qu'ran*, text and explanatory translation by Muhammad Pickthall, Muslim World League, 1977.

2. It should be noted that the word 'Allah' has been used throughout, because there is no corresponding word in English. The word 'Allah' is neither feminine nor plural, and has not been applied to anything other than the unimaginable Supreme Being. The word God is used in the translation corresponding to the word 'ilah' in Arabic. The verses presented in this paper, in English translation, are samples of the verses of the Holy Qu'ran which include more than six thousand verses. The verses presented are those dealing with and expressing the creation of the human being created man in the best form and the best stature by Allah. Allah stated in Surah 30, v. 41, that "corruption will occur and appear on land and sea by men's hands". Surah 10 (Jonah), verse 24, states that "when the Earth has taken on her ornaments and is embellished, her people deem that they are her masters. Our commandment cometh by night or by day and we make reap the Earth like we reap a mature corn field. Thus, do we expound the revelations for people who are reflective".

19

Islamic Ethical
Sensibility to Posterity

ABUBAKER A. BAGADER

As we are about to enter the 21st century, it is urgent and appropriate to reflect and act on the future existence and survival of this planet. Since it is future generations who will live then, it becomes our shared duty and responsibility to hand over to them a more promising and a better life. To achieve this goal, we ought to take all available measures and means to secure satisfactory results. Since world religions exert a major directing and moralizing influence on their followers, and their traditions provide guidelines for them on many issues of conduct, they will provide us with some ideas to help future generations to have a promising future. What modern social sciences, physical sciences and technological advances provide are valuable and should enhance what religions offer rather than confront or negate them.

My reflection takes off from the fact that Islam pays much attention to the social, psychological, legal, ecological, political and economic welfare of human beings in general and future generations in particular. The chapter will explain briefly how Islamic tradition addresses the major issues related to future generations. But before doing that, allow me to introduce to you some general notions about Islam.

Islam is a monotheistic religion; it stresses that God, the Creator, is different from and unlike all creatures. Islam presents itself as *Deen Al-Fitrah,* the natural religion for all human beings. Actually, it is the same religion that all the prophets came to deliver to their respective audiences. Islam, as such, presents itself not as a new religion, but as the religion people should have known all the time. It is for their welfare in this world and the other world. It is a gift from God to humanity to make them happier and more content. Its teachings are simple, without mysteries, and it is accessible to all, believers and non-believers. It has no formal or established Church or institutions, whether official or unofficial, that claim to represent Islam, nor a priesthood to claim sole authority on how religion should be practised or understood. Of course, there are well-known scholars who either graduated from established high institutes of learning or studied directly with scholars in learning circles in mosques or traditional schools.

These scholars are better equipped to present Islamic sciences. Usually they do that using the accumulated scholarly works, which are traceable to the Qu'ran, the traditions of the prophet and mass consensus of early Muslim generations. If any scholar deviates from these standards, his views are rejectable. So the *Ulema* (Islamic scholars) are not themselves representatives of the faith, but their scholarship may be! These scholars do not have to be members of a formal set-up. The grand *Mufti* (the highest religious authority) cannot present himself as the sole representative of Islam, as he is fallible and his views reflect his scholarship and as such can be criticized. Islam's teachings provide the believers with guidelines that encompass almost all aspects of life. The main objective of the believer is to worship Allah, and all he does or says is some kind of *Ibada*, worship, done in accordance with the teachings of Islam. So one's worldly activities and one's ritual prayers and other religious rituals and duties have, in the eyes of Allah, the same value. These teachings direct one's behaviour and deeds in general for the welfare of the self, the community and humanity.

The purpose of the *Shariah* (Islamic Law) is to protect and preserve the soul, mind, body, material wealth and to maintain personal and collective honour and security of human beings. Allah gives man the ability to reason and to distinguish between good and evil. Allah created human beings with the ability to pursue either and holds them responsible for their deeds and actions.

The Family and the Social Environment

Islam gives the family an important place in society. The prophet Muhammad was a family man, and named marriage as his *Sunnah* (tradition). Islam recognizes human sexual drives and desires and channels them into the institution of marriage. It not only encourages marriage, but also considers celibacy undesirable and against human nature. The prophet called on the young to get married when they are able to afford having a family; if they cannot yet they are advised to fast and refrain from any illegal and unlawful sexual relations.

Islamic teachings stress religious commitment and high standards of morals as the most important qualities to be sought in any future wife. These qualities precede beauty, class, wealth, etc. As much as Islam seeks to channel human sexual desires into marriage, it realistically looks at sexual pleasure. It also respects and protects human life. It gives the unborn an independent legal status. The unborn child is entitled to inherit, to have its *Nasb* (being declared as a legal child) despite any objection from anyone, provided it was born from a legal relation. The unborn is entitled to custody and to physical and emotional care. It is the parents' duty to protect their children from all sorts of hazards, and do their best to bring them up well. It is reported that the prophet said that whoever has three daughters and took good care of them until they got married, will have a guaranteed place in paradise. Parents are supposed to provide a rich and comfortable family atmosphere as a religious vocation and duty, and they should do that not expecting any material or worldly rewards in return.

It is incumbent on fathers to choose healthy, well-bred, religious women as wives for their sons, in order to secure healthy offspring free from diseases and so that they will be able to provide a suitable family environment for upbringing. The newly born is entitled to a good,respected, and socially accepted name. Parents are encouraged to spend time with their children and to live for them.

Islam considers sex outside marriage unlawful. Islam is against all forms of infanticide and the termination of life. Islamic traditions encourage the bearing of children: the prophet advised his followers to marry fertile women. Islam does not object to personal use of contraceptives, provided there are good reasons for doing so. But it is against national birth control policies. It is against deliberate abortion, except when the mother's life is in danger.

Islam provides guidelines on how to sustain the best relations between parents and children. It is common wisdom that "Beneath mothers' feet lies the paradise!" It is indicated in the Qu'ran (the holy book of Islam), that children should respect and take care of their parents, even in the case of different faith, creed or views. Parents are not allowed to abuse their children physically or emotionally. Parents are ordered to work hard and to provide their children with an education in order to enable them to do well. It is reported that Ali the fourth caliph said "Teach your children what suits their times and not yours." Teaching children is an important individual duty, the prophet said: it is a personal duty for every Muslim to be educated. Muslims should spare no means to get an education.

Traditions dictate that they should pursue knowledge even if it were in China, the most distant place then from Arabia. Islam encourages upward mobility and considers worldly activities to be part of one's *Ibada* (fate). Parents should help their children to achieve the best.

Islam is against discrimination or differential treatment. Best among human beings is the one who is best in the eyes of Allah.

Islam values family life and cherishes its strength and continuity. The laws of inheritance, for example, are directed towards that end. Within the family, Muslim traditions stress the importance of caring for and protecting the young, and respecting and helping the elderly.

The young play a major role in Islamic history. Several of the earliest Muslims were young men and women. Many of them played leading roles in spreading, presenting, and protecting Islam and the Muslim community. Islam encourages the young to contribute to the welfare of the community. Many of those young men and women played major roles in *Ijtihad* and *Fatwas*. Age is never considered a barrier; talent, ability, knowledge and piety are a basis for scholarship.

Demographically speaking, the Muslim community, world-wide, is youthful, with a high percentage of members under twenty years old. The teachings and traditions of their faith provide them with incentives and opportunities to contribute to the welfare of humanity.

Humanity's Relations with Nature in Islam

Allah created the universe and all it contains in due proportion and measure, and did that for a purpose. We are part of this universe, whose elements are complementary to one another, and together constitute an integral whole. We play a distinctive role, as *Khaleefah* viceroy, in the universe. We are supposed to build and cultivate this planet as part of our vocation in life. However, we are merely managers and executors on earth and not disposers or ordainers.

Human beings are granted the right to manage and utilize the earth's resources, but is required that they maintain and preserve them as honestly as possible. The sustainable use of the earth's resources is the right and privilege of all human beings. Hence, we should take every available precaution to ensure and protect the interests and rights of all creatures. They are equal partners in these resources. We should not regard this use as limited to one generation but rather think of these resources as a joint property of which each generation must make the best use without disrupting or upsetting the interests of future generations. Every generation is entitled to benefit from these resources, but none can claim permanent ownership.

Islam has a positive attitude towards nature in general. Such an attitude necessarily entails commitments on our part to conserve and protect natural resources and the environment from excessive, irrational and destructive abuse. It also involves taking measures to improve all aspects of life including the hygienic, nutritive and psychological. In this connection, Muslim jurists developed legislative rules. The protection, conservation and development of the environment and natural resources are a religious duty to which every Muslim should be committed. This commitment emanates from the individual's responsibility before God to protect himself or herself and the community. Any deliberate damage to the environment or abuse of natural resources is considered improper and is forbidden in Islam. It is dictated by Muslim traditions that he who does not show concern for the interest and good of the community is not a Muslim. Muslims are encouraged to improve and cultivate nature. The one who removes whatever obstructs a public road, or cleans it, for example, has done good. Another Muhammadan tradition states that if somebody were told that the world was at its end while planting a tree, that person would still be obliged to carry out the task.

Muslims are required to deal with environment and natural resources in accordance with morals and manners dictated by Islam. That means no extravagant or excessive use of resources. Muhammad teaches one not to use water excessively, for example, even if one is by a riverside! We should use the resources with respect and moderation. They are Allah's gift and we should be thankful rather than abusive.

The natural resources are *Amanneh;* trust for man to use and hand on to successive generations. This trust is also common to all human beings to share. In case of violation of the above-mentioned general regulation for dealing with the environment, Islamic law stipulates that the ruling authorities have the right to intervene to establish the good and interest of the community and to eliminate mischief or abuse. However, it should be realized that if the community's interests led to damage or sitaution worse than what was there before, the juristic rule indicates that avoidance of dispoliation be given preference and should come before the achievement of interests. The state should not only work to prevent damage to the environment, but also work to remedy it whenever it happens. The task of developing and improving the natural resources and the environment is also owed to both the state and the individual.

Islam encourages Muslims to co-operate and work to achieve these goals with other nations and faiths in peace and war. Allah's benevolence is for all human and non-human beings and they should not be prevented from using their rights. In war, for example, Islam instructs its followers not to destroy plants or natural resources as a means to force the enemies to surrender. Muslims are instructed to share these resources with other creatures. Muhammad is reported to have said that a woman entered paradise for feeding a cat, and another was doomed to hell for not allowing a thirsty dog to drink!

This positive and practical attitude towards the environment allows for the provision of a healthy, rich, renewable environment for coming generations. It also provides them with the practised and proven wisdom and traditions that will enable them to carry on for many generations to come.

Values and Traditions

In a world of relativism and materialism, the best future generations could get are values and traditions that, in the past, have proved their worth in preserving and respecting nature, life and human existence. If such traditions and values were bequeathed to future generations, they would at least inherit the natural resources on which to survive. In an era where we no longer have a clear meaning and vocation in life, religious traditions can provide future generations with meaning and something to live for. As world religions spokespersons, we should re-emphasize the significance of religious values and traditions for humanity. We should also stress that each religion should be respected without any compulsion or negation. One's freedom in adhering to a particular religion should be fully respected. Islam teaches tolerance of and respect for other faiths, and Muslims are ordered to debate gently and respectfully with the followers of other faiths. Diversity in cultures, colours, nationalities is only a sign of Allah's greatness; it should be celebrated rather than become a reason for hostility and intolerance.

We should work together to provide future generations with a stable and just social order. We should, firstly, without any discrimination, provide them with the right to learn and improve their cognitive, affective and psychological abilities. Education should be directed to produce a better human being able to live in fellowship with other human beings and not merely a professional specialized to fix or do things.

Economic opportunities and a just distribution of goods should become a common goal for humanity to achieve in the new world order. This matter should not be left only in the hands of politicians or professionals who look at the matter from non-religious and non-moralistic perspectives. Actually, the present disparity between the rich North and the poor South should not be accepted as a norm, and our joint efforts should be coordinated to ensure that a more just and balanced economic distribution be realized. We should realize that, without harmony, global tension will continue and might lead to destruction that could jeopardize future generations' chances for life.

Future generations ought to be helped to protect themselves and communities from the dangers of weapons of mass destruction, violence, drugs and venereal diseases. Faiths, nations and communities should work together to ban nuclear arsenals and declare our planet free from weapons of mass destruction to save it for future generations and to allow for a peaceful life among nations. It is also our responsibility to work together to stop abuses of drugs. We should all co-operate to have a world free of drugs. Aids constitutes a threat to humanity. It is our responsibility to fight the disease by the morals provided by our traditions and by teaching our young people how to escape the dangers of venereal diseases.

Let us work jointly to develop interfaith global ethics that could help our youth and the coming generations to face today's serious environmental and drug problems. We will, for sure, benefit from our traditions, but this does not exclude openness to the new achievements of modern social and behavioural sciences.

20

The Rights of the Unborn in the Muslim Tradition

M. A. ZAKI BADAWI

Can the unborn be accorded rights? A pedantic lawyer might answer in the negative, suggesting that rights are always coupled with duties. Clearly this cannot apply to the unborn. Further it might be said that a prerequisite of a right is the actual existence of the rightful. Our pedantic lawyer may advise that the use of the word "rights" in the title should refer to a religious or moral concept rather than to a legal one. I would like to argue that, while the religious and moral connotations are certainly present, the legal one need not be excluded for it is possible for members of present generations to claim on behalf of the coming ones just as States sign treaties that bind future generations. The rights here are also duties on each generation in respect to succeeding ones.

In the Muslim tradition, the rights of the unborn originate from the whole question of the relationship of human beings with the Creator and their position in the scheme of things. The Qu'ran tells that God addressed the angels thus: " I am about to establish a vice-regent on earth" (S2,29). Adam was thus made a trustee of all that is on the earth. He and his descendants were enjoined to care for their trust and to hand it down from generation to generation. The Qu'ran tells us to use and not abuse the resources of the earth. It says: "Eat and drink but waste not by excess for Allah loves not the extravagant."

The Islamic tradition places great emphasis on maintaining and enhancing the environment, considering it as an act of worship. In a *Hadith* from the Prophet he says: ""Should the end of the world come upon you and there is just enough time for you to plant a tree, do so at once."

The sanctity of the environment is further enshrined in the rules of war. Islam recognizes that human beings have aggressive tendencies and that wars are bound to take place among them. In conflict, each side is tempted to inflict the maximum damage on the other people's material resources. In the Muslim rules of war the destruction of basic resources such as orchards, water wells and religious buildings is forbidden. Indeed these rules extend immunity from harm to women, children, the old, the disabled and ministers of religion.

Each generation, therefore, must bequeath to the unborn an environment suitable for healthy growth and a safe life. The concern for the unborn was expressed in the early revelation of the holy Qu'ran. The Arabs like many ancient nations regarded human life as dispensable. Their pagan gods required human sacrifice and they were only too ready to provide it. The sacrificial victims were always children. The Holy Qu'ran says: "Thus the pagan gods enticed their worshippers to slaughter their own children" (6v137). The Holy Qu'ran condemns the practice outright and states: "Lost indeed are those who in their weakmindedness and ignorance slay their children" (S6,140). It was not unusual for a man to promise an unborn child to the god as a thanksgiving for a favour from the god.

We are told that the grandfather of the Prophet Muhammad vowed that if he was favoured with ten sons he would sacrifice the tenth child to god. When the tenth son was born, however, he did not have the heart to kill the baby. He consulted the priest, who suggested that he gamble with the god by offering a hundred camels against his son. If he wins he gains his son and the god would gain a hundred camels. Should he lose, the god would take the baby and the camels. We are told that he played and lost. Every time he lost he raised the number of camels by one hundred until in the end the god lost the infant but gained one thousand camels.

Islam came with a message of the unity of God, the Beneficent and the Merciful, who sanctifies life and prohibits the shedding of human blood. It was difficult for the Arabs to understand how an Almighty God should be so squeamish about human sacrifice. They used to kill their children for fear of poverty. But the Holy Qu'ran said to them: "Do not ascribe divinity in any way to aught beside Him the Lord, Allah. Do not treat your parents unkindly but do good unto them. Do not kill your children for fear of poverty for it is We who shall provide for you and for them" (S6,151).

The Arabs, like many ancient peoples, preferred male progeny and considered them a favour from the gods. Female progeny, however, was regarded as a disaster. The Holy Qu'ran describes their reaction to the birth of a daughter thus: ""When news is brought to one of them of the birth of a girl, his face darkens and he is filled with inward grief. With shame he hides himself from the people because of the bad news he has had and debates with himself whether to retain it on sufferance and contempt or to bury it in the dust. Evil indeed is what they decide" (S16,58-59). The custom of burying the infant female in the sand was so common that they were shocked when they heard the words of the Holy Qu'ran telling them of the Day of Judgement when the female infant buried alive would be questioned for what crime she was killed (S81,8). Modern medicine is able to identify the sex of the foetus and many women, especially in Asia, abort the foetus if it is known to be a female. This practice is not dissimilar to the old practice of infanticide so strongly condemned in the Qu'ran.

The right of unborn generations to life is absolute. Abortion is not permitted except in circumstances where the life of the mother is threatened. Some Muslim scholars argue that for the first sixteen weeks the foetus is part of the mother and she is free to abort it if she so chooses. They reasoned that up to that time the foetus would have no independent movement and thus may be seen as less than an independent person. There was a belief amongst them that prior to the sixteenth week the foetus was without a soul. The vast majority of scholars in all Schools of Law, however, rejected this judgement as well as the reasoning behind it. They pointed out that the foetus is a living being from the moment fertilization occurs and its life is sanctified and that any violation against it is a crime which Islamic jurists have listed together with an appropriate punishment.

It is the duty of each generation to procreate through marriage. The Muslim tradition considers marriage as a gift from God that should be gratefully enjoyed. Celibacy is not instituted in Muslim tradition. The Holy Qu'ran refers to the Christian tradition of monastic life as something that was instituted by pious persons and not decreed by God.

When a man once vowed to devote himself to God forsaking marriage, the Prophet angrily told him: "Marriage is my Sunna (way) and those who shun my Sunna are not of me."

Objectives of Marriage

Marriage in Islam has its objectives in a shared happiness, love and comfort. Marriage's fundamental aim is to multiply and bring forth new generations. Marriage is, therefore, a social as well as an individual responsibility. Society must regulate this important relationship and these regulations in the Islamic tradition are directed at bringing forth a healthy and vital new generation. Hence, Islam lists the qualifications required of the husband and wife. The Prophet said that a woman is sought in marriage because of her beauty, wealth, noble birth and piety. He advised: "Let your choice be the pious one. And he said: Do not reject a suitor who is upright and pious for to do so would cause disorder and corruption." Islam gives great importance to piety and good manners, noting that to disregard them in favour of material success or influence would plunge the community into a social order devoid of moral principles and prone to disintegration. For, without ethical values arising from a deep faith, harmonious human society could hardly survive.

The selection of the spouse to be worthy as a partner in the act of procreation is emphasized in numerous *Hadiths*. The Prophet warned the male from falling for the allure of beauty disregarding the more fundamental qualities of moral rectitude, and he warns the female not to favour looks, wealth and power over sincerity, piety and uprightness. The Prophet saw this as an obligation on the parents towards their unborn children. Islam recognizes the human desire to have children. The Holy Qu'ran tells us that the early Prophets who were without children longed to have them. It states that Zachariah prayed unto his Sustainer: "Bestow upon me out of Thy Grace goodly offspring for Thou indeed hearest my prayer" (S3,38). Muslim tradition recognizes this deeply seated desire for offspring and it notes also the fears that some parents experience of poverty and the inability to look after them. So He reminds humanity of the example of Abraham, who having placed Hajar and her son Ishmael in a treeless land turned to his Lord and said: "Oh, our Sustainer behold I have settled some of my offspring [i.e. Ishmael and his descendants] in a barren valley [that of Mecca] close to your sanctified temple so that they might devote themselves to prayer. Cause Thou therefore people's hearts to incline towards them and grant them fruitful sustenance" (S15,17). He trusted his Sustainer to turn the inhospitable valley of Mecca into a bountiful market to which all goods are brought.

The choice of habitat for the unborn is a fundamental responsibility accorded to society and to the individual. Amongst the rights of the unborn is a suitable place for healthy growth and development. I have already mentioned that the environment is a trust that we are enjoined to protect and enhance. But the needs of coming generations might be more specific to that particular culture. It is the right of the unborn Eskimo to have a clean and healthy environment and not to be forced out of its habitat to a different climate or to be enslaved by an imported social order just as it is the right of the desert dweller to have his environment ready for his unborn in a manner which would ensure a fulfilling existence. This, to be sure, is not a call for freezing humanity into a mould that turns it into an artifact suitable for a museum but a recognition of the intrinsic value of each and every culture.

The death of a valid and viable tradition is tantamount to genocide. Islam, while recognizing, respecting and absorbing varieties of culture, also appreciates that there is always a process of change alongside continuity. It seeks to encourage and enhance the changes necessary to uplift each culture and enshrines the continued elements that distinguish it from all others and reflects the history and spirit of the community. Thus Islam as a universal religion is enriched by many cultural expressions all of which are valid and worthy for they are all manifestations of God's grace. The Holy Qu'ran says that: "One of His signs is the varieties of your tongues and of your colours." Linguistic, cultural and racial variations are gifts to humankind and are not barriers or fault-lines. The Holy Qu'ran says: "We created you from a man and a woman and made you into nations and tribes so that you may know each other" (S4,91). The alternative to the variety of races, languages and cultures is a uniform existence in which every individual looks, speaks and lives like every other individual, in other words a world of clones. What a dull world it would be!

There are those who wish for a world inhabited by one cultural tradition based on one religious faith and one race. Some societies committed extreme cruelty against those who were different and weak. The case of the original inhabitants of Tasmania comes to mind. There, the white Christian settlers set out to annihilate the entire Tasmanian race without mercy. Such a crime is not only morally reprehensible but it may prove to have been a disservice to the settlers themselves.

We live in an age when our knowledge has reached such a high level and our technology has given us such power that surpasses even the imagination of our ancestors. We now know more about the causes of diseases and the means to prevent or cure them. We know further that the varieties of human races are a source of strength and the means to ensure survival against sudden disaster. Certain races and communities, for instance, may be immune to illnesses that gravely affect others. Their genetic traits and cultural habits may be the salvation of threatened communities. Botanists mourn the disappearance of plant species as a danger to the existing ones. Surely, the same should apply to the human race.

Cultural Habits Die Hard

There is, of course, the possibility that certain cultural habits may be damaging to the race or may perpetuate certain genetic defects. Such cultures need to be modified in the light of modern knowledge. Marriages between cousins that are common in many Muslim and non-Muslim societies often produce unhealthy offspring. It is our duty to the unborn to protect them against such an eventuality. Not surprisingly, the Prophet advised against marriage between relatives and warned that such a marriage may bring forth weak offspring. But old traditions die hard and many Muslims still prefer marriages between cousins despite the known risk. This raises another issue, namely, the right to marriage of those afflicted with a defect likely to be transmitted to their offspring. There is no question as to their right to enjoy the comfort and love of a spouse but do they have the right to procreate?

In the last century, eugenics was the vogue amongst politicians and even amongst the common people. The afflicted, the inferior and the backward were regarded as not deserving to live let alone to procreate. The vagaries of the philosophy were demonstrated in the mass sterilization which was practised in some Asian countries against certain undesirable sections of the population. In its extreme form this philosophy led to the mass destruction of those regarded as alien to the main culture. Against this philosophy and its resultant practices, Islam stands firm. It places its faith in God's mercy and man's skill. It also decries man's ambition to play God, and fiercely opposes those who set themselves up as judges and executioners in matters so vital as the right to live and to procreate. To be different is no crime and the denial of difference is a denial of freedom.

Freedom is the most precious gift that a culture can grant its members. The absence of freedom dehumanizes society and turns its members into zombies. Uniformity of ideas impoverishes intellectual life. The suppression of religion by another harms the oppressor just as much as it harms the oppressed. The killing of a cultural tradition by a more powerful one limits the chances of the victorious culture to learn and to develop. Islam sanctifies the freedom of belief and of conscience through its declaration in the Qu'ran: "No compulsion in religion" (S2,256). It rejects as an objective the obliteration of other religions. The Qu'ran says: "Had God wished to make all mankind into one religious community He would have done so. But they shall always differ" (S11,119). To seek to force others into a faith is a breach of the divine law and to attempt to eliminate other religions is a challenge to the will of God.

Cultural freedom is respected in the Muslim tradition and is exemplified by the Prophet's recognition of the different behaviour pattern of the early Muslims, who came from various tribal and social origins.

Freedom, however, can be ensured only if there is a system of justice to protect it from those who want to deny it to others. Islam brought forth a legal system that grants equality to all. It ensures that the victim would be compensated by the aggressor. The distribution of justice in the Islamic system is affected by neither fear nor favour. The Qu'ran says: "God commands you to render back your trusts to those to whom they are due and when you judge between people judge with justice" (S4,58). The Qu'ran further warns against denying justice to those who are hostile. It says:"Oh you who believe stand out firmly as witnesses to fair dealing and let not the hatred of others to you make you swerve to wrong and depart from justice" (S5,9).

To summarize: Muslim tradition grants the unborn the right to have a healthy life in a suitable environment enjoying freedom of conscience and ideas in a just world. These rights lead directly to that most elusive and important right that the unborn deserve, that is peace. Wars are caused by the assertion of racial or cultural superiority. They can also occur as a result of an unjust distribution of resources. Islam seeks to eliminate the causes of conflict and thus clear the way for peace between nations and communities.

The greatest gift to the unborn is to bequeath to them a world at peace. This is the ultimate aim of Islamic faith, whose very name means surrender to God and peace.

21

Religions, Nature and Technology in the Mediterranean

HILAL ELVER

The theory developed here focuses on future generations and the intergenerational relationship in view of religions, nature and technology in the Mediterranean culture. Within this framework, this chapter examines three topics: first, international law principles and some implementations on future generations, intergenerational justice and equity; secondly, the concepts of nature and future generations which have found a place in the various Mediterranean religions and cultures; and finally, the Islamic principles on nature, technology and future generations.

Theory of Intergenerational Justice and Future Generations in International Law

Intergenerational equity arises in the context of fairness amongst all generations. As custodians of this planet, we have certain moral obligations to future generations which we can transform into legally enforceable norms. Our ancestors had such obligations to us.

Law and philosophy provide a basis for analyzing the normative relationship among generations and the instruments for transforming normative values into rights and obligations.

The notion that each generation holds the earth as a steward or in trust for its descendants strikes a deep chord with men and women of all cultures, religions and nationalities. Nearly all human traditions recognize that we, the living, are but sojourners on earth and temporary stewards of its resources.[1]

The theory of intergenerational equity outlined here asserts that all peoples have a set of intragenerational planetary rights designed to implement justice between generations. The central issue is what intergenerational fairness means in the context of using the common patrimony of natural and cultural resources of our planet.

There are two extreme cases defining the boundaries of intergenerational equity. In the first, present generations do not consume anything; rather they save all resources for future generations. This is the preservationist model. This model supports the socialist model of economic development applied by Stalin, in which citizens were urged to sacrifice today for a better tomorrow. This attitude was common to the Calvinists as well.

The other extreme is the opulent model, in which present generations consume all that they want today and generate as much wealth as possible, either because there is no certainty that future generations will exist or because maximizing consumption today is the best way to maximize wealth for future generations.

In order to define what intergenerational fairness means in using and conserving our common patrimony, it is useful to view the human community as a partnership among all generations. Although all generations are members of this partnership, no generation knows before it is a living generation at what point in time it will be the living generation, nor how many members it will have, nor even how many generations there will ultimately be.

In conclusion, the theory of intergenerational equity calls for a minimum level of equality among generations. This theory finds deep roots in international law. Since World War II, states have begun to express concern in international legal documents for the welfare of future generations. A growing number of international agreements, declarations, charters and United Nations General Assembly resolutions express such concern and set forth principles or obligations that are intended to protect and enhance the welfare of both present and future generations. The United Nations Charter affirmed the universal concern for the welfare of future generations in its opening paragraph, "We the peoples of the United Nations, determined to save succeeding generations from the scourge of war ...".[2]

The Preamble to the Universal Declaration of Human Rights, the International Covenant on the Prevention and Punishment of the Crime of Genocide, the American Declaration on the Rights and Duties of Man, the Declaration on the Elimination of Discrimination Against Women, the Concention on the Rights of the Child and many other human rights documents affirm that human beings are fundamentally equal and protect the dignity of all people and the equality of their rights.[3] The Declaration of the Principles of International Cultural Co-operation provides in Art.1 that "each culture has a dignity and value which must be respected and preserved" and that "all cultures form part of the common heritage belonging to mankind".[4]

International law has always been concerned with justice. States have made general claims for international justice in relatively few areas, but these are significant: the debates over a new international economic order[5] and the negotiations for the law of the sea convention regarding exploitation of seabed minerals.[6]

Sustainable development rests on a commitment to equity with future generations. Concern for justice to future generations regarding the natural environment first emerged in the preamble of the Stockholm Declaration on the Human Environment which expressly refers to the objective of protecting the well-being of future generations: "To defend and improve the environment for present and future generations has become an imperative goal for mankind - a goal to be pursued together with, and in harmony with, the established and fundamental goals of peace and of world-wide economic and social development." [7] The declaration's first principle provides that "man ... bears a solemn responsibility to protect and improve the environment for present and future generations."

Other international agreements in the last two decades have contained language indicating either a concern for sustainable use of the environment or concern for future generations, often by reference to the common heritage of humankind.[8]

And finally, in the 1990s, we are faced with defining and implementing this commitment to future generations in the context of environmentally sustainable development. Moreover, the concept of future generations was one of the most important new areas for the Rio Declaration.[9]

Besides these "soft law" materials, the principle has been subsequently applied in a number of cases before the International Court of Justice.[10]

On the other hand, the difficult issue is to define justice between countries in the context of generations. Does one country have an obligation to the future nationals of another country? It is clear that a country has obligations to its own existing nationals and to its own future nationals.

The proposed theory of intergenerational equity postulates that all countries have an intergenerational obligation to future generations as a class, regardless of nationality. This means that, even to protect our own future nationals, we must cooperate in the conservation of natural and cultural resources for all future generations.

The most urgent problem today, however, arises from the present economic inequality among countries and among communities within countries. How can we expect an impoverished community to care about future generations, if it cannot even care for its own people today?

Poverty is a primary cause of ecological degradation. Moreover, as an ecosystem begins to deteriorate, the poor communities may suffer most because they cannot afford to take the measures necessary to control or adapt to the degradation, or to move to more pristine areas.

In the intragenerational context, intergenerational equity requires wealthier countries and communities, which will benefit from protecting the general planetary environment for future generations, to contribute to the cost incurred by poor countries and communities in protecting these resources, to help them gain access to the economic benefit from them, and to help protect them from suffering a degraded environmental quality. As beneficiaries of the planetary legacy, all members of present generations are entitled to equitable access to the legacy. Intergenerational justice requires wealthier communities to assist impoverished ones in realizing such access.

From Past to Recent Civilizations, Religions and Nature in the Mediterranean

It is useful to address the issue of sustainability through law and philosophy in addition to economics. Concerns about equity are central in the legal tradition. Law and philosophy provide a basis for analysing the normative relationship among generations and the instruments for transforming normative values into rights and obligations. Legal instruments provide a means of ensuring that those who hold power follow the ideals of justice held by society.[11]

Recent Civilizations, Customs and Religions

All traditional cultures and religions are familiar with future generations. The great world religions have systematized ecological and environmental understanding in their holy books and scriptures. Philosophers from diverse cultural traditions have recognized that we are trustees or stewards of the natural environment. The fundamental thesis that we have obligations to conserve the planet for future generations and rights to have access to its benefits is deeply rooted in the diverse legal traditions of the international community. There are roots in the common and civil law traditions, in Islamic law, in African customary law and in Asian non-theistic traditions.

Many useful analogies in legal systems set forth rights of access to and use of property, which are coupled with obligations to conserve the property. For example, tenants have the right to a reasonable use of property but must return it in good condition for future tenants to use. Similarly, beneficiaries of a charitable trust in common law have the right to enjoy the benefits of the trust, but there is an obligation not to dissipate the *corpus* of the trust for future beneficiaries. Citizens have a right to use national parks and an obligation to future users not to desecrate them, which is usually embodied in enforceable regulations.

In the Judeo-Christian tradition, God gave the earth to his people and their offspring as an everlasting possession, to be cared for and passed on from generation to generation. This has been carried forward in both the common law and civil law tradition. The basic thesis that we are trustees or stewards of our planet is deeply embedded.[12]

In the civil law tradition, this recognition of the community interest in natural property appears in Germany in the form of social obligations that are inherent in the ownership of private property. Rights of ownership can be limited for the public good, without the necessity to provide compensation to the owners. Thus legislatures can ban the disposal of toxic wastes in ecologically sensitive areas and invoke the social obligation inherent in property to avoid monetary compensation to the owner of the land.[13] In common law countries such as the United States, local governments can do this through the exercise of police power - the power to protect the health and welfare of its citizens - or the public trust doctrine.[14]

The socialist legal tradition also has roots which recognize that we are only stewards of the earth. Karl Marx, for example, states that all communities, even if taken together, are only possessors or users of the earth, not owners, with obligations to protect the earth for future generations.[15]

According to African customary law we are only tenants on Earth, with obligations to past and future generations. Under the principles of customary land law in Ghana, land is owned by a community that goes on from one generation to the next. The chief of the community or head of the family is like a trustee who holds it for the use of the community. Customary laws and practices of other African communities, and indeed of peoples in other areas of the world, also view natural resources as held in common with the community, promoting responsible stewardship and imposing restrictions on rights of use.[16]

The non-theistic traditions of Asia and South Asia also stress a respect for nature and our responsibilities to future generations as stewards of this planet. In most instances they call for living in harmony with nature. Moreover, Hinduism, Buddhism and Jainism indirectly support the conservation of our diverse cultural resources in their acceptance of the legitimacy of other religious groups.[17]

The Mediterranean Ecosystem

Throughout the Mediterranean Basin and the adjoining Near East, the ruins of ancient civilizations stand amid the evidences of depleted environment. The conclusion seems inescapable that the natural environment and the course of civilizations were interrelated.[18]

The art and literature of all civilizations are full of motifs inspired by the natural world. Philosophy was likewise influenced. Religion was deeply imbued with nature. Most early religions emphasized fertility and honoured certain animals, plants and locations. Christians use wine and bread in the eucharisic sacrament because these were the staple food and drink of the land of Christianity's birth. This list of influences of the natural environment on civilizations is far from complete. The theme of environmental influence on civilization is vast and pervading, and has been the subject of many prior studies.

The ecosystem of the Mediterranean Basin and adjoining river valleys, within which the ancient civilizations of the West arose, is varied. It can be harsh to those who live there, and even violent at times, but all things considered, it is one of the most pleasant areas of the earth. It is also an area which has felt the results of human actions as long and as extensively as any place on earth.

The geographic area described here comprises the theatre of ancient Western civilization, the Mediterranean Sea and its immediate coastlands; and the adjacent river valleys. Such an area is called an ecosystem, and in another sense, the Mediterranean area is made up of many communities of animals and plants, each of which could be considered, with its physical setting, to be an ecosystem.

The Mediterranean is the largest inland sea in the world, surrounded almost completely by the land masses of Europe, Asia, and Africa, and penetrating deeply into them.

An amazing variety of living things flourishes in the Mediterranean ecosystem. Various parts of the basin support different communities of animals and plants, interacting with one another, each adapted to its particular location and climate.

This brief description is meant to be suggestive of the size, beauty and variety of the Mediterranean ecosystem, its place in the light of the energy-giving sun, its alternating yearly cycle of climate, its unique mixture of mountainous, unstable land and sparkling inland sea, and its living, growing, interacting balance of animals and plants. The human species was once simply one of the strands in this ecosystem, held in delicate relationship to all the other strands, physical and biological. But humankind went beyond that. The developing civilizations were in one sense adaptations to the ecosystem, but in another sense, they were ways of using and controlling the ecosystem and enabling humankind to achieve a dominant status over all other forms of life. Human beings played a changing, growing and increasingly complex role, sometimes constructive, but more often destructive.

Ancient Civilizations and Religions in the Mediterranean

From the beginnings of human society on earth, human beings have struggled to survive and flourish and they have used technology as an aid in that struggle. But early humanity's attitudes towards nature and technology were fundamentally different from our own. Nature was accepted as an all-encompassing environment and many of its manifestations were worshipped and looked upon with awe.

Throughout history, people have argued about what distinguishes us from the other animals. For most philosophers and their cousins the theologians, we have been *Homo Sapiens*, distinguished from other animals by having the ability to reason. For others we have been *Homo Ludens* or "man the playing animal".[19]

Human beings have always been users of nature and technology. Early civilizations tried in various ways to deal intellectually with nature and technology. Religions also played a major role in human attitudes towards technology and, above all, towards nature.

In time, the people of the Mediterranean established their place in history. Both the Egyptians and the Mesopotamians regarded nature as basically nurturant and, above all, subject to human ends.[20] Nature was represented in Mesopotamian mythology as "monstrous chaos", and it was the proper task of humankind to tame wild things. The Egyptians were clearly more dependent on their natural environment than their neighbours. Egypt was "the gift of the Nile". To the Egyptians, "all nature was animate and filled with gods". In all these ancient civilizations, religion provides the major focus for the concept of nature.

The Greeks discovered nature as a concept, as part of their discovery of philosophy. All Greeks agreed on one thing: what was natural was in some sense more basic, more ancient, and therefore more venerable than and superior to what was ever made by humans. The universe of nature, moreover, was not a chaos but a cosmos, governed by laws of nature that people must obey: "Nature had become the sum of all that was divine".[21]

But the order of nature can be broken in many ways. To the Greeks, religion was not an isolated aspect of life; it included and permeated everything else. The gods, offended by human injustice on what would now be called the social level, could manifest their wrath in natural disasters.

Justice, to the Greeks, was not simply fairness among people; it was keeping the proper relationships among people and between people, the natural environment, and the gods, so that the whole universe might stay in balance.

The Greeks, unlike their predecessors, sought to understand nature in a rational way. They were much concerned about the interaction between people and their natural environment. They saw the natural environment as the sphere of activity of the gods. Greek religion recognized humankind's oneness with nature. The Greek's belief that the gods, in upholding the order of nature, would punish the transgressor supported an impressive list of taboos against pollution of various kinds.

The Roman mind was marked by its practicality, and Roman attitudes towards nature were distinctly utilitarian.[22] The Romans generally believed that the world is here for human use and they proceeded in a very pragmatic way to find uses for its components. This dominant Roman characteristic is reflected in religion, literature, philosophy and science.

Roman religion was not much concerned with careful definition of the nature and role of the gods, or with matters of ethics. It was concerned with ritual, and the ritual was designed for a specific practical end, that is, to control the natural environment through enlisting the cooperation of the unseen powers which control it.

One attitude towards the natural environment which is of the greatest importance to ecology is curiosity, the desire to understand how nature works.

Romans tremendously destroyed the environment. The loss of forests was the most widespread and noticeable change made in the natural environment by Roman activity. The lumber trade was very important to the military; the Roman government promoted and regulated it. State forests were rented out to private exploiters. Cutting off shipments of timber could be a weapon against actual or potential enemies, and was used against Rhodes in the first half of the second century B.C. The deforestation of much of Italy and the Roman provinces was unfortunately permanent. Among the results of this permanent deforestation were flooding and greatly accelerated erosion. Rome suffered serious floods from time to time in the low-lying areas of the city.

Rome demanded wild animals from the provinces of the empire and beyond. But the entertainment industry of Rome, which included the display and killing of countless animals, was more wasteful and destructive of wildlife than any other feature of Roman culture.

Roman mining had many environmental effects. It caused major erosion, removing hillsides and clogging streams. Government policy did not prevent disasters, and may even have produced some.

Noise, air and water pollution was familiar to the Romans because of the high density of cities.

Roman ability to affect the natural environment was the result of technology and Roman technology was one of the wonders of the ancient world. The Roman government did not support technological advance. If the Romans had developed their technology further without much change in their attitudes towards and knowledge of nature, their impact upon the natural environment would probably have been swifter and more destructive.

The importance of ancient Israel in the history of the relationship of humankind to the environment results from the wide influence of the Judaic religion and its implicit attitudes towards the natural world. The major distinctive contribution of Israel to humankind is, of course, the idea of ethical monotheism. The god of the Jews was one God only, and tolerated no other gods beside him. God was the creator of all the earth and all that is in it, and the sky and stars as well. But God was above and beyond his creation, ruling it from on high.[23] The Judaic teaching was that God is the ruler of the universe and retains the ultimate dominion over the natural environment. He not only created the world, but afterwards maintained his sovereignty over it.

The Judaic emphasis upon ethical conduct in obedience to God's law applied also to human treatment of the natural environment. The grant of dominion was not a licence to kill, exploit heedlessly, and pollute, and was not understood as such by the ancient Jews, although later Western thought did indeed take it in that distorted sense.

Christianity came into existence in the womb of Judaism and adopted most of the Judaic ideas about the nature of God, humanity and the universe.[24]

Islamic Rules and Future Generations

Islam's Attitude towards the Conception of
Future Generations and Natural Resources

The conception of future generations and intergenerational equity rights are deeply rooted in the Islamic attitude towards the relation between human beings and nature. Islamic law regards human family as having inherited "all the resources of life and nature" and having certain religious duties to God in using them. "Each generation is entitled to use the resources but must care for them and pass them to future generations." The utilization and sustainable use of these resources are, in Islam, the right and privilege of all people. Hence, each one of us should take every precaution to ensure the interests and rights of all others since they are equal partners on earth. Similarly, we should not regard such ownership and such use as restricted to one generation above all other generations. It is rather a joint ownership in which each generation uses and makes the best use of nature, according to its needs, without disrupting or upsetting the interests of future generations. Therefore, we should not abuse, misuse and distort the natural resources as each generation is entitled to benefit from them but is not entitled to own them permanently.[25]

Islamic law supports collective restrictions, which are to be observed under a principle of good faith, and collective rights, which are rights of the community of believers as a whole.[26]

In Surah 6,38 of the Qu'ran we read: "There is not an animal that lives on earth, not a creature that flies on wings but forms part of the communities like you. Nothing have we omitted in our books, and all will be gathered before their Lord in the end." Here is a sense that everything created is good, beautiful and holy.

Later in the same Surah we read of God's hand in creation: "It is He who produces gardens with trellises ... and dates and tilth with produce of all kinds, and olives and pomegranates ... eat of their fruit in their season, but render the dues which are proper on the day that the harvest is gathered. But waste not by excess; for God loveth not the wasters."

Also the Prophet has shown us, through his commandments and teachings, how to rear and conserve these creatures. The prophet of Islam has forbidden leaving animals to starve and damned a group of people who used a bird as a target.

Islam looks upon these creatures in two ways:

- as living creatures in themselves attesting to God's wisdom and omnipotence;
- as creatures subjected in the service of men and women, and playing a vital part in the development of this world.

In one of the traditions (*hadith*) of Muhammad, we hear that: "It is an act of charity to plant trees or plough land where birds or man or animals come and eat its plants." This is done not for oneself but for the people who come after. There is a story of Muhammad travelling with his friends. The friends decided to catch birds for their own amusement. When Muhammad saw this he was angry, and ordered the bird to be freed. Selfish pleasure had caused great unhappiness. Any notion of using other species for selfish purposes is, for Islamic tradition, disastrous and destructive.[27]

Whatever God has created in this universe was created in due proportion and measure. God says, "Verily, all things have we created by measure"(S54,49) and "everything to Him is measured" (S3,8). God says, "And produced therein all kinds of things in due balance" (S15,19). In the universe there is diversity and variety of forms, colours and functions. In the universe and its various elements there is fulfilment of man's interests and evidence of the Creator's greatness; it is He who ascertains and determines all things, and there is not a thing He has created but celebrates and declares His praise. "He who has spread out the earth for you and enables you to go about therein by roads (and channels) and has sent down water from the sky. With it have we produced diverse pairs of plants each separate from the others. Eat (for yourselves) and pasture your cattle; verily, in this are signs for men endowed with understanding" (S20,53).

We are part of this universe, whose elements are complementary to one another in an integrated whole. However, we are a distinct part of the universe and have a special position among other parts of the universe. Islam speaks of humankind as God's "Vice-regent".[28] The relation between man and the universe, as defined and clarified in the Glorious Qu'ran, is as follows:

- a relationship of utilization, development and subjugation for man's benefit and for the fulfilment of his interest;
- a relationship of mediation, consideration and contemplation of the universe and what it contains.

God's wisdom has ordained to grant humankind inheritance on earth. Therefore, in addition to being part of the earth and part of the universe, we are also the executor of God's injunctions and commands. And as such we are only managers of the earth and not proprietors; beneficiaries and not disposers or ordainers. We have been granted inheritance to manage and utilize the earth for our benefit, and for the fulfilment of our interests. We, therefore, have to keep, maintain and preserve it honestly, and act responsibly within the limits dictated by honesty.[29]

In conclusion, the attitude of Islam to the environment, the sources of life and the resources of nature is a positive attitude in as much as it is based on protection and prohibition of abuse and destruction. This positive attitude involves taking measures to improve all aspects of life: hygienic, nutritive and psychological, for the benefit and the maintenance of the welfare and well-being of present generations, as well as for the improvement of the quality of life for all future generations.[30]

Nature and Technology in Islam

With a billion of the world's population holding allegiance to the tenets of Islam, its outlook on nature, future generations and technology is of the utmost importance to the future of the planet. Some authors think that Islam and the West are two different civilizations. Some argue that Islam is in effect a heresy from the Christian tradition. Historian Arnold

Toynbee considered Islam, like Christianity, a "deviated Judaic religion". Lynn White speaks of it as "a Judeo-Christian heresy", a view that is vigorously rejected by a leading contemporary Muslim scholars.[31] I think that while all three religions in question have the same environment (in this case the Mediterranean) and are equally affected by it, each religion might be influenced in a particular way by that same environment.

In A.D.613, a native of the trading city of Mecca, Muhammad, began preaching a new religion to his polytheistic fellow tribesmen. The new religion spread rapidly, impelled both by voluntary conversion and by the sword, first through Arabia, then North Africa, Asia, and even as far away as France. Not only did the Muslims threaten Western Christendom militarily, they threatened it intellectually as well. The thinkers of the West were still under the spell of the ancient Greeks, above all Aristotle. Now the Muslims, who had retained the original text, had the source of many of the ancient texts that now appeared and were eagerly devoured in the West.

During the four centuries from A.D. 750 to 1150, "Islam held the lead in scientific activity", with original works appearing especially in mathematics, optics, astronomy and medicine; and geography and history were well developed as well.[32] Despite these promising beginnings, in a few centuries Islam lagged far behind Europe in scientific knowledge and technological application. The problem of accounting for the "relative passivity towards technology" is accentuated by the fact that Islam and the Western world were closely related societies. But, in Islamic thought, "science was not separated from philosophy, nor philosophy from theology", a position which in the long run could be counter-productive from a scientific point of view.

The Islamic position not only requires that science and religion be kept together, but automatically precludes the Baconian use of socio-economic consumeristic nature. Science and religion cannot conflict as they did in the West. Science in Islamic philosophy is, like everything else, judged on moral grounds, and real science is by definition almost good, since it must exist for the sake of social good.[33]

It is impossible to understand the Islamic attitude towards science without understanding the Islamic attitude towards nature. Nature was created by God not simply for our use but as "man's testing ground". We are enjoined to read its "signs". Nature has therefore been created in an orderly and knowable fashion. "Man has, of his own accord, accepted nature as a trust and theatre for his moral struggle ... Man is but the deputy of God possessing no authority save that of a steward." This view, of course, differs basically from that often attributed to Christianity.[34]

As the Prophet so beautifully put it: "The whole of the earth is a mosque". Yet despite their alleged differences about the value of nature, Islam and Christianity - at least a major part of medieval Christianity - are united in stressing that contemplation rather than manipulation should be the primary way in which nature is approached. It was this contemplative attitude towards the unity of science and religion that enabled the Muslim world to accept much from the sciences of others. It also makes it difficult for contemporary Islam to deal with modern Western scientific tradition, which rejects the unity of knowledge and primacy of contemplation and moral judgements in scientific activity.[35]

Why did Muslims, after a distinguished beginning, fall behind in the sciences? Philosophers argued that because life is so short, preference should be given to the sciences that could help men save their souls rather than to secular sciences. The Muslim attitude towards technology, like the Muslim attitude towards science, was shaped by the importance that Islamic thought placed on reverence for nature and service to humankind. As one Muslim scholar describes it, Islamic philosophy already sets up the framework for assessing technology: "Such concepts as *adl* (all-pervasive justice), *islah* (public interest), *khalifah* (trusteeship) and *iotisad* (moderation) and Shariah injunctions, for example in environmental areas such as *ihy* (land reclamation), *harim* (conservation areas) and *hima* (public reserves), can accurately map the circumference of technological activity."[36]

There is disagreement among non-Muslim and Muslim scholars as to the contemporary attitude about science and technology in Islam. Europeans and Americans tend to assume that the Qu'ran and modern sciences and technology are basically incompatible. One Western scholar typically asserts that "a regime seeking to be true to the Koran had difficulty in coping with twentieth-century technology since those who mastered the technology of the West were unlikely to remain fanatically faithful to Muhammad's revelation."[37]Many Muslim scholars would strongly reject this whole perspective, however. Starting with the last century, "modernist" Islamic scholars have argued that true Islam is not incompatible with modern science and philosophy.

Paradoxically, Muslim-oriented thinkers about science and technology identify with the West's concern about nature and the environment. The widespread publicity that has been given to the environmental crisis in the Western media in the 1970s and 1980s has convinced many Muslim scientists that they were right about science's responsibility to society and our stewardship of nature. This, despite the fact that the actual record of Muslim countries was, if anything, worse than that of the rest of the world, in part because they have been "importing Western technology uncritically and blindly", since "the leaders of many wealthy Muslim nations have become completely separated from their religion and their roots in the land." Ironically, one observer notes, given the terrible problem of desertification in many Muslim countries, "it is the tiny state of Israel which is coming up with virtually all the new scientific developments in turning the desert green". Note is taken again, in a contemporary context, of the extent to which Islam has always made people not the masters but simply the stewards of nature. Islam has a code of environmental values that would prevent such debasement, and the fact that Islamic nations are no better than the West in terms of the environment indicates that they have ignored the Shariya law for the last three or four hundred years because they assimilated the value system of the Occidental colonizers. Islam has many concepts to show that the environment, "in all its kaleidoscopic richness, must be preserved".[38]

As Muslim nations continue to rely on their religious heritage for guidance, one can expect these concepts to become more refined and play a major role in the planet's future.

Notes

1. Brown Weiss, E. (1993). 'Intergenerational Equity: Toward an International Legal Framework' in Choucri, N. (ed.), *Global Accord*, Cambridge, Massachusetts Institute of Technology Press.

2. UN Charter (June 26, 1945), 59 Stat. 10331, T.S. 993.

3. Brown Weiss, E. (1989). *In Fairness to Future Generations: International Law, Common Patrimony, And Intergenerational Equity*, New York, Transnational Publishers.

4. UNESCO Declaration of the Principles of International Cultural Cooperation, Resolutions, General Conference (Nov 4, 1966), session 14.

5. Charter of Economic Rights and Duties of States (December 12, 1974): p. 14; International Legal Materials (1975): p. 251; 'Declaration on Establishment of a New International Economic Order', *International Law Monthly* 13 (May 1, 1974): p. 715.

6. Bellow, E. G. (1980). 'International Equity and The Law of the Sea',*Verfassung und Recht in Uebersee* 13: pp. 201-12.

7. U.N. Document A/Conf. 48/14 (1972).

8. For a review of the extent to which international agreements concerned with conservation of natural and cultural resources contribute to the protection of future generations, see Brown Weiss, E. (1984), 'The Planetary Trust: Conservation and Intergenerational Equity', *Ecological Law Quarterly* 11: p. 495.

9. Panjabi, R. K. L. (1993). 'From Stockholm to Rio: A Comparison of Declaratory Principles of International Environmental Law', *Denver Journal of International Law and Policy* 21.

10. Brown Weiss, E. (1989). *In Fairness to Future Generations*, see note 3 above.

11. Choucri, N. (ed.) (1993). *Global Accord*, see note 1 above: p. 333.

12. Genesis: 1,1-31; 17,7-8.

13. Dolzer, R. (1976). *Property and Environment*, Geneva, IUCN Publications.

14. Garton (1971). 'Ecology and the Police Power', *S.D.L. Review* 16: p. 261.

15. Marx, K. (1985). *Collected Works* .

16. Brown Weiss, E. (1992). *Environmental Change and International Law*: pp. 385-412.

17. Kenneth, C. (1994). 'World Religions and Intergenerational Responsibilities', pp. 177-193 in Agius, E. and Busuttil, S. (eds.), *What Future for Future Generations?*, Malta, University of Malta.

18. Churchill, E. S. (1931). *The Geography of the Mediterranean Region: Its Relation to Ancient History*, NewYork, Henry Holt.

19. Ferkis,V. (1993). *Nature, Technology and Society: Cultural Roots of the Current Environmental Crisis*, New York University Press.

20. *Ibid.*

21. *Ibid.*

22. Rostovtzeff (1957). *Social and Economic History of the Roman Empire*, London, Oxford University Press.

23. Hughes, J. D. (1975). *Ecology in Ancient Civilizations*, University of New Mexico.

24. Ferkis, V. (1993). 'To Serve Man or to Serve Nature', p. 11 in *Nature, Technology and Society*, see note 19 above.

25. Ba Kader, A. B. A. (1984). *Islamic Principles for the Natural Environment*, Geneva, IUCN Publications.

26. *Justice* (1984), John Hopkins University Press: pp. 137-139, 219-220, 233-239.

27. Kenneth, C. (1994). 'World Religions and Intergenerational Responsibilities', see note 17 above.

28. Qu'ran Surah 2.30.

29. Ba Kader, A. B. A. (1984). *Islamic Principles for the Natural Environment*, see note 25 above.

30. *Ibid.*

31. Ferkis, V. (1993). 'Nature and Technology in Islam', p. 119 in *Nature, Technology and Society : Cultural Roots of the Current Environmental Crisis*, New York University Press.

32. Al Hassan, A. & Hill, D. (1987). *Islamic Technology*, New York, Cambridge University Press.

33. Nasr, S. N. (1968). *Science and Civilization in Islam*, Harvard University Press.

34. Al Faruqi, I. & Naseef, A. O. (1981). *Social and Natural Science:*

An Islamic Perspective, Jeddah, King Abdulaziz University/Hodder and Stoughton.

35. Sardar, Z. (1985). *Islamic Futures: The Shape of Ideas to Come,* London, Oxford University Press.

36. Rahmen, F. (1982). *Islam and Modernity: Transformation of an Intellectual Tradition,* Chicago University Press.

37. Al Faruqi, I. (1967). 'Science and Traditional Values in Islamic Society', *Journal of Religion and Science* 2: pp. 231-246.

38. Ferkis,V. (1993). 'Nature and Technology in Islam', see note 31 above: p. 119.

22

Environmental Obligations towards Future Generations in Monotheistic Religions

SAADIA KHAWAR KAN CHISHTI

The proposition advanced in this chapter is that from an Islamic perspective, if future generations are to live in harmony with nature, then present generations must realize that, ultimately, the 'environmental crisis' is caused by our reluctance to perceive and internalize the God[1] of Abraham as *Al-Muhit*. *Al-Muhit* is one of the attributes of Allah as stated in the following Verse[2] of the Holy Qu'ran: "But to Allah belong all things in the Heavens and on Earth and it is Allah who encompasseth (*Muhit*) all things."[3]

It is of utmost significance to realize in one's inner being that *Muhit* also means environment. It implies perceiving Allah everywhere and being fully aware of the Divine Environment which surrounds and permeates both the world of nature including natural phenomena, the non-human part of creation and all living species including humankind. The traditional Islamic view of the natural environment is based on an intrinsic and permanent relation among what is today called the human and natural environments and the Divine Environment, which permeates and sustains all kinds of environments.

Islam postulates that Allah created all, including man and woman, to whom Allah gave a special place in His creation. He honoured the human pair to be his Vice-regent, and to that end, endowed the pair with understanding and spiritual insight, so that human beings should understand nature, understand themselves and know Allah through his wondrous signs, and glorify Him in His absolute Unity with reverence and sincere heartfelt devotion.

For the fulfilment of this great trust of Vice-regency, Allah created the human pair in the best of moulds and endowed man and woman with intellect and will so that their acts should reflect Allah's Universal Will and Law. Thus they may experience the sublime joy of being in harmony with the Creator on the one hand and His creation on the other. Several *Ayats* of the Holy Qu'ran and the corresponding *Ahadith*[4] of the Prophet of Islam bring to the fore the relationship between Allah as the creator and His creation, which includes all kinds of creatures. Allah loves his creation and a genuine lover of Allah who is inflamed with Divine love loves the creator and cares for his creation; a true lover instinctively reveres nature and puts it on a pedestal of preservation and motherly care to be passed on to posterity as a heritage and not as personal property handed over from parents to their children.

Alas! On the contrary, modern man has raped virgin nature with animal ferocity, desiring its conquest. In his hideous venture, he turned a deaf ear to the wailing whales, crying birds and many other dying species which not only adorned the natural scene but also provided man with physical nourishment, mental recreation and spiritual bliss. Ironically, what seemed to modern man, stooping to indulge in all kinds of immorality, the conquest of nature, became ultimately the conquest of his own sublime nature by the infra-human elements within him. Consequently, the current generation is now finding itself plunged in crises and suffering from the accompanying perturbed state of mind.

In order to save future generations from falling prey to infra-human elements or the lower self, *Nafs* (or to use the modern psychological term , *Ego*) we must arrange to sit together in the near future, to trace out a programme to bring home to our generation a message to this effect: If today's people are really desirous of improving their environment and are in search of the Creator, the Truth and everlastingpeace, then they should follow the way of Muslim sages who contemplate the wonders of nature and natural phenomena just for understanding the nature of 'Nature' and to benefit spiritually from it and for being ultimately in tune with the Universe. In such a state of being, the true contemplative person would never even think of conquering nature, for it is a sanctuary which represents the handiwork of its ultimate Creator and serves as a vast book of Divine wisdom, an image of the Divine word, which in Islam is the Qu'ran, in Christianity Christ and in Judaism the Ten Commandments.

Spiritual Significance of Nature

The point is that a Muslim sage following in the footsteps of the Prophet of Islam (who used to retire to the cave of Hira where he began receiving the perfect code of life) retires temporarily from the humdrum of this materialistic world to be in conversation with his beloved creator - Allah. Through the reading of the Book of Allah and with the beads of his rosary, the sage immerses himself in the celestial beauty and majesty of the Divine Unity by imprinting it on the tablet of his purified heart, which is the real throne of the King of kings - the God of Abraham.

The Muslim sage, immersed in Divine Unity and having imbibed even a tiny speck of the mighty and immeasurable attributes of Allah, returns to serve humanity as an *Abd* - servant of Allah. He strives to disseminate the Divine message to his fellow beings. It is for this reason that the Islamic tradition holds saints and sages as the salt of society who keep it together and who leave the message of goodwill to all as a heritage, to be passed on to posterity - the future family of the Creator - Allah.

It is noteworthy that as far as the question of the spiritual and metaphysical significance of nature or to be more specific, the natural environment, is concerned, Islam has placed more emphasis upon it than any other religion of the world. To be precise, it can be asserted that Western Christianity (not Christianity as a religion) did fail to emphasize the spiritual significance of nature in its mainstream theology even before the advent of the Renaissance, which resulted in the success of the forces of secular science and environmentally unfriendly aspects of technology as opposed to the Sacred Sciences.

This, in turn, depleted nature of its sacred quality and caused the human pair to forget its origin and vocation to be the custodian of the Earth and its natural treasures. A secular approach to nature made men and women oblivious of their obligations as preservers of both renewable and non-renewable resources of the planet Earth to be handed over to each successive generation as gifts of the Creator - the ultimate owner of everything.

Suffice it to say that a pristine monotheist sees virgin nature in the form of snow-covered mountains, gushing springs, rivers and seas finding their way into endless oceans (providing humanity with countless benefits through its hidden and manifest resources), starry skies, dawn and dusk saturated with the tunes of the chirping birds, gigantic forests with their wildlife and grazing cattle as direct symbols of the power of Allah from whom he comes and to whom is his return.

Islam asserts that nature is among the highest blessings of Allah to humankind. It seems that the bliss of the enjoyment of virgin nature is an advance payment of the rewards of Paradise. In this context, it becomes relevant to realize that not only is the Islamic paradise constructed of precious stones and metals from the mineral realm but the heaven also contains plants and animals. Shirazi speaks at length of the resurrection of not only human beings but also of plants and minerals.[5]

The Islamic love of nature as manifested in the signs of Allah and being imbued with the Divine presence must not be confused with Naturalism as understood in Western philosophy and theology. However, it was left to St. Francis of Assisi to express Christian spirituality with a profound insight into the sacred quality of nature. One finds in the figure of St. Francis of Assisi an awe-inspiring reminder of the possibility of a reverential attitude towards nature. St. Francis is truly a patron saint of ecology, who, amongst all the great medieval saints, comes closest to the Islamic concept of love of nature and the natural environment and its emphasis upon nature's role as a means to gain access to the Creator's wisdom as manifested in His creation. Consequently, the true lovers of St. Francis of Assisi have striven to preserve nature and to pass it on as a heritage to future generations. The followers of the monotheistic religions must ponder the message of the Abrahamic tradition as propounded in the *Ayat*: "Withersoever ye turn, there is the face of Allah". And therefore we are morally obliged to obey Allah's commandments. It becomes our ethical duty to be fully aware of the Divine Environment - *Al-Muhit* - which surrounds and permeates both nature and the human family and all that exists in this world.

Modern people have forgotten the reality that although the Universe is immersed in the Divine *Muhit*, they are unaware of it. This is mostly due to an overall secular system of education imparted in the schools and higher seats of learning and a similar kind of upbringing given at home which may block awareness/perception of *Al-Muhit*. In other words, the modern person, who seems to be in search of the Soul, is unaware of the omnipresence of the Creator of our own souls, for our learning and upbringing are devoid of a spiritual dimension, and are cut off from their roots - spirituality/ proximity to the Divine - *Al-Muhit*. Consequently, the secularly minded society ignored ethical and moral values and indulged in the Pleasure Principle of life till it found itself in danger of extinction due to the havoc which can be caused by the depletion of the ozone layer, the greenhouse effect and pollution. Now, modern society, struck by panic, is desperately attempting to find solutions but is finding itself unable to remedy these environmental ailments.

Present Generations' Moral Obligation

In the context of the Islamic perspective and environmental degradation, it is the moral obligation of current generations to re-orient their thinking towards ideals and realities of the Abrahamic tradition and leave a legacy of knowledge and style of life based on faith and righteousness, to be inherited by future generations. Once they are tuned to invoke Allah as *Al-Muhit* and through their invocation realize the reality of the God of Abraham, in the truly Abrahamic tradition, they see Allah everywhere in His creation. Through its captivating influence they experience Allah's reality as *Rab-il-Alamin* - as one who creates, owns, surrounds and nourishes - the One Being from whom we come and to whom we return; where and when we'll be questioned as to whether or not we followed the code of life spelled out clearly by the Prophet of Islam, but unfortunately ignored by the modern, secular-minded society which is eventually lost in the labyrinth of environmental darkness and is now desperately searching for light.

It is the responsibility of present generations to convey to future generations the fact that we human beings are insignificant beings on a small planet on the periphery of a minor galaxy and that our sense, perception, experience and rational powers are limited and preclude our vision of the beyond. Therefore, absolute rationalists should come out of the web weaved by the school of Rationalism. The adherents of Rationalism used nature as a means of satisfying their greed and their epicurian lifestyle, which, in turn, contributed towards bringing about the current environmental crisis. As such, the strangulating hold of Rationalism needs to be replaced by Sacred Sciences in our system of education at all levels.

A study of Sacred Sciences unveils for its ardent students the esoteric aspects of the Divine revelation. They keenly experience the need to rediscover virgin nature as a source of Learning the Truth - *Al Haq* - and experience nature as an aid in living a spiritual life and as a means of attaining *barakah*.[6] It must be remembered and conveyed to posterity that Islam has always strongly opposed the absolutization of what one might call the Promethean and Titanic human being. Islam does not permit the glorification of the human being at the expense of the creator - Allah and His creation other than humans. The Islamic perspective holds that only Allah is Absolute. Therefore, the Titanic art of the Renaissance, created for the glorification of humankind in rebellion against the supernatural or the Divine and the Sacred, is detestable to the sensibilities of traditional Muslims. In other words, the Islamic perspective excludes the possibility of deification of the earthly human being or of the total securalization of nature. Consequently, *Homo Islamicus* has always lived in awareness of the rights of the Creator and our duties towards him as his Vice-regents, which include the rights of others, comprising also the would-be generations and all other non-human species and realms.

Islamic Science is based upon the particular genius of the Islamic perspective, which, as mentioned before, is centred upon Unity - *Tawhid* - the Oneness of Allah - *La illa-ha-illallah*. This doctrinal principle is manifest in Islamic Natural History in many ways, e.g. in the vision of the Unity of Nature and the interrelations of all things. Muslim historians of nature asserted this intertwining relationship so often when they affirmed the presence of the signs of Allah in nature and studied plants and animals for the purpose of seeing Divine wisdom therein and thereby benefited mankind through an overall wise and balanced planning, keeping the interests of future generations as important as those of their own generation.

Nowadays we hear a lot about paradigm shifts. In the light of Islamic perspective, the logical step would be shifting to the *Tawhidic*[7] paradigm, which takes its guidance from the Quranic philosophy, is formulated in the light of the Sacred Sciences, philosophy, and is based on a deep and realistic understanding of the Divine Environment - *Al-Muhit*. The *Tawhidic* paradigm would lead its adherents to hold on to the primordial Truth; they would spend their earthly life in the conscious-presence of their creator, who watches their every moment and every breath of their earthly lives and to whom they are finally responsible for their deeds in this temporary state of life. If such a belief is implanted in the heart of future generations, then it will, in turn, leave this planet, if not a lovable, at least a livable place for succeeding generations.

Excerpts from the Qu'ran

Before concluding, I would like to voice to our brothers and sisters from the Abrahamic tradition, some excerpt from the Holy Qu'ran:

We believe in Allah
and what was revealed to us
and what was revealed to Abraham and Ismael
and Isaac and Joseph and the Tribes
and what was given to Moses and Jesus
and what was given to the prophets from their Lord
and we do not make any distinction
between individuals among them
for we submit to Allah
We gave Moses the Book
and caused messengers to follow after him
and we gave clear proofs to Jesus Son of Mary
and we strengthened him with the Holy Spirit

Also, the Holy Book adds:

Allah sent to you the Book with the Truth
Confirming the truth of what preceded it

and Allah sent the Torah and the Gospel before,
as guidance to humankind and Allah sent the criterion

The Holy Book also tells us:

Be they Muslims, Jews, Christians or Sabians,
those who believe in Allah
and the Last Day and who do good have their
reward with their Lord

The Holy Qu'ran also declares:

Who can be better in religion than one
who submits his whole self to Allah,
does good and follows the way of Abraham the true in faith?
For Allah did take Abraham for a friend.

The above *Ayats* impress on us that the Judeo-Christian tradition remains incomplete if we were to exclude Islam. Therefore, the appropriate term should read the Judeo-Christian-Islamic tradition.

If we sincerely believe in the above *Ayats*, then we must unite and pledge true allegiance to Abraham, the father of all religions, and unite our efforts to save our planet earth, make it livable for future generations who, in turn, by following the faith of Abraham and the code of life revealed to Muhammad, would make out of planet Earth a holy sanctuary that is welcoming to succeeding generations.

Notes

1. Henceforth, the personal name of the God of Abraham - Allah, as mentioned in Allah's Book - The Holy Qu'ran, will be stated in the place of the word God, for the obvious reason that the word God has been used for deities other than Allah - the One and Absolute Supreme Being - the Living and Eternal God of Abraham.

2. The Arabic word for the Verse of the Holy Qu'ran is *Ayat. Ayat* is the true unit of the Holy Qu'ran. Therefore, an *Ayat* is different from the poetic verse in its diction, rhythm and other parts of its composition. An *Ayat* is the word of Allah and not the word of the Prophet of Allah to whom it was revealed through the archangel Gabriel. Therefore, it is erroneous to call an *Ayat* a verse.

3. The Holy Qu'ran, Sura IV, *Ayat* 126.

4. Sayings and Doings of the Prophet of Islam, which form a source of Islamic Law.

5. As cited by Sadr-al-Din Shirazi in his *Asfar-al-Arbeah*. The basic concepts in this article are taken from the works of Dr. Sayyed Hussain Nasr.

6. *Barakah* is an Islamic term which means much more than Divine grace in having components of other attributes of Allah.

7. *Tawhidic* is based on *Tawhid* - the Unity and Oneness of God of Abraham - Allah - the foundation stone of the structure of Islam. It is noteworthy that Islam is not Muhammadanism, for the Prophet of Islam revived the Abrahamic belief in the Unity and Oneness of God - and Allah in his infinite mercy revealed to the Prophet of Islam a perfect code of life to be practised by humankind for all times to come.

Declaration on the Responsibilities of the Present Generations towards Future Generations

The General Conference of the United Nations Educational, Scientific and Cultural Organization, meeting in Paris from 21 October to 12 November 1997 at its 29th session,

Mindful of the will of the peoples, set out solemnly in the Charter of the United Nations, to 'save succeeding generations from the scourge of war' and to safeguard the values and principles enshrined in the Universal Declaration of Human Rights, and all other relevant instruments of international law,

Considering the provisions of the International Covenant of Economic, Social and Cultural Rights and the International Covenant on Civil and Political Rights, adopted on 16 December 1966, and the Convention on the Rights of the Child, adopted on 20 November 1989,

Concerned by the fate of future generations in the face of the vital challenges of the next millennium,

Conscious that, at this point in history, the very perpetuation of humankind and its environment are threatened,

Stressing that full respect for human rights and ideals of democracy constitute an essential basis for the protection of the needs and interests of future generations,

Asserting the necessity for establishing new, equitable and global links of partnership and intra-generational solidarity, and for promoting intergenerational solidarity for the perpetuation of humankind,

Recalling that the responsibilities of the present generations towards future generations have already been referred to in various instruments such as the Convention for the Protection of the World Cultural and Natural Heritage, adopted by the General Conference of UNESCO on 16 November 1972, the Framework Convention on Climate Change and the Convention on Biological Diversity, adopted in Rio de Janeiro on 5 June 1992, the Rio Declaration on Environment and Development, adopted by the United Nations Conference on Environment and Development on 14 June 1992, the Vienna Declaration and Programme of Action, adopted by the World Conference on Human Rights on 25 June 1993, and the United Nations General Assembly resolutions relating to the protection of the global climate for present and future generations adopted since 1990,

Determined to contribute towards the solution of current world problems through increased international co-operation, to create such conditions as will ensure that the needs and interests of future generations are not jeopardized by the burden of the past, and to hand on a better world to future generations,

Resolved to strive to ensure that the present generations are fully aware of their responsibilities towards future generations,

Recognizing that the task of protection of needs and interests of future generations, particularly through education, is fundamental to the ethical mission of UNESCO, whose Constitution enshrines the ideals of 'justice and liberty and peace' founded on 'the intellectual and moral solidarity of mankind',

Bearing in mind that the fate of future generations depends on decisions and actions taken today, and that present-day problems, including poverty, technological and material underdevelopment, unemployment, exclusion, discrimination and threats to the environment, must be solved in the interests of both present and future generations,

Convinced that there is a moral obligation to formulate behavioural guidelines for present generations within a broad, future-oriented perspective,

The General Conference therefore, solemnly proclaims on this twelfth day of November 1997 this Declaration on the Responsibilities of the Present Generations towards Future Generations.

Article 1: Needs and Interests of Future Generations

The present generations have the responsibility of ensuring that the needs and interests of future generations are fully safeguarded.

Article 2: Freedom of Choice

It is important to make every effort to ensure, with due regard to human rights and fundamental freedoms, that future as well as present generations enjoy full freedom of choice as to their political, economic and social systems and are able to preserve their cultural and religious diversity.

Article 3: Maintenance and Perpetuation of Humankind

The present generations should strive to ensure, with due respect for the dignity of the human person, the maintenance and perpetuation of humanity (recognizing that the role of women is central to this process). Consequently, the nature and form of human life must not be undermined in any way whatsoever.

Article 4: Preservation of Life on Earth

The present generations have the responsibility to bequeath to future generations an Earth which will not one day be irreversibly damaged by human activity. Each generation inheriting the Earth temporarily shall take care to use natural resources reasonably and ensure that life is not prejudiced by harmful modifications of the ecosystems and that scientific and technological progress in all fields does not harm life on Earth.

Article 5: Protection of the Environment

In order to ensure that future generations benefit from the richness of the Earth's ecosystems, the present generations should strive for sustainable development and preserve living conditions, particularly the quality and integrity of the environment.

The present generations should ensure that future generations are not exposed to pollution which may endanger their health or their existence itself.

The present generations should preserve for future generations natural resources necessary for sustaining human life and for its development.

The present generations should take into account possible consequences for future generations of major projects before these are carried out.

Article 6: Human Genome and Biodiversity

The human genome, in full respect of the dignity of the human person and human rights must be protected and biodiversity safeguarded. Scientific and technological progress should not in any way impair or compromise the preservation of the human and other species.

Article 7: Cultural Diversity and Cultural Heritage

With due respect for human rights and fundamental freedoms, the present generations shall take care to preserve the cultural diversity of humanity. The present generations have the responsibility to identify, protect and safeguard the tangible and intangible cultural heritage and to transmit this common heritage to future generations.

Article 8: Common Heritage of Mankind

The present generations may use the common heritage of mankind, as defined in international law, provided that this does not entail compromising it irreversibly.

Article 9: Peace

The present generations should ensure that both they and future generations learn to live together in peace, security, respect for international law, human rights and fundamental freedoms.

The present generations should spare future generations the scourge of war. To that end, they should avoid exposing future generations to the harmful consequences of armed conflicts as well as all other forms of aggressions and use of weapons, contrary to humanitarian principles.

Article 10: Development and Education

The present generations should ensure the conditions of equitable, sustainable and universal socio-economic development of future generations, both in its individual and collective dimensions, in particular through a fair and prudent use of available resources for the purpose of combating poverty.

Education is an important instrument for the development of human persons and societies. It should foster peace, justice, understanding, tolerance, equality and health for the benefit of present and future generations.

Article 11: Non-discrimination

The present generations should refrain from taking any action or measure which would have the effect of leading to or perpetuating any form of discrimination for future generations.

Article 12: Implementation

States, the United Nations system, other intergovernmental and non-governmental organizations, individuals, public and private bodies should assume their full responsibilities in promoting, in particular through education, training and information respect for the ideals laid down in this Declaration, and to encourage, by all appropriate means their full recognition and effective application.

Bearing in mind UNESCO's ethical mission, the Organization is requested to disseminate the present Declaration as widely as possible, and to undertake all necessary steps in UNESCO's fields of competence to raise public awareness concerning the ideals enshrined in this Declaration.

Index